The History and Politics of Latin American Theology

Volume I

Mario I. Aguilar

scm press

© Mario I. Aguilar 2007

The Author has asserted his right under the Copyright, Designs and
Patents Act, 1988, to be identified as the Author of this Work

British Library Cataloguing in Publication data

A catalogue record for this book is available
from the British Library

978 0 334 04023 1

First published in 2007 by SCM Press
9–17 St Alban's Place,
London N1 0NX

www.scm-canterburypress.co.uk

SCM Press is a division of
SCM-Canterbury Press Ltd

Typeset by Regent Typesetting, London
Printed and bound in Great Britain by
William Clowes Ltd, Beccles, Suffolk

Contents

To Louise J. Lawrence

Cras amet qui numquam amavit;
Quique amavit, cras amet

Acknowledgements

There is no doubt that the genesis of this work can be traced back to June 2004 when the University of St Andrews conferred an honorary doctorate in Divinity on Gustavo Gutiérrez. Being consequent with his life of commitment to the poor, Gustavo rejected the offer of staying at a grand hotel in St Andrews and stayed at my home instead. I thank him for his enthusiasm and the many unanswered theological questions he left with me. He had a poignant meeting with my doctoral students and during that conversation it was very clear that Latin American theology had developed into a complex phenomenon and that its history and politics was still to be developed.

During those conversations Gustavo asked me about my impressions of the theology of Marcella Althaus-Reid, currently Professor of Contextual Theology at the University of Edinburgh, whose work he was reading at that time. I am thankful to Professor Althaus-Reid, and to Professor Alistair Kee also based in Edinburgh, for their encouragement, support and ongoing friendship. If theological works could have more personalized titles, my attempt to systematize the history and politics of Latin American theology in the twentieth century could be called 'From Gustavo Gutiérrez to Marcella Althaus-Reid: between liberation and indecency'.

I am grateful to Professor Philip Esler, Professor Ron Piper, Dr Ian Bradley and Dr Esther Reed for encouraging this kind of research and for their friendship. I have discussed parts of this book with my postgraduate students – Dr Cheryl Wissman, Dr David Wilhite, Jennifer Kilps, Jeff Tippner, Rob Whiteman, Joshua Edelman, Jonathan Rowe, David Brannan,

Yumi Murayama, Casey Nicholson, George Hargreaves, Gordon Barclay, Alissa Jones Nelson and her husband Matt, Breanna Cranfield and Joanne Wood; I thank all of them for their ideas and challenges. My family in St Andrews and Edinburgh has been always supportive and I thank Laurel and Sara for hosting Gustavo Gutiérrez and making him feel at home during his stay in St Andrews.

This book is dedicated to Dr Louise J. Lawrence, fellow academic and dear friend. Her ongoing encouragement and friendship over the past few years have been crucial for the development of many of my research projects, and her personal generosity and happiness have been crucial within ongoing challenges and personal developments.

Finally, a word of thanks to Barbara Laing, SCM Senior Commissioning Editor, for believing that an idea over a glass of wine could become an academic work.

Mario I. Aguilar   *St Andrews, January 2007*

Introduction

Generational Paradigms in the Theologies of Liberation

The end of the military regimes in Latin America and the collapse of the Soviet Union during the early 1990s gave rise to new utopian dreams of a democratic nature in Latin America. Those social manifestations of hope together with political processes of democratization, provided the Latin American Church, predominantly Roman Catholic, with new agendas and new dreams of centrality. Those theological aspirations coincided with the emergence of liberation theology as a challenge to social injustice and of new democracies perceived as solutions to economic deprivation and social inequality. By the late 1990s it was clear that new democracies based on old localized democratic principles did not have the same social power that they previously held or claimed to have had. In an ongoing process of social change, the very centralized relation between the Catholic Church and the state had been erased, the monolithic perception of Christianity had been diversified with the official recognition of Pentecostalism, and the world, shocked by the events of 9/11, was being defined not by crumbling nation/states but by the hegemonic power of the United States.

In this work I argue that neither massive conversions to Pentecostalism nor the contemporary relation between Church and state set the appropriate context for a theology that narrates God's work among Latin Americans. Instead, political and liberationist theologies are faced with a new divided context, a chaotic scene of opposition between those in the margins of a larger process of globalization and communities taking part in contemporary cultural phenomena such as individualism, hedonism and consumerism. However, for the first time social categories of 'the marginalized' also include democratic governments, despised by indigenous activists as well as by international agents of globalization that do not seek their destruction but trigger a process of sub-empowerment and cultural annihilation. In re-examining the contemporary work of some Latin American theologians I argue that as the context changes any theological engagement with social realities on behalf of God also changes, and that instead of declaring that liberation theology is dead, one can expect more actions, reflections and questions regarding neo-colonialism and globalization, the politics of conversion and the anti-globalization movement in Latin America arising out of the actions and writings of Latin American liberation theologians. In the words of Enrique Dussel: 'Each generation must start from its novel situation; it must use its liberty created in order to effect and live out a new moment in the one and only history there is: the history of messianic liberation, the history of salvation.'[1]

From Religious Utopia to Theological Opposition

Religious change within Latin America in the twentieth century was a social phenomenon that had started in the early part of the century.[2] In countries such as Chile, for example, where there was still a large European presence and where the majority of the poor and marginalized workers did not find a place within the aristocratic Catholic Church, conversions to Pentecostalism had already taken place.[3] Those converts did not find a home in the Catholic Church dominated by clergy chosen from well-to-do families and who had studied in private Catholic schools. The number of Pentecostals could not be large because of the close ties between the state and the Catholic Church; however the life of itinerant preachers and mobile evangelical congregations suited the insecure lifestyle and the discrimination suffered by migrants and those who neither belonged to rural communities nor to urban centres. Those in the margins of society found their place either in branches of political parties, particularly socially oriented parties, or within small churches led by a Pentecostal preacher. Within lives of disorder, excess drinking, home violence and economic deprivation the marginalized found new avenues of bettering themselves and a place to express their emotions either in Pentecostal churches or, as in the case of Brazil, within the possession cults of African origins.[4]

In some cases, such as Chile and Brazil, the Catholic Church had managed to provide a clear organizational pattern for those in the margins, communities that after all constituted the majority of Latin Americans.[5] The period of the military regimes created a social moment of cohesion through Basic Christian Communities that, inspired by the biblical text, developed social cohesion, growing literacy and political consciousness, and eventually became central actors in the recovery of human rights taken away by dictatorial regimes that used force and violence for their means and ends.[6]

The response of the Catholic Church was different in different countries but, for the most part, bishops and priests challenged the nation/states ruled by military regimes with the tools provided by a post-Vatican II consciousness for the poor and those who suffered, and the theological reflection of clergy involved with the poor – theologies of liberation.[7] The response by Pentecostals and other born-again Christians was of support for the military who were perceived as bringing God's order to society, who were anti-Marxist, and who gave Pentecostals their first official recognition of social existence and social worth. For example, Pinochet attended the inauguration of an evangelical cathedral in Chile while Ríos Montt fostered the development of a national Pentecostal movement in Guatemala.[8] The military stressed order and individualism through hard work, and therefore Pentecostalism provided an alternative to Catholic communities because 'Pentecostalism's great theological achievement in Latin America is freedom of expression and the affirmation of the individual's worth within the community'.[9]

Within that period those outside the state and outside the Church, for example, indigenous populations, relatives of those persecuted by the state, women, and even socialists and communists, found a place of safety within the Catholic Church and were part of a revival in church activities that made the Catholic Church an alternative state that protected citizens and provided social welfare and education. However, with the end of the military regimes those natural political allies of the Church left the Christian communities in order to pursue their own agenda, while Pope John Paul II continued appointing conservative bishops who fostered issues of family and life and did not feel inclined to involve the Catholic Church in any kind of challenge to the emerging democratic regimes. For those new bishops, democratic regimes were not to be challenged as long as the Church was allowed her freedom to influence policies against abortion, contraception, and divorce within nations still considered by those bishops to be 'Catholic societies'. As a result, pastoral areas and their communities became more isolated from economic and political issues and there was an increase in separation between religion and politics.

However, there were further changes related to significant changes in traditional models of nation/states and their relation with the Church and with the theologians, particularly with the liberation theologians. The indigenous populations continued their fight for indigenous rights to language, culture, and land outside the Church, helped by some priests but without the solidarity of the Basic Christian Communities, as was the case in Brazil.[10] Some of those indigenous activists started using violence in order to push for the removal of multi-national corporations from their lands, and the Church left them to their own devices. Globalization affected the nation/state as the World Bank and the International Monetary Fund (IMF) scheduled economic targets that required privatization. The Church lost the central role it had previously enjoyed, and the Basic Christian Communities lost their grassroots involvement in local politics, local economics, and movements for solidarity.

Despite those changes, new movements outside the Church

arose out of the economic disasters triggered by international economic policies. In the case of Argentina, for example, during the 2001–2 economic crisis the *piqueteros* – a group of protestors against the Argentinean economic collapse – took control of areas of Buenos Aires, while the solidarity of many kept feeding starving middle-class Argentineans who had lost all their savings and their investments due to the collapse of the banking structures in a phenomenon that surely can be deemed as the death of the nation/state.[11] Some of those groups, particularly the relatives of the disappeared, strengthened their international networks and became part of international efforts to apply international law in order to capture and to bring to trial torturers and assassins who had led the military regimes and their systematic violations of human rights.[12]

Further changes in the context of a Latin American political response and a changing liberation theology took place after 9/11. The terrorist attack against the twin towers in New York and the war on terror declared by President Bush caught the attention of liberation theologians who had not found a new role within the economically controlled new democratic regimes in Latin America. The attack took place on the 11th of September, the annual anniversary of the military coup in Chile. For theologians, like myself, the attack was a despicable act of murder on innocent civilians and we condemned it. Nevertheless, it also brought a sad realization that the world media were focusing on the United States rather than on the search for truth, reconciliation and memory in Chile and Latin America where the memory of 'the 11' (*el once*) was central to the reconstruction of democratic and just societies.

With the international push led by President Bush for a war on terror and the pre-emptive war on Iraq, the context of theology changed once again. The nation/state had become secondary to the international concerns of a powerful government that was pushing for international interventions on Third World countries that posed a threat to the democratic values upheld by the United States, values supposedly shared by most people of the world. The memory and history of Latin America showed that any American intervention in the continent had brought suffering and pain for the poor and the marginalized. President Bush allied, by pressure and diplomacy, the support of the majority of the Latin American nations, with the exception of President Chávez in Venezuela and Fidel Castro in Cuba. In ten years the hopes of Latin Americans of forwarding peaceful democracies without war or revolutions had collapsed. It was within that changing social and historical context that traces of new political and liberation theologies started to arise out of the challenges of globalization and within theological circles and churches that were no longer central to the state but were forcefully located within the social political periphery of weak Latin American nation/states.

The Changing Faces of Latin American Theology

After the collapse of the Soviet Union many proclaimed the death of liberation theology. In particular, those who associated liberation theology with the politics of Marxism expected it to die with the end of the gross injustices that Marxism as Leninism brought to the Eastern Bloc. Indeed, those who forcefully proclaimed the death of Marxism as a social theory wanted only one social option to remain alive – that of capitalism and the free market economics. It is clear that liberation theologians used Marxism as a social tool not as a political ideology, with the consequence that Marxism as a social tool of analysis could only die if made to die by the media, or be forcefully suppressed, as previously attempted by the Latin American military regimes. Contemporary theologians such as Gregory Baum have insightfully argued that, 'the ideas of Marxism . . . have, in one way or another, become part of the Western intellectual tradition and hence are not likely to lose their validity. The modification of these ideas in the light of faith has greatly enriched theology and helped to enrol theology in the service of God's coming reign.'[13] Enrique Dussel has re-read Marx in the context of theological systems and has argued that his reading of history remains an important social tool in order to challenge post-modernism and create a new utopia of 'trans-modernity'.[14] Dussel has further argued that there is the possibility of those suppressed parts of social action coming together in the future allowing for a diversity of social and cultural narratives.[15]

Liberation theologians continue using the tools of social theory in order to carry out their pastoral involvement with the marginalized, and in doing so they assert the hermeneutics of love, of distrust, and of continuous enquiry. In that sense, liberation theologians' hermeneutics and general methodology have not changed, while particular social tools for reflection and their own involvement with different groups of society could have taken a different focus. The changing conditions of the Catholic Church, for example, have made theologies *ad intra* to become theologies *ad extra* with a challenging and creative dichotomy of exclusion/inclusion within that process of solidarity with those outside the Church. A theology that desires the liberation of human beings from social injustice and from structural sin continues challenging the narratives of the powerful, and continues reading human history from the point of view of the poor, the marginalized and those in the fringes of society. In proclaiming an option for the poor the theologians of liberation have continued asking rude questions about their disbelief in the face of injustice. For example, in April 1999 Jon Sobrino asked the following question: 'How is it possible that after so many scientific discoveries the world does not know that 40 million people die of hunger every year?' For Sobrino it is clear that there is a cover up by those who are interested in profit and wealth so that contemporary human beings know a certain amount but they do not know the realities of life and death in our planet.[16] Others, such as Gregory Baum, have continued distrusting the possibility of accepting that capitalism provides a social recipient for the values of the kingdom of God.

Most of the current practices of theological engagement have assumed social protest as a traditional way of social consciousness, and most of those protests have isolated social problems and social injustices at the local level in Latin America that have arisen out of the globalized policies of a free-market capitalistic economy pushed as the way forward by the United States and its global corporations. Baum's description of the contemporary context for a global political theology resumes the theological *res* in a sobering and post-romantic fashion:

> The collapse of communism has led to a new world order. Because of the absence of an alternative, capitalism, it would seem, is now able to show its ugly face, promote a global economy based on competition and the quest for gain, and become indifferent to the growing sector of people excluded from society's wealth – massively in the poor countries, and significantly in the rich ones. A single, unchallenged military superpower is now protecting the ongoing globalization of the self-regulating market system. Thanks to the power of the large corporations and the international financial institutions, national governments have lost the capacity to protect the material and cultural well-being of their citizens. The dominant neo-liberal ideology persuades people that the ideas of Marx have lost their relevance.[17]

A Generational Theological Paradigm

If the context has changed, the theological minds behind the production of a Latin American theology have also changed. A first generation of theologians who engaged themselves mainly with the roots of rural poverty have biologically aged, while they still support the poor and the marginalized, and they also support a second generation of liberation theologians who arose out of the time of the military regimes and the social injustice of the Cold War. A third generation of liberation theologians is beginning to emerge in the fringes of the churches while still overshadowed by the first generation, and mostly by the second generation.

Let me make clear that theological generations do not follow the accepted biological patterns of a cycle of 25 years – an expected cycle of biological reproduction related to parent–

sibling, brother–sister, or grandparent–grandchild. Instead, generations of theologians respond to a breaking paradigm of faith–action–reflection that marks a group of actors/writers/ theology makers. I have previously used this application of social generations forwarded by Karl Mannheim in order to isolate common patterns of sociability and meaning-sharing capabilities in another Third World context.[18] Indeed, for Mannheim 'the teacher-pupil relationship is not as between one representative of "consciousness in general" and another, but as between one possible subjective centre of vital orientation and another subsequent one. This tension appears incapable of solution except for one compensating factor: not only does the teacher educate his pupil, but the pupil educates his teacher too. Generations are in a state of constant interaction.'[19]

For Mannheim, sociology is a human endeavour that tries to understand contemporary reality (the challenging present) rather than the past, and within that particular task the sociologist works within a structure understood as a dynamic entity.[20] However, within that structure there are no static relationships but social conflicts, so that according to Kecskemeti, for Mannheim, 'antagonism and conflict was of the very essence of structure; the structure of social reality *was* the configuration of antagonistic forces which contended for supremacy and mutually shaped and influenced one another while locked in combat'.[21]

Thus, I have argued, social actors are located in history and cannot be expected to be somewhere else. They do not have genetic information that conditions their thinking and their heritage does not count because they move and think according to the challenges that communities define for themselves in their response to God's action in the world and, in this particular case, within Latin America. Thought coming out of action is naturally socially constructed and all theology is contextual because it arises out of a theological, social, and political context sometimes expressed as theological canon.

The first generation of liberation theologians include the most well known in the English speaking world, such as Gustavo

Gutiérrez, Jon Sobrino SJ, Leonardo Boff, Juan Luis Segundo SJ, José Miguez Bonino. Following Gutiérrez's attempt to use the theoretical metaphor of liberation within theology they produced a body of theological writings that engaged faith, revelation and the biblical text with the historical and pastoral realities of Latin America.[22] Their context was an immediate response to the Second Vatican Council (1962–65) and its encouragement for a clear engagement with the contemporary world, the pastoral conclusions of the general meeting of Latin American bishops in Medellín (Colombia, 1968), and the following meeting of Latin American bishops in Puebla (Mexico, 1979). The general socio-political situation of those years was the proliferation of a series of military regimes, and the efforts by the United States to foster development on the one hand, and to fight revolutionary efforts in the context of the Cold War on the other hand by applying the doctrine of the national security state.[23]

The second generation of liberation theologians included those who had studied with the first generation of theologians or who had been influenced by their ideas within their own pastoral, human and social concerns. As argued previously, they constitute a different social and intellectual group but they do not depart from a continuity of aims, methodologies and theological objectives. Among this group there are biblical scholars,[24] those who explore feminist critiques of the Church structures, those involved with indigenous movements and, for the first time, those who are able to think and create theological models that can function outside the Church.[25] The critique of this second generation expands to the areas of biblical criticism, in which the category of the poor is too lose, too general, and has a lack of coherence outside a Marxist critique.[26] This generation contests the fact that the majority of first-generation liberation theologians are male, Catholic priests, and that they functioned within a very cohesive and successful community of believers even when in the midst of suffering.

The third generation of theologians is dependent on the second generation but has an epistemological agenda of rupture, chaos and hermeneutical development. These theologians share the theological methodologies of the first generation and they admire those great intellectuals but have a wider affinity with the breaking grounds of the second generation. This generation wishes to continue exploring new methodologies and theoretical tools, while their theology is located among the people in the fringes of society, culturally poor, rejected and questioned by society, and those who are not traditionally central to discourses of nationhood and fatherland.[27] One of the major criticisms of this third generation relates to the popularity and marketing abilities of the first generation of liberation theologians. Liberation theology has become a victim of its own success and therefore has bowed to the commercial enterprise of academia by fighting an intellectual war of intellectual acceptance. In my opinion, liberation theology by its very nature can never be a systematic theology, even when first-generation liberation theologians have produced one, and indeed a further series of theological explorations that attempts to systematize the subject for a North Atlantic theological consumption.[28] Most of the third-generation theologians' works have not been translated into the English language.

For some of the contemporary liberation theologians of the third generation, such as Marcella Althaus-Reid, the project of theology is a materialistic one, not necessarily grounded in a particular church, and not necessarily grounded in an institutional Church at all. She writes: 'This is a concrete materialist theology which understands that the dislocation of sexual constructions goes hand in hand with strategies for the dislocation of hegemonic political and economic agendas.'[29] The context for theology has changed because the Catholic Church has become more traditional; however, its context has remained similar because there are still people oppressed and marginalized for the sake of greed, selfishness, and profit. However, the Church has not managed to welcome groups such as gay, lesbian, and queer, forgetting that Jesus of Nazareth himself welcomed all, including women, destitute, rejected human beings, and repentant sinners from all ways of life.

Despite those efforts, it is clear that the aspirations of

indigenous peoples have not been met, and the movements for land and indigenous rights have taken a central place in theological discourses about land rights and biblical lands. It is Diego Irarrázaval who brings the biblical paradigms into the concrete through the textualization of a theology of inculturation.[30] A previously African theological development, a Latin American theology of inculturation develops the possibility of a political manipulation of Christianity by indigenous populations in order to be themselves indigenous and Christians, mixed races of mixed identity, in opposition to any resurgent ideas of a Christian empire in the past or in the present. For some, a Latin American theology of inculturation is a new development outside liberation theology – in my analysis clearly one of the many emerging and challenging liberation theologies for the twenty-first century.[31] Attached to those theologies of the land are the concerns for ecology and justice and all the contemporary issues related to the stewardship of the land and the crisis of global warming.[32]

It is clear from these developments that liberation theology has become a diversified subject that contains in a theological umbrella many diverse theologies that use the social metaphor of liberation in order to stand with the marginalized in the name of God and which, through their writings, sustain a defence of human rights and the rights of those in the fringes of society. Their tools include cultural theory, anthropology, history, literary criticism, and mostly a simple way of life that challenges the centrality of profit and consumption within a contemporary capitalistic society and the globalized hedonistic phenomenon of consumerism.

Globalization, Neo-Colonialism and Terror

As previously argued, one of the greatest contributions to twentieth-century social and political processes made by liberation theology was the possibility of establishing a credible diversity within Christianity. While the North-Atlantic world perceived liberation theology as a unified phenomenon, the action and commitment to the poor by liberation theologians provided a new experience of diversity that challenged the unified experiences of traditional nationalism and the perception of social groups as unified, and based on divisions of ethnicity and race. Thus, for Gutiérrez 'reflection on the word of God is linked to the way this is experienced and proclaimed within the Christian community. When a theology becomes deeply and courageously involved in the situation in which the Church finds itself at any given moment of its history, then it will continue to be meaningful even once the context in which it arose has passed.'[33]

Globalization as a model of society remains a universalistic model in which social action is reified through the exaltation of individualism.[34] Individual choices, including a sort of detached individual Christianity, provide the necessary means to wider access. Freedom of choice is perceived as the ultimate goal of a free democratic society. Capitalism remains the central means to achieve order and stability by activating relations of demand by consumers who, in turn, dictate the most important trends of society and the market.[35] Democracy, understood in a single way, as experienced by the United States, remains the only possible goal of a crying humanity that wants peace and justice and does not find it. Evangelical Christianity, closely allied to the market economy, with a single-minded possibility of individual salvation, provides the Christian model for that kind of globalization – a Christianity that does not accept diversity but that dogmatically emphasizes the separation of religion and politics, of economic causation and salvific effect. In the case of Pentecostalism, that kind of Christianity 'offers individuals a psychological sanctuary in an otherwise chaotic and hostile world'.[36]

Within that individualistic model it is difficult to accommodate the Christian utopia of communalism, solidarity, evangelical poverty as a value, and a Christian way of life that aims at liberating human beings not only from personal sin, but also from sinful structures that impede the proclamation of good news to the poor, the afflicted, and the marginalized.[37] Within a capitalistic discourse of development and freedom of choice, as reified by President Bush, it is difficult to see how the Third World is not going to become an experimental ground for a new colonial phenomenon. After all, colonialism was a phenomenon in which oppressors transformed the minds of the oppressed through their own brand of colonial education, through the explorer, the missionary, and the colonial officer. There was a colonization of minds and bodies in which Africans, Asians, and Latin Americans were expected to become Europeans because their own cultural values and their own perceptions of the world were considered uncivilized. They were seen as 'other' and there was no place for otherness within the colonial structure.[38]

Hegel and Kant reasserted that European centrality by suggesting that the development of the Spirit was not plausible for Africans. Hegel, in his Lectures on the Philosophy of History, asserted that:

> The realm of the Absolute Spirit is so impoverished among them [the Africans] and the natural Spirit so intense that any representation which they are inculcated with suffices to impel them to respect nothing, to destroy everything . . . Africa does not have history as such. Consequently we abandon Africa, to never mention it again. It is not part of the historical world; it does not evidence historical movement or development . . .[39]

Post-colonial theology fought that oppressive paradigm and helped to construct new symbolic systems that were local expressions of God speaking to his own people.[40] It is that ongoing theological project that is at stake in contemporary liberation theology.

Liberation theologians of the first generation already shared the beginnings of a universalistic understanding within Third World theologians that suggested that realities of poverty and oppression were common to all their countries and continents. They challenged ideological systems that became so unified that they in turn didn't allow people to have a localized and diversified experience. Biblical scholarship, particularly, showed the potential of God's Word read in context and God's deep experience among the poor and marginalized. However, it was the second generation of liberation theologians who were able to push forward the need to accept God's own diversity in human experience, through a common experience. Liberation theology came of age when theologians realized that they themselves were different from others; and Gutiérrez spoke of liberation theology as 'an attempt to make the word of life present in a world of oppression, of injustice, of death'.[41]

Those features of a contemporary and, indeed, a past world have not been eradicated. The oppressive military regimes of Latin America and the Leninist societies of Eastern Europe have been exchanged for democratic regimes; however within those democratic regimes there is still social oppression, injustice, and death due to lack of medicines, employment, and human dignity within societies still divided by class, race, and economic status. Instead of despairing liberation theologians continue their journey with the poor and the marginalized and with their own writing tools continue to alert others of the need to change lifestyles and international policies in order to embrace the reign of God in which those marginalized within society, and those at the fringes of any society, are always at the centre.

Liberation theologies after 9/11 have an important role to play because the terrorist attacks on New York and Washington had the impact that the terrorists wanted: an armed response towards an invisible terrorist world that could not be controlled, a world in chaos as the terrorists wanted it.[42] Thus, triggering an imperial response of further globalization not only on trade and economics, but also involving armed intervention in order to prevent further violence – a reminiscence of Vietnam and the Indochina war is in place here.[43] 9/11 marks a new era for Latin America because it marks a new era for the globalized community under constant economic pressure from the United States. President Bush becomes the head of a globalized crusade for morality and democracy, a crusade that presumes a globalized universality under American influence – a reminiscence of British and French colonialism is in order here.[44] President Bush represents a political administration but his words speak of the religious politics of neo-conservatism, with God at their side, and with a massive task of rallying people around them.[45] Iraq is invaded – or 'liberated' – in order to prevent further terrorism, while weapons of mass destruction are never found. The Blair government follows the lead in order to become great among the nations – a reminiscence of the partition of Africa in the late nineteenth century is in order here, as well as the connections with 1492 and the encounter of two different worlds in which, finally, the European empires crushed all indigenous American civilizations because of greed and the need for gold.[46]

The response by Elsa Tamez, a liberation theologian based in Costa Rica, resumes the new challenges and the new steps taken by liberation theologians. In a letter to the Christians of Latin America she cancels all of her academic engagements in the United States and pleads for Christian solidarity with Iraq through the pages of *Voices from the Third World*, the journal of the Association of Third World Theologians.[47] North-Atlantic feminist theologians in response speak of the academic isolation faced by American academics and the need to organize a globalized peaceful protest against war – once again a reminiscence of the period of the Vietnam War. The recipients of the letters are diverse: Christian communities in Latin America and university professors in the United States. It is clear that the stakes are high: the American presence in Afghanistan represented the possibility of helping others to rebuild their own existence after years of Soviet occupation; however, a second 'liberation' indicated that Iraq was part of a concerted effort of empire rather than an isolated humanitarian effort. The vision of American troops at the palaces of Iraq spoke of conquerors rather than liberators and, for some of us Latin Americans, it subjected us again to the vision of military boots and the feeling of them – certainly not a vision of hope and solidarity with the poor and the marginalized.[48]

The context for Latin American theologians has expanded as the world has expanded. The injustice, oppression and death of the Latin American slums still remain despite the private economic successes of some Chilean companies. The context for theologizing has expanded to the realms of a globalized empire that for profit and economic expansion is able to compromise the Christian values represented by the poor and made into text by liberation theologians. With a weak nation/state and a weak United Nations there is only one mighty player, the one who can provide the ideological structure for a symbolic construction of reality. A nation is becoming empire or, for theologians such as Walter Wink, it has already become an empire.[49] The consequences of that change are worrying for Latin Americans as well as for Christians in the United States because as Wink has pointed out 'when a nation aspires to empire, it tends to become virulently evil, no matter how hard individuals may try to prevent it . . . For empires live from the lust of power, and that lust is insatiable.'[50] Within that new unfolding context liberation theology in Latin America has new challenges to face, challenges that provide the continuity of Christian praxis but invite to a rediscovery of the hermeneutical circle within new forms, new contexts and new meanings.

New Utopias, New Theologies

Within the first generation of liberation theologians in Latin America there was a tingling utopian touch that made them take part in many social movements and many Christian reflections on a new world closer to the values of the kingdom of God. Those utopian visions were triggered by a whole renewal within the Catholic Church during and after the Second Vatican Council. The implementation of Vatican II in Latin America through Medellín and Puebla created a body of action and theological literature that was impressive in theory and practice.

The challenge of the following generation of liberation theologians has been to act, reflect, and produce theology within a less dramatic context, without military regimes, without martyrs, without challenges from the Vatican. In this new context suffering and poverty are more present in Latin America but that poverty is forgotten in the context of globalization. The local has become less prominent as a vehicle of knowledge and the powerful of this world have opted to follow models of universal knowledge, universal communication, and universal action by assuming that the world is better because we all drink Coca-Cola or can have access to the Internet.

Contemporary events have reminded theologians that not all is well. The tragic attacks of 9/11 on New York and Washington are markers of symbolic significance because they devolve in a material and empirical way the suffering of others – of course using the wrong means and for the wrong ends. The Tsunami disaster has reminded theologians that even when millions of people open their hearts to suffering human beings they do not have absolute control over the earth and its complexities. The planet cries out because of our own destruction of the atmosphere through the emission of gases, most of them arising from our need to consume, and to be comfortable, while still millions die of poverty, hunger, and disease.

New Christian utopias and new liberation theologies arise out of this context: theologies of inculturation, feminist and queer theologies, ecological theologies, and ultimately theologies of liberation and freedom. Those Latin American theologians continue using the methodologies of Gutiérrez or Sobrino in order to address new injustices, new suffering worlds, with hope and with the utopia of the kingdom of God in mind. Liberation theology is not dead; it has diversified in order to accompany the suffering people of God, located in many churches, many mosques and many secular spaces. The God who liberates his people is not dead; she lives among us, even within processes of war and globalization. After all, those processes of social change and globalization were already present in 1492 when the empire brought new social structures to the indigenous populations, by bringing to them a new religion as well as the sword.

The following chapters provide a general look at some of those theologies and the theologians that, out of Christian praxis, have stressed important areas of theological engagement and subsequent political action.

Part 1

Ecclesial Theology

I

Gustavo Gutiérrez

Liberation theology seeks to be a way of speaking about God. It is an attempt to make the word of life present in a world of oppression, of injustice, of death.[51]

The adoption of a spiritual perspective is followed by a reflection on faith (therefore, a theology) as lived in that perspective.[52]

For the past 40 years Gustavo Gutiérrez has been at the centre of discussions related to the place and mode of engagement between the Church and the world.[53] Born in Peru, he trained for the priesthood in Europe and was raised within the intellectual tradition of the French *nouvelle theologie*. Gutiérrez's seminal work *Teología de la liberación* became one of the most read and discussed theological works of the twentieth century.[54] Within that particular context of the Latin America of the 1960s and an ongoing Cold War between the United States and the Soviet Union, Gutiérrez made an epistemological statement that was to bring together several ecclesial and theological developments within the Catholic Church triggered by the Second Vatican Council (1962–65).[55] For Gutiérrez, theology is a second act and a narrative that uses language in order to understand God's presence in the world. Thus, for Gutiérrez: 'Theology is a language. It attempts to speak a word about the mysterious reality that believers call God. It is a *logos* about *theos*.'[56]

Theology is not a first act for a theologian; the first act is clearly faith, expressed in prayer and commitment within the Christian community.[57] However, that clear statement had been the product of many years of theological disputes, doctrinal misunderstandings, interpretative projects, engagement with Marxists and neo-liberals, and all within a changing Latin American Church that became fully engaged with the world of politics, economics, and development.[58] In other words, for Gutiérrez theology is a textual narrative that arises out of a practice within a particular context of a Christian community engaged with the world, and particularly within the world of the poor and the disadvantaged of society.

This chapter explores ideas of religion and politics within the writings of Gustavo Gutiérrez. In its first part it outlines greater ecclesial and social influences within his early theological period; in its second part it focuses on the centrality of human history in his theological framework of his second theological period; and in its third part it examines some of Gutiérrez's post-1992 writings in relation to religion and politics in a wider social context.[59] It is clear that Gutiérrez's treatment of religion and politics presupposes God's presence in human history through a Church engaged with the world, in which it is necessary to participate actively in the political in order to act religiously. Religion as the ritual and social practices of a rule of life (*religio*) produces theology as a narrative. That narrative as a text allows practitioners (and others) to follow historical interpretations of the rule of life and those interpretations also affect the way in which practitioners understand practices within that way of life. Therefore, and according to Gutiérrez, religion and politics are embodied in religious ritual and secular governance respectively through a constant dialectic of interaction, contradiction, and solidarity.

Theology as Commentary

Gutiérrez's major work arose out of his religious commentary on political events. The Latin America of the 1960s, as the one of today, had a majority of people living in economic deprivation and the European educated Peruvian priest challenged the sole possibility of a God that wanted an established order that was socially unjust. Gutiérrez, the student of theology, was influenced by a new theological trend present in France in the 1950s and 1960s arising out of French democratic ideas and by the sociological theories that had challenged the functional and non-changeable world portrayed by Emile Durkheim and Marcel Mauss.[60]

A post-war European world was rebuilding itself on new paradigms that arose out of suffering and the annihilation of the Jews, in which Marxism and a Marxist critique of society was playing an ever-increasing role, particularly in France. Gutiérrez's favourite European theologian of that time was M.-D. Chenu, who had asked questions about the given scientific nature of theology as a science rather than as an interpretive project, and from whom Gutiérrez was to learn the centrality of spirituality within the construction of any theological edifice.[61] It is at that moment that the roots of three kinds of Catholic theology became collateral as scholars posed questions about religion as a ritual practice and the following of Christ as a rule of social life. Those three types of theology were neo-scholastic theology, a transcendental-idealist theology and a post-idealist theology.[62]

Neo-scholastic theology based itself on a religion associated with a ritualistic piety, its acolytes returned to the sources of scholastic philosophy of the Middle Ages and they produced a narrative theology based on 'a theology of antiquity'.[63] As a result, neo-scholasticism was unable to deal with social change, secularism, atheism, and with suffering. Religion and politics were separated as far as religion and political governance were separated, with the hope that they could become one in order to return to a past union between God, the Church, and the governance of society. Neo-scholasticism remained a European phenomenon as far as religious practice remained sectarian and did not engage with other faiths or indeed with atheists and with the possibility of the freedom of conscience proclaimed by the Second Vatican Council. Gutiérrez did not partake of this paradigm and did not include it as a possibility in his dealings with religion and politics.

Transcendental-idealist theology based itself on a religion associated with the sources of the Church Fathers and with scholasticism; however, its acolytes engaged themselves with the challenges of modernity in Europe through the production of a theological narrative of community. They tried forcefully but positively to engage themselves with the use of subjectivity rather than classical metaphysics, the critical encounter with Kantian narratives of the self, German idealism, existentialism, secularization, and the narratives of truth and method of scientific discourses. Gutiérrez studied those challenges and addressed them in his studies but decided later to leave them and to search for paradigms of religion and politics that used other social contexts.[64]

Post-idealist theology based itself on a practice of religion that addressed three new challenges to theology as a narrative: (1) the end of theological innocence *vis-à-vis* secularization and the ideological and social challenges to a practice of religion devolved from social and political life[65]; (2) the end of theological systems that did not include the individual self and the person, triggered by the post-holocaust theological narratives of the survivors, the 'irruption' of the Auschwitz catastrophe,[66] and the 'irruption of the poor' rather than the development of theologies about poverty; and (3) the end of a practice of religion based on cultural mono-centrism and superseded by a social governance related to an ethnically and culturally poly-centric world in which ethnic and cultural characteristics can no longer be part of an ideological superstructure based either on Marxist or neo-liberal terms.

It is in that response to religious practice in the contemporary world of the 1960s and within that framework of a *post-idealist theology* that Metz and Gutiérrez articulated a theological narrative that described and challenged the possibility of theologizing outside the social structures of political governance and indeed of people's lives.[67] Metz's context is European and he develops a strong political theology while Gutiérrez's context is Latin American (and the Third World) and he develops a theological framework known as liberation theology.[68] For both theologians, religion and politics are not separate entities because they come out of actions carried out by Christians who involve themselves with those in need within society, involvement that arises from their religious selfhood and their Christian life in community. The place of the Church in history is not as establishment but as people, and the place of theology is of narrative rather than doctrine.

The influence of those ideas was enormous in Catholic theological circles not because those were new ideas (it must be remembered that the social doctrine of the Church had already been articulated since 1891), but because they were the first theological fruits of the Second Vatican Council. The 'post-idealist' narrative of God's work in the world had returned to the biblical and doctrinal sources that had been confused by European philosophical epistemologies within European theology. The works of Metz in Europe and of Gutiérrez in Latin America became catalysts for pastoral models centred on the concept of the 'people of God' rather than on the Church as the only place where God could or should intervene within the contemporary world.

Gutiérrez's talk to a group of priests in Chimbote, Peru, in 1968 and the subsequent publication of his seminal work did not end theological discussions on pastoral matters related to the implementation of Vatican II, but activated a clear theological exploration of the place of religious practitioners within society.[69] The European context of secularism and atheism was changed into a theological narrative that explored the religious practices and beliefs of Christians within a heavily religious environment that questioned the political governance offered within their own societies. Theological works spoke of the 'irruption of the poor', of oppressors and oppressed, of liberation from personal sin as well as from sinful structures of governance.

The impact of Gutiérrez's work was enormous because he relocated a majestic God from a triumphant Church into an anthropomorphic and incarnate deity closer to the Hebrew Scriptures than to Greek thought and platonic ideals. The rediscovery of the Scriptures as authority within the Catholic Church at Vatican II helped to question the possible dichotomies of the neo-scholastics by returning to the Old Testament where relations within society were part of a social practice in which there was no clear separation between religion and politics. North American and European theologians took the challenge of Gutiérrez and organized conferences and seminars in order to examine their own theological presuppositions and the diversified contexts in which those theological statements were being made. The students of the University of Chicago, for example, organized a conference in 1979 where the new Shailer Matthews Professor of Divinity, Langdon Gilkey, addressed their concerns with the following statement:

> Surely there can be no doubt that the important later symbols of the New Covenant people, the messianic reign, and even the Kingdom itself repeat and develop, rather than abrogate, this union of the social and the religious, the historical and the ideal, which begins here in the original calling and establishment of the people of God. This interrelation and interdependence of the religious and the social, the individual and the communal – and the providential constitution of both – was re-expressed in classical, Hellenistic form in Augustine's *De Civitate Dei*, and variously – and often unfortunately – in the subsequent concepts of Holy Christendom and in the Calvinistic views of the Holy Community.[70]

Within Latin America, Africa, and Asia theologians explored their commitment, their religious practices, and the political world in which they lived. In North America, the oppressed of the past and of the present asked questions about their role in society (their religion), God's involvement in the world (their theology), and their politicians' governance of society (their politics).

However, while most theologians, academics and politicians have explored some of Gutiérrez's ideas related to his first period of work, he continued his practice of religion and his ministry as a priest in a slum of Lima, where the politics of Peruvian society required him to reflect on his practice through two further research periods: one on the place of history in God's plan of salvation, and another one on the place of political events and the teaching of the Church as its response. Gutiérrez found a companion in the anthropologist, novelist, and poet José María Arguedas (1911–69), who wrote about the poor and challenged the oppression towards the poor within Peruvian society. They met at Chimbote, a coastal fishing port to the north of Lima, while Gutiérrez was giving conferences and Arguedas was finishing his novel *El zorro de arriba y el zorro de abajo.*[71] Arguedas was influential on Gutiérrez and vice versa because both found that God was present in the poor of Peru, either in Chimbote or in Rimac, a Lima slum where Gutiérrez ministered through a parish and through his Las Casas Institute.[72] It is difficult to imagine, but it was at the Rimac slum that Gutiérrez wrote most of his theology, teaching only part-time at the university.[73]

Theology as History

If during his first theological period Gutiérrez asked questions about social and divine processes of underdevelopment and poverty, during his second period of research he asked questions about God's involvement in human history.[74] Gutiérrez's understanding of human history followed the Second Vatican Council in its document on the Church in the Modern World, where the Council Fathers assert that 'The Lord is the goal of human history, the focal point of the desires of history and civilization, the centre of mankind, the joy of all hearts, and the fulfilment of all aspirations.'[75] Those thoughts had been applied to the Latin American pastoral reality in his seminal talk to the meeting of the National Office for Social Research in Chimbote (July 1968) when he stated that:

If there is a finality inscribed in history, then the essence of

Christian faith is to believe in Christ, that is to believe that God is irreversibly committed to human history. To believe in Christ, then, is to believe that God has made a commitment to the historical development of the human race. To have faith in Christ is to see the history in which we are living as the progressive revelation of the human face of God.[76]

His main source for this second period was the Bible and he argued for one major theological presupposition: God became human through the incarnation and therefore one of us. The outcome of such theological presupposition is that God acts through human history in order to save and he administers graces for human beings in order to interact in the world and be part of it. As a result, religious practice (religion) takes place within a particular society that is governed not by others but by the same 'people of God' with the Church as a community immersed in a particular society. However, that incarnation as theological principle was relevant to the people of Israel in the Old Testament. Yahweh led his people out of oppression at an early stage of their history, he gave them the land, and he asked them to keep a covenant that included just and equal relations between all. Within those just relations, the prophets reminded Israel of her obligations towards the poor, the needy, the widows, the orphans, and the stranger.[77] The demands by God in the history of Israel point to the fact that 'the history from which biblical faith springs is an open-ended history, a history open to the future'.[78]

Gutiérrez moved to a re-reading of Latin American history by assuming God's involvement in human history throughout the Hebrew Scriptures. The history of Latin America was no different from that of Israel because within that human history there were God-fearing people who asked questions about history in order to understand questions about God. If the liberation of Israel through the Exodus made a people, Gutiérrez explored the 'encounter' between Europeans and indigenous peoples in 1492. Christians led a colonial conquest based initially on ideals of civilization and evangelization but that subsequently was driven by human greed and an ongoing strife for riches and power.[79] Those who suffered poverty and social annihilation under the conquistadors became part of a society that proclaimed itself Christian and, in the name of an unjust Christian relation between colonizers and colonized, subjected indigenous peoples to slavery, genocide, forced conversion, and inhuman conditions of life.[80] Nevertheless, for Gutiérrez, God was in Latin America in pre-Columbian times and he remained with the suffering indigenous peoples while many atrocities were taking place.

In reading Latin American history Gutiérrez isolated the example of some Christians who did not comply with the *status quo* of colonialism and degradation and became themselves defenders of the poor for the sake of the gospel. One of them, Bartolomé de las Casas, was an example of a full conversion to the poor in colonial Latin America that allowed their voice to be heard within the Spanish Courts and the learned universities of Europe.[81] Las Casas's attitude and his Christian attitude made a difference in God's action in history because he defended the poor and the needy, and in return he became a sign of contradiction that had to suffer attacks from philosophers, theologians, and conquistadors alike.[82] Those attacks came upon him because Las Casas not only exercised Christian charity towards the indigenous population but constructed a theologically informed defence of their human rights because of their condition as children of God made in his own image.[83]

In his defence of the indigenous populations Las Casas resembled Job, another biblical figure important for Gutiérrez. If Gutiérrez dwells on the suffering of the innocent by examining the book of Job, he does so by associating the person of Job not with a passive sufferer but with an example of suffering-trust in God and his love for all.[84] Job in the Bible and Bartolomé de las Casas in the Latin American context become prototypes of Christian history. They are able not only to empathize with those suffering but, because in enduring physical and emotional suffering themselves, they also see God not through a general depersonalized historical narrative, but through the poor as protagonists of that history. Thus, they develop a theology that speaks once and again of the love of God in a human history in need of liberation and not in a theology ridden with clauses, argumentations, and intellectual discourses attached to the learned and to the philosophers. In the case of Las Casas:

> Bartolomé welds faith to what we today would call social analysis. This enables him to unmask the 'social sin' of his time. That, doubtless, was his forte – and also the difference between him and the great majority of those in Spain who were concerned with the affairs of the Indies . . . Those who had not seen the abuse and contempt to which the Indians were subjected, those who had not suffered in their own flesh the aggression of the mighty ones of the Indies, those who had not counted dead bodies, had other priorities in theology.[85]

During this period of biblical and theological reflection Gutiérrez brings together the concept of the God of history, already present in his *A Theology of Liberation*, with a shift in Latin American ecclesial history towards the place where the God of history makes his presence felt: the world of the poor. The 'irruption of the poor' within Latin America suggests that the centrality of the poor within the practice of religion should bring a change in the political understanding of social, economic, and power relations. If the Christian communities of Latin America, and therefore the Latin American Church, decided to strive for the world of the poor because it was among the poor that the incarnate Son of God decided to dwell, the political world should do the same, particularly in a continent where most politicians declared themselves Christians and are part of that servant Church of the poor. The 'preferential option for the poor' forwarded by Gutiérrez and others and sanctioned within the pastoral options of the Latin American Church constitutes not a change in pastoral orientation but 'is nothing short of a Copernican revolution for the Church'.[86]

Gutiérrez explores God's involvement in human history

through the religious practice of his Church in the past, but in doing so he moves with theological, religious, and political questions that take place in the present of Latin America. The publication of A Theology of Liberation takes place after the implementation of the Second Vatican Council in Latin America through the second meeting of all Latin American bishops in Medellín (Colombia), while his second period of theological reflection coincides with the third meeting of Latin American bishops in Puebla de Los Angeles (Mexico) in 1979. It is at Puebla that the 'preferential option for the poor' is publicly declared by the meeting of bishops within the political climate of a number of military coups, including those in Chile (1973) and Argentina (1976), while the force of Medellín remains the crucial impact for Gutiérrez's theology. It is at Medellín in 1968 that the theological movement of a Latin America driven by lay unpublished theologians began.[87] The Church in Latin America had to ask hard questions about its religious practice within difficult political circumstances and, aided by the theological reflection of Gutiérrez, the bishops did not separate religion and politics, but provided a political response of commitment to political change and the defence of human rights. However, the subsequent pastoral implementation of Medellín was very different so that, in the case of Chile, the bishops challenged the military regime, while there was an avoidance of any prophetic denunciation in the case of Argentina.[88]

Gutiérrez provides a clear biblical and theological reflection that does not differentiate between religion and politics because those processes are neither separated in the Hebrew Scriptures nor in the history of the Church in Latin America. The politics of religion that a local church decides to implement cannot be influenced by theology as a second step but it reflects the first step of commitment and practice with the poor, in the case of Gutiérrez, to the wealthy and powerful, in the case of many clergymen and bishops of Argentina. Gutiérrez's return to the biblical sources follows from his own commitment to the poor, his own involvement with the reading of contemporary history in Latin America, and his own involvement with important ecclesiastical figures such as Helder Camara, Pedro Casaldáliga, Oscar Romero, Evaristo Arns and Manuel Larraín.

Religio and the *Polis* in Post-modernity

During a third period of action, reflection, and writing Gutiérrez asked questions about the response to God's actions in history by the Latin American poor and marginalized. They, after all, are the majority of theologians because they reflect on the Scriptures together allowing for narratives on the action of God in the world to be articulated. Their religious response through their Christian life produces different localized ways of responding to the work of the Holy Spirit, thus it produces new spiritualities.

Spirituality for Gutiérrez does not relate to a pious individual response to God in order to acquire security; on the contrary, an honest response to God creates insecurity, persecution, misunderstanding, and suffering. The actions of those who respond to the Holy Spirit do not always please the powerful and the rich; thus the poor become ever more dependent on God, not on their own means. Religion as a way of life based on the Spirit produces men and women who trust and wait for God's promises while sharing solidarity with the poor and the marginalized within communities. Thus, Gutiérrez challenges the idea of a self-sufficient individualistic spirituality that creates prosperity and security. On the contrary, he systematizes the possibility of a distinct Latin American spirituality closer to the values of the kingdom and distant from the security of riches, power, and social acceptance.[89]

Spirituality for Gutiérrez is a way of life that moves towards the poor because the poor are the ones who show more trust and need of God, not because they are better than other human beings. Spirituality becomes a method for theology because a way of life close to the poor comes before any theological thinking or theological writing. Thus, religion as a practice informs the involvement of Christians within politics because all actions that precede theology are enacted within society, within the *polis*, and therefore they are all political. Even those who practise a spirituality that agrees with the *status quo* express opinions within society, and therefore within the realm of political governance; they elect politicians, professional governors, according to their beliefs, according to their spirituality, according to their theology, according to their preferences that rationally cannot be contrary to their way of life.

For Gutiérrez, God is at the centre of that social and religious change that allows human beings to be liberated from their own personal sin but, most importantly, from sinful structures that do not allow them to be fully human and in God's image. Thus, in his later work Gutiérrez who so far has not allowed for a separation between religion and politics returns to the theme of liberation by returning to reflections on the action of God in the Bible as liberator within a particular history. God is the God of life because he liberates. However, Gutiérrez makes very clear distinctions about the fact that God is a liberator when he writes:

> God is not a liberator because God liberates; rather God liberates because God is a liberator. God is not just because he establishes justice, or faithful because God enters into a covenant, but the other way around. I am not playing with words here, but trying to bring out the primacy and transcendence of God and to remind ourselves that God's being gives meaning to God's action. According to the Bible, God's interventions in the life of God's people do not imply any kind of immanentism or any dissolution of God into history; rather they emphasize that God is the absolute and transcendent sort of being.[90]

In this late reflection on God and his work Gutiérrez synthesizes his theology by integrating the Latin American context and the action of the absolute being much preferred within European discourses on transcendence and immanence. The difference in his discourse in relation to other theologians is that any discourse about God arises out of a communal practice of social justice within the *polis* and not in isolation from those social realities. For Gutiérrez is not making an attempt to inte-grate two separate realities – religion and politics; the separation is in the mind, while the practice indicates that theological dis-courses and the act of contemplation constitute a political act of prophetic solidarity, defiance, and a social pronouncement. It is at the end of his theological book on God that Gutiérrez discloses the possibility of a relation between aesthetics, poetics, and God's option for the poor by outlining the hope that comes out of suffering in the poetic works of César Vallejo.[91] He does not return to theological aesthetics and instead continues an exploration of history within a Latin American post-modernity.

Gutiérrez's later theological work, always a reflection on his pastoral work, is influenced by the preparations for the 500th anniversary of the encounter between indigenous peoples and Europeans. As the Latin American Church prepared for the Fourth General Meeting of Latin American Bishops in Santo Domingo, Gutiérrez, as a theological expert, realized that for some 1492 meant a great moment of discovery, for others a great moment of evangelization but for the indigenous peoples of Latin America it meant an encounter with a colonial machine that destroyed, enslaved, and did not differentiate the religion and politics of empire. While historians such as Enrique Dussel explored the chronological periods and changes of the Church in Latin America, Gutiérrez delivered an uncompromising Christian manifesto for solidarity with the indigenous peoples of Latin America, but within the context of the Church.

The context of the Latin American Church at Santo Domingo was already post-modern and post-romantic. The military regimes in Latin America had ceased to exist, civil wars in Guatemala and El Salvador were coming to an end, and the influence of a neo-liberal economic system that fostered indi-vidualism, economic prosperity, and personal salvation was felt throughout the continent. The rise of Protestantism pointed to a refreshed Christianity for Latin America but in many cases the individual salvation supported by those Christian groups coming from North America undermined the pastoral aims and objectives of the Christian communities. The violence of the military regimes had ended but the violent protests by indigenous peoples against the state had brought new challenges associated with indigenous rights, international laws of cultural protection, and the recovery of indigenous sacred landscapes and political spaces.

Gutiérrez took active part in the 1992 meeting of bishops in Santo Domingo and together with others he challenged the neo-conservatism coming out of the Vatican and the newly appointed bishops, most of them of a more neo-scholastic way of thinking. If for some of them religion and politics could be separated Gutiérrez returned in his theological writings to the social doctrine of the Church and to the pastoral achievements of Medellín and Puebla. If Vatican II had prepared the way for a clear engagement of the Church with the contemporary world, it was the reflection on ecclesial praxis at Medellín and Puebla that had provided the theory and method for being religious in Latin America. The epistemology of Medellín, particularly, had indicated that it was not possible to do theology without a commitment to the poor and that to be committed to the poor a religious practitioner had to engage with the political in order to influence it for the sake of the poor. Thus, democratic or non-democratic institutions did not perceive the poor as the recipients of Good News but as a social and political problem. Economic growth and successful economic policies did not take into account the human value of the poor but were geared to maximize profit in order to implement successful economic models of development that benefited few and punished the majority that did not have resources for economic growth or investment.

For Gutiérrez, the newly centred reflections on the religious, the social and the political stem from the centrality of the human person. Political systems that are not person centred fail to understand the beauty of God's creation of man and woman in his own image. For example, on the subject of work, and coinciding with John Paul II's encyclical letter *Laborem*

Exercens, Gutiérrez argues that the dignity of the person who works comes from the fact that a human being is recreating the earth and not from the type of work undertaken – a clear break from the Spanish colonial understanding that there was a higher type of work, a more intellectual one, that left a lower type of manual work to slaves and servants.[92] However, Gutiérrez recognizes that for some commentators the Pope seems to be speaking about the Third World only and that is not the case. The encyclical recalls the dignity of every human being everywhere and the absolute primacy of the human over technological discoveries, economic and political systems that place profit over workers and economic growth over human dignity. As already argued at Medellín, the call of the Church is to denounce poverty but also to show through material poverty that human beings remain at the centre of passing systems, policies and social structures, be they just or unjust. Thus, Gutiérrez argues forcefully that:

> The encyclical clearly describes the universality of the social problem, the depth of the injustice and the abandonment suffered by the poor today, the responsibility of leaders of socio-economic systems which violate the rights of workers, and the urgent need for the whole Church to make the cause of the dispossessed her own.[93]

To be religious within that society that violates human dignity and favours markets over people requires a return to the body of social teaching of the Church in order not to foster solely academic study, but in order to give further authority to the already plentiful commitment by Christian communities towards the poor. It requires a return to the idea articulated by the Church Fathers that a Christian life needed a style of life that visibly spoke of the religious. Therefore words and confessions do not match a style of life in solidarity with the poor, in which what is given is not only the excess gained but the goods acquired by human and divine right. A style of life and a spirituality of poverty do not become an exception to ordinary life but the norm of the life of all Christians and of the Church. Thus, Gregory the Great wrote that:

> The earth is common to all men, and therefore the food it provides is produced by all in common. Thus they are wrong to believe themselves innocent who demand for their private use the gift that God gave to all . . . when we give what is indispensable to the needy, we do not do them a favour from our personal generosity, but we return to them what is theirs. More than an act of charity, what we are doing is fulfilling an obligation of justice.[94]

It is that theology of the daily life, of a style of life, of a social morality of connection with other human beings, which makes Gutiérrez's theological agenda meaningful as well as central within a post-socialist world. Those who understood his agenda as a religious commitment to socialist ideas rather than to Christian ideas saw an end to liberation theology after the collapse of socialist states in Eastern Europe during the 1990s. However, the religious preoccupation for the poor and the oppressed can only end when there is no more poverty. Until then the voice of the poor in theology, in the practice of religion and in politics is to be heard as a central commitment to the building of the kingdom of God now and for the future. The Church as the body of believers and as a signifier of God's presence altered the role of the poor at Medellín, where they became theological and political actors in society. The task remains, according to Jon Sobrino, to make the Church of the poor a reality in order to continue challenging the centrality of wealth and profit in the running of society.[95] Sobrino, as well as Gutiérrez, points to the fact that the Christian utopia of religion and politics has not been realized; however, both of them remain committed to bridge any separation between religious practice and governance, between the world of the poor and the neo-liberal world that dominates Latin America at the beginning of the twenty-first century.[96]

Theological Solidarity

As already argued, within Gutiérrez's writings there is no clear separation between the religious and the political. Theological narratives about God textually re-create understanding of a divine history that it is expressed through human history, following Nicholas Lash's theological dictum: 'All human utterances occur in a context. And the contexts in which they occur modify their meaning.'[97] Thus, Gutiérrez provides a challenge to any privatization of theological reflection concentrated in academia but he also assumes that a few within the theological community and the Christian community exercise their Christian mission within universities and theological colleges through an ongoing ministry of teaching and research.

For Gutiérrez, the relation between the practice of religion and the practice of politics needs to be articulated through the Christian faith. Within that relation, commitment to the poor and the marginalized in the name of God provides the first step of involvement by Christians in the world, and particularly within the social context of Latin America. That commitment to justice and to the poor is the first step in any theological reflection about the world and its relation with God. Faith comes first, and reason follows because 'theology is an understanding of the faith. It is a rereading of the word of God as that word is lived in the Christian community' so that 'we can separate theological reflection neither from the Christian community nor from the world in which that community lives'.[98]

Gutiérrez's reflection on the relation between religion and politics presupposes an ongoing commitment to God through the poor of society that is inscribed much later in theological narratives about the love of God for human beings and the need for theologians to immerse themselves in that extension of the incarnation in contemporary human history. Thus, his theologizing differs from political theology, theologies of development and theologies of revolution because in all those theological movements the articulation of ideas and writings comes first, the practice of religion and politics comes second.

What unites all those theological models is a Christian response to individualistic models related to romantic movements, post-enlightenment ideas, and the post-modern condition.

Religion as the practice of faith becomes politics because Christians involve themselves in their own contexts in solidarity with the poor and the marginalized. If the response to modernity had been to reject the world and to establish immanent truths with the help of reason and philosophy, Gutiérrez provides continuity to Bonhoeffer's theological commitment by assuming that at the root of a Christian response to modernity is the search for a life in Christ that is lived 'irreligiously' by expressing solidarity with others.[99] For Bonhoeffer, to practise religion was to assume the life of the weak and suffering God of the cross; for Gutiérrez, to practise religion is to assume the politics of the weak and the suffering human beings who represent the face of God.[100] Thus, solidarity with the oppressed presumes a critique to the political establishment that in most cases has failed to protect the poor and where Christians had failed to practise the ethical values of religion within the social spheres of political influence. If initially Gutiérrez could have followed some of the Latin American theologians calling for a socialist-oriented society, his methodological critique of the possibility of a single political model and a continuous solidarity with the poor have made Gutiérrez's forceful assessment of the religious and the political even more important in understanding the involvement of Christians within the contemporary world in a post-Soviet Union and post-9/11 world.[101] In the words of Gutiérrez:

> We shall not have our great leap forward, into a whole new theological perspective, until the marginalized and exploited have begun to become the artisans of their own liberation – until their voice makes itself heard directly, without mediation, without interpreters – until they themselves take account, in the light of their own values, of their own experience of the Lord in their efforts to liberate themselves. We shall not have our quantum theological leap until the oppressed themselves

theologize, until 'the others' themselves personally reflect on their hope of a total liberation in Christ. For they are the bearers of this hope for all humanity.[102]

The conclusion is simple: the sole practice and advancement of theology depends on the right relation between religion and politics; thus, the theological project is to be realized as a second act of solidarity rather than as the only possible intellectual response to human solidarity – and therefore becoming a selfish individual act. Thus, 'in searching for this meaning, the theologian knows that, as Clodovis Boff says, everything is politics but politics is not everything'.[103]

2

Enrique Dussel

Dussel, an Argentinean and a descendant of a German family that immigrated to Argentina, has been one of the most prolific thinkers of Latin America. If Gutiérrez is better known among English-speaking circles, Dussel has had an enormous intellectual impact in particular areas of Latin American Christian practice and scholarship, such as philosophy, ethics, history and economics. He has been called the 'father of Latin American philosophy' due to his re-elaboration of philosophical paradigms, culturally constructed but accessible to a universal philosophical discourse of post-colonialism and the historical materialism of an engaging material economics.[104] He later became the spokesman of a new Latin American movement known as liberation philosophy and worked on wider issues of the politics of liberation within the contemporary world.[105] His latest work has criticized post-modernity because of its lack of a future project and he has forwarded the concept of trans-modernity arguing that in this utopia the colonially suppressed sides of culture would come together.[106] While challenging the failure of socialist political systems in Eastern Europe Dussel has also criticized those who have discarded Marx and he has focused once again on the theological and the liturgical in Marx's work.[107]

The Thinker and the Exile

Dussel was born in Mendoza, Argentina in 1934, a descendant of a German Lutheran and a socialist, Johannes Kaspar Dussel, his great grandfather. J. K. Dussel was a poor carpenter and in 1870 arrived in Buenos Aires, escaping poverty and persecution, raising a family and dying in Argentina.[108] Enrique Dussel studied philosophy in Mendoza completing his undergraduate degree in 1957 at the Universidad Nacional del Cuyo. He continued his philosophical studies in Europe and he completed a doctorate in philosophy at the Universidad Central of Madrid in 1959. Further postgraduate studies included a licentiate in religious sciences at the Catholic Institute of Paris in 1965 and another doctorate in history at La Sorbonne, Paris in 1967.[109] In his academic career he has been Professor of Ethics at the Universidad Nacional de Resistencia (Chaco, Argentina 1966–68), Professor of the Instituto Pastoral of CELAM (Quito, Ecuador, 1967–73), and Professor of Ethics at the Universidad Nacional de Cuyo (Mendoza, Argentina). Due to political circumstances in Argentina, in 1975 he left for exile in Mexico, where he eventually took Mexican nationality while he was Professor of Church History at ITES (Mexico, DF, 1975–85), Professor of Philosophy at the Universidad Autónoma Metropolitana/Iztapalapa (1975–) and Professor of Ethics and Philosophy at the Universidad Nacional Autónoma de México (UNAM, 1976–).

Dussel is one of the few Latin American theologians of the first generation who did not work as a parish priest or as a theologian and because of that his contribution has been even greater within wider academic and political circles.[110] He influenced others by a wide-raging reinterpretation of methodological paradigms that reinvented the understanding of the role and objectives of an ethical and political project for Latin America at a time when the military regimes aligned themselves with capitalist policies.[111] The military regimes used a common doctrine of the national security state in order to prevent the influence of communism and in order to implement their policies the Argentinean government, for example, violated human rights on a massive scale. The first official reports regarding forced disappearance in Argentina by the Comisión Nacional sobre la Desaparición de Personas (National Commission of

Disappeared Persons, CONADEP), established by President Raúl Alfonsín, suggested that there were 9,000 documented cases of forced disappearances while the human rights organizations have pointed out over the years to 30,000 cases.[112]

Dussel recognized that his intellectual project about the suffering of Latin America started 30 years ago when he had a conversation with the philosopher Emmanuel Levinas. Dussel asked Levinas why he thought only about the Jews and did not think about the suffering of the indigenous peoples and the Black populations of Latin America. Levinas looked at him and said: 'That is for you to think about.'[113] However, his intellectual project brought him under suspicion by the right-wing paramilitary groups in Argentina and on the 2 October 1973 a large bomb destroyed part of his home.[114]

On 20 June 1973 Juan Domingo Perón and his new wife María Estela Martínez de Perón had returned to Argentina after 18 years of exile and subsequently on 23 September 1973 Perón was elected president of Argentina, but he failed to reach an understanding with the trade unions and the business organizations. The situation in Argentina became very violent after a full economic crisis unfolded. Inflation rocketed and by 1974 the European Common Market had already closed down meat imports from Argentina. However, the main political crisis took place within the movement that followed Perón (*peronistas*) in which more revolutionary factions were not happy with economic practices and the alliance of Isabel Perón with private businesses that took place after Perón's death in July 1974. Within 1975 there was a full economic crisis and the displaced left-wing groups within the followers of Perón – the revolutionary wing of the Peronist Party *Montoneros* and the Marxist *Ejército Revolucionario del Pueblo* (ERP) – continued the armed struggle through attacks on military barracks, kidnappings of well-to-do people and assassinations. In response to those events the right-wing military groups, organized through the *Alianza Argentina Anti-Comunista* (AAA), targeted opponents, particularly those supporters of the left-wing organizations who, because of their professional positions, didn't go into hiding, for example, teachers, lawyers, university professors, medical doctors and middle-class professionals. The Minister for Social Welfare, José López Rega, had organized the AAA as a neo-fascist group in order to cleanse the Peronist Party of Marxist elements and their supporters.

Given the context of that time, it is plausible to suggest that Dussel would have been killed if he hadn't sought refuge in Mexico. Mexico offered shelter to highly qualified professionals and intellectuals escaping the military regimes of the Southern Cone as well as to the leaders of the ERP who left Argentina after the death of the ERP leader Roberto Santucho in July 1976. Argentinean pastoral agents suffered heavy casualties due to political persecution while the Argentinean bishops did not speak openly about the gross human rights violations by the military junta and its leader Jorge Videla, who became president of Argentina in March 1976.[115]

The History of Christianity

Dussel's better-known works *History and the Theology of Liberation* and *Ethics and the Theology of Liberation* came out as series of lectures delivered to an audience comprised of those involved in the process of liberation of Latin America in the 1970s.[116] The lectures written for *History and the Theology of Liberation* were delivered orally at the Latin American Pastoral Institute in Quito and the Liturgical Institute in Medellín and finally written for delivery in Buenos Aires in 1971. On the following year Dussel delivered another series of lectures that were collected into the book *Ethics and the Theology of Liberation*. Dussel stressed the importance of that oral delivery and the interaction with an audience as a methodological tool of spoken discourse recognizing that written texts can never convey the whole depth of spoken lectures: 'They are words *spoken* to people, not words *typed* in the privacy of a comfortable study. They are spoken discourse, not textbook material.'[117]

Dussel used history in order to set the context for a liberating project that included the liberation from economic structures *ad intra* as well as the liberation from a Christian situation of empire symbolized by the historical development of Christianity from a persecuted religion to a colonizing system of Christendom. The 'Christendom of the Indies' as spoken by the Bishop of Lima Toribio de Mogrovejo at the Third Council of Lima (1582–83), remained for centuries in the periphery while the European Christendom remained at the centre. However, for Dussel there were signs of a Latin American cultural identity suppressed and forgotten by the centre. The aim of a historical reconstruction of that Latin American history, an academic project undertaken by Dussel, was to rediscover a Latin American Christian identity that in his words would discover 'theologically, philosophically, and historically – who we are as Latin American Christians'.[118]

Dussel gave central importance to the Christian communities within a process of renewal in a post-Christendom era and challenged those who were embracing single political options as social embodiments of the gospel message. If he challenged the Christians for Socialism, a radical movement of Catholic priests and lay Catholics in the early 1970s, he also challenged the possibility that the Christian Democratic Parties, either European or Latin American, could embody all gospel values. For Dussel, 'the problem is that while Christianity can criticize a political system, it can never be identified with any one political system. When it is, we end up with some version of Christendom and all the ambiguity it entails'.[119] Nevertheless, Dussel recognized that those examples of Christendom expressed as political parties did not rule out the possibility that Christians could be involved in helping establishing certain forms of socialism in Latin America. Indeed, in 1971 the Peruvian bishops had in their Synod opted for socialism by stating that 'Christians ought to opt for socialism. We do not mean a bureaucratic, totalitarian, or atheist socialism; we mean a socialism that is both humanistic and Christian.'[120]

Within a Latin American history of dependence there were different political models that tried to correct social injustice by using particular shades of international dependency theory. As outlined by the Latin American bishops in Medellín, those political models used for their analysis the so-called 'developmental theory of dependence' of the 1960s.[121] Within those political models history became a process of analysis of human and social relations that challenged the principles of creation in which the earth and the economic resources belong to all. It is in this sense that Dussel's ethical model of social justice and international dependency becomes a whole model of action and life in that he systematizes a material reading of complex relations using his wide knowledge of history, philosophy, economics and ultimately of Marxian writings.[122]

The Ethics of Society

Dussel has summarized his vision of social ethics in *Ethics and Community*.[123] In the first part of the book he outlined major presuppositions of that area of critical reflection within liberation theology and in the second part of the book he outlined particular areas of enquiry that concern ethics and community. The book, while summarizing his main ideas and presuppositions concerning social ethics, was prepared in order to facilitate reflection by Christian communities that were already involved in practical social ethics. Therefore he requested those listening to him or reading the book to chose a piece of a newspaper clipping in order to reflect on a particular act of daily or communal sociability. Thus, for Dussel, 'theology is a reflection on daily, current, concretely Christian praxis'.[124] After reading that newspaper clipping Dussel proposed to those listening to him to find a biblical passage related to that piece of news, a process that could ultimately highlight the relation of Scripture to real life while providing members of a Christian community with a concrete reflection on social morality and ethics.

Social morality understood in the social sciences and as followed by Dussel refers to the social norms that are accepted by a group of people, so that in some cases Christian morality would equate social morality but in other cases it could be agreed that an act could be moral but not ethical. Therefore, for Dussel, ethics refers to 'the future order of liberation, the demands of justice with respect to the poor, the oppressed, and their project . . . of salvation'.[125] Further, for Dussel, society refers to individual relations within a social morality of domination and sin while community embraces the just relation between face-to-face relationships by people through justice. Thus, the praxis of liberation requires the acceptance that the world produces systems of sin that are reinforced by the desires of the flesh and that have mechanisms that justify a tranquil conscience and a principle of universality that tends to accept social morality as good and ethical. In turn, the moral conscience of a society is shaped by a reinforcement of practices that are moral and therefore perceived as just – private poverty or the prohibition to steal. However, social practices that prevent a worker from having enough to feed his family become solely moral but unethical within what Dussel calls 'the Jerusalem principle'. The same social reality remains moral and ethical within a system that uses what Dussel calls 'the Babylonian principle' of social exclusion, which within the 'Jerusalem principle' is challenged as an ethical principle always guided by the biblical text.

Social morality in a conservative and traditional Christianity, according to Dussel, dictates the values of a morally ordained divine order, which does not change, even when in reality the poor and the marginalized are not included within that moral order, while those who sustain the structures of sinful exclusion assure others that the socio-political and economic system cannot be changed and it is morally acceptable because it comes from God. A close reading of the biblical text, that is, the preference for the poor by God in the biblical text and the preference for the poor by Jesus of Nazareth within the New Testament, challenged that established view of social order and deemed the given-cohesive stratified social order as unethical and immoral.

However, within those 'given' parameters of social ethics there is the possibility of a gospel challenge towards the institutionalized welfare and charity that perceives the poor as unable to function, dependent and ultimately lazy. The role of the Christian and, by extension and collateral association, of the Church, is to be able to discern social injustice, unethical paradigms and to challenge the possibility of remaining within a social morality to the exclusion of a social ethics. Indeed, it is the mandate of all Christians to look after the poor and the marginalized in the first place, regardless of the possibility of an unjust social morality. Further, Christians are to engage their reflections and their actions with the poor at the centre.

Dussel's work remains within the more theoretical contributions within liberation theology because he connects and builds up processes of thought combining Scripture and tradition. His contribution has that force of engagement with European thought and with European theology, while others, for example Gutiérrez, provide the force of the pastoral engagement with the poor and the marginalized. Thus, Dussel's development of a liberating engagement provides particularities of action within a philosophical reflection on thought, while Gutiérrez perceives that liberating process through the action of engagement and learning from the poor and the marginalized in context.

Thus, the characteristics of a new Latin American way of thinking were described by Dussel as creative, historical, concrete, committed, asystematic, prophetic and anguished.[126] *Creative* because it cannot be imitative, otherwise it ceases to be thought; this characteristic excludes the possibility of copying other systems of thought as in the case of a Marxist who applies the ideas of a modernist philosopher, Karl Marx, in order to assess all reality around him. However, while the projection of Marx's ideas provides the possibility of assessing reality, his historical context of modernity within a particular European modernity responded to a particular context requiring action within the nineteenth century.[127]

For Dussel, *historical* thought requires an 'ontological horizon of comprehension' where ideas come out of Latin American works that reflect the context of the poor and the marginalized, such as the Argentinean classic *Martin Fierro*. Latin American thought also requires a form of *concrete* thought that is able to bridge the foundational ideas and Christian praxis, thus providing a sobering moment of self-assertion: thought and action take place within a climate of oppression. *Committed* thought in turn requires a very difficult mode of existence, particularly for intellectuals and thinkers: a commitment to action from thought and an awareness of concrete realities around us. This is difficult because those who treasure a mode of existence in which they think and therefore in which they exist forget and eventually are unable to connect with the realities outside their thought, in this case, those of the poor and the marginalized. Thus, pointing to Sartre, Dussel provides a sobering warning for all those working in areas of life that create thought and ideas:

> Thinkers who uproot themselves from the praxis that engages their thinking are also totally uprooted, without being aware of it, from their existence. They begin to be sophists, mere academicians; they adopt less risky but also less inciting attitudes; they fail to fulfil their historical function.[128]

Further, *asystematic* thought requires rejecting a given structure because structures impede the acceptance of those areas of knowledge and reality that we cannot understand but that remain open to the possibility of further knowledge. Thus, for Dussel 'to systematize is to build a scaffolding that impedes the growth of life. But leaving the question open is never easy.'[129] Thought can be left open as to constitute *prophetic* thought that speaks about where we are going but with the reality of the past as constituent of the present, rather than a utopian future that never comes, and it has nothing to do with the past and therefore with the present. *Anguished* thought arises out of situations in which people do not know where they are going and the task of Christians is to show the way forward, not to the left or to the right but forward through the centre, not through a centrist position towards life but through a position forward.

The result of such heading forward through the centre is that neither Marxists nor traditionalists would find a way to understand and support such Christian thought and action. Marxists would not like that kind of Latin American thought because it would not reflect a particular foreign import to Latin America and it would not relate to a particular type of revolution. Traditionalists would not like this prophetic thought either because they would see it as not following the orderly social structures already 'given' by God, nation and society.

Dussel's criticism of Moltmann, Metz and other European theologians, who have labelled themselves as political, is that they provide a centrality for a European self that exists in experience and in society however, that lives in hope for the future, for that kingdom of God that is already here but not yet. That European self does not provide a third place to be. That third place relates to a theological 'I' who lives in the present and awaits the future but in the meantime is involved in a full theological critique from within of economics, politics and all other systems and structures that socially locate the poor at the periphery, not at the centre where those with money, commodities and privileges are located. Within European theology the self and the Christian self are separated from the world outside and not within the world. For within Dussel's periphery to be poor is a blessing because the poor have already experienced some realities of the kingdom and from those realities they challenge the centre and the world that does not recognize their blindness, the world that cannot and doesn't want to change. Therefore, the periphery acts in an ongoing class struggle not because it recognizes human injustice arising from a problem of classes but because the theologian of the periphery recognizes that all social injustice arises out of sin, individual, social and structural sin, to be redeemed by God who marches and remains within the periphery of society and within the realities of the poor and the marginalized.

For Dussel, action and thought go together and it is not action that maintains thought but the other way around, so that it is possible to suggest that the philosophy of liberation permeates the pre-class struggle and the active life of the periphery in relation to the kingdom of God. For philosophy remains a tool in order to analyse and recognize the 'Other' in relation to a totality while theology remains the tool to recognize God's revelation within a periphery in which a new and ongoing theological thinking remains as the activator of those who live and reside with the God of the periphery.

A Philosophy of Liberation

Dussel's system of social and intellectual engagement has a complexity that remains at times difficult to assess. For Gutiérrez, theology arises out of a biblical paradigm in which God reveals himself to the poor and in turn the poor teach others about the realities of the kingdom. Dussel gives more centrality to the self; however, this is a peripheral self as part of a social reality that creates a theology closely related to a theodicy in which the knowledge of self leads to the knowledge of God and of others that like all those who live in the periphery are marginalized and oppressed.

Philosophy does not become a Latin American project of liberation because there is an intellectual occasional project of rethinking the world. Philosophy becomes a liberating project when the philosopher is in union with a historical subject so that 'concrete articulation from within a people is a *conditio sine qua non* for the philosophizing of liberation' and the actualization of that project can mean for the philosopher 'losing one's freedom in prison, enduring the pain of torture, losing a professorship at a university, and perhaps being killed, given the situation in Latin America'.[130] However, the oppression of the philosopher because of his life of liberation is also connected with an exclusion of non-European philosophies, peripheral to the centrality of European philosophy. Dussel concluded his work on the philosophy of liberation with the following statement: 'Respect for the other's situation begins with respect for the other's philosophical discourse.'[131]

In his 1992 Frankfurt lectures Dussel returned to the land where Hegel had advocated the erasing of African history due to the fact that, according to him, only cultures of the East had any history and therefore any importance for the world. Dussel reiterated the role of the philosopher of history as the one who could engage with other histories, other lives and other thoughts and he marked the entry of Latin American philosophy within a challenge to modernity associated with colonialism, ignorance and Eurocentrism.[132] The return of Dussel to Germany, being a descendant of German immigrants, also marked his own return to wider discussions of otherness in Europe and to the problems that such concept and practice of exclusion had created for other people, other human beings with rights and obligations attached by nature to any human being, regardless of their race, class, religion or social status. Thus, following the personal challenge that Levinas posed to Dussel and his writings on philosophy Dussel returned to a wider problem of the global and the challenges of modernity. Within those challenges, and always using a multi-disciplinary approach, Dussel has raised questions about the possible replacement of post-modernity by the notion of 'trans-modernity', a utopian vision of multiculturality.[133]

For Dussel, post-modernism has two central limitations: (1) it is a Eurocentric critique of an included negation, and (2) it cannot include those aspects of culture already excluded by a European modernity. Therefore post-modernity as a movement within ideas fails because it is not radical enough – it does not reconstruct the possibility of many worlds instead of one single European world created by the philosophers of modernity and a world totally centred and enacted within Europe and its European paradigms of self-representation.

It must be remembered that within the world-systems theory Europe has been perceived as central to the world around the conquest of the Americas in 1492 and after.[134] Dussel's previous work has challenged that Eurocentric view by suggesting that before the encounter ancient civilizations existed in Latin America and were self-contained, not needing the European route for commerce.[135] Instead, European powers needed the opening of China and India, again self-contained civilizations, in order to trade and increase the flow of goods, particularly spices, precious commodities within European markets. Thus, for Dussel Europe only achieved global importance much later with the industrial revolution and with the openings of Japan, China, India and Africa.

Within those parameters of colonial exclusion of cultural paradigms outside Europe modernity as a response to colonial processes remained a European phenomenon, once again self-centred to the exclusion of philosophical, ethical and religious systems that existed within ancient civilizations outside Europe. Post-modernity, as a reaction to modernity, challenged the stand of the modern self but could not bring back those excluded elements, cultural elements not based or found in European thought, society and cultural paradigms. Therefore, post-modernity did not go far enough and Dussel's theological conclusion is that there is a new utopia outside post-modernity that challenges cultural exclusions and that creates in turn a new utopia, that of trans-modernity, in which the new creation does not emerge from the old (modernity, post-modernity) but from nothing, from a model to be created, from an inclusive trans-national system in which all components have importance and in which European theological and philosophical systems are not at the centre but remain part of a new world system. Indeed, in his latest lectures Dussel has surprised North American audiences by arguing that such a new world system, trans-modernity, is in turn created from nothing – *ex nihilo*.

The utopian dream of Dussel for the twenty-first century with the *ex-nihilo* proviso is consistent with his ongoing use of Marxist analysis as a tool that remains foundational in order to understand the theologians of liberation of the first generation.[136] Therefore, in re-reading the theological and the liturgical in Marx, Dussel has been consistent with his use of a historical reading of ecclesial and non-ecclesial documents using the tools of Marxist analysis.[137] From that point of view, Dussel has not negated the ongoing necessity of using Marxist analysis and the debt that liberation theology owes to Marx's reading of history, regardless of whether Marxism remains fashionable or not. It is Marx's historical analysis that challenges the possibility of any system being an actualization of the human and divine utopia of the just society. Indeed, Christendom as a term of an oppressive type of Christianity of a Eurocentric variety came out of an analysis of Christianity as a form of trans-cultural capitalism that left out all traces of the option by God for the poor and the marginalized in history (see the chapter on Pablo Richard in this volume).

Dussel has spent many years reading and re-reading the work of Marx since he started his own seminar on the writings of Marx in 1977 at the Universidad Nacional Autónoma of Mexico (UNAM). Within that seminar Dussel and a team of students, divided into small groups, dedicated years of study trying to analyse the writings of Marx as a totality, with an archaeological interest in finding out if there were manuscripts that had not been published, particularly those that were still located in libraries of Germany. Dussel himself edited and published some manuscripts such as a draft of *Capital*, work that went through four drafts from 1857 to 1880.[138] Since his three major works on Marx have been published Dussel has reminded readers and scholars of Marx that if one does not use the German originals there is the need for caution regarding the semantic use of particular words, such as 'money', 'surplus' or even 'capital'. However, in those works by Dussel the connections with the individualism and the humanism of Hegel become apparent, as well as his critique of Althusser's commentaries that depart from Marx, by the fact that Althusser deals with the fragmented Marx rather than with the Marx *in toto*. For Dussel, the second century of Marx has just begun because if one leaves the Soviet dogmatism and goes back to Marx himself issues of hunger, surplus and greed have not been resolved and therefore while there is still hunger there is still a need for a revolution, be it social, ethical or political. Thus, he wrote: 'It is a question, then, of a complete rereading of Marx, with new eyes: as a Latin American, from the growing poverty of the peripheral world, the underdeveloped and exploited of capitalism at the end of the twentieth century. Marx, in the periphery, today, more pertinent than in the England of the mid-nineteenth century.'[139]

Within all those new insights into history, ethics, philosophy and the work of Marx, Dussel has used his seminal model of centre/periphery. The same model appears in his new and latest venture of trans-modernity and it reflects a significant and consistent theoretical framework that he has used throughout his writings and his critiques of European historiography, philosophy, ethics and economic theory. Due to his many and varied academic appointments Dussel has remained within a small circle of liberation theologians who have bridged the cloisters of theology into theoretical discussions taken by the other disciplines and other worlds. As a result, Dussel together with Gutiérrez and Boff remain members of the first generation that have transcended global socio-political changes over the past 40 years.

3

José Míguez Bonino

During 2004 José Míguez Bonino celebrated his eightieth birthday and during that same year a volume of essays in his honour was published in Argentina by the Instituto Universitario ISEDET.[140] The essays outlined ideas and thoughts related to Míguez's work over a period of 50 years as a teacher of several generations of Christians, activists and pastoral agents. Among the contributors, Elsa Tamez and other theologians who were influenced by José Míguez Bonino provided a three-part theological expansion of his thought and work under the following themes: (1) globalization and ecumenism, (2) theology and context and (3) ethics and history. These themes summarize the pastoral and theological concerns of José Míguez Bonino, Argentinean, theologian, Methodist and, foremost, a teacher.

If Dussel delivered most of his books as lectures where he could get feedback and return to the text, Míguez Bonino preferred to test his own ideas and theological understandings within the milieu of group work, that is small groups that after a short exposition on ideas developed their own conversations focusing on their contextual experience and later reporting their main contributions to the larger group. I would argue that such modus vivendi made Míguez Bonino into a teacher of liberation rather than a lecturer or a writer. Within that sustained group work he made possible the encounter and dialogue between Christians of different traditions and ways of life, and he also stressed the dialogue between Christians and atheists, and within those atheists with Marxists, all within a context in which Míguez Bonino continued teaching critically a pastoral theology of liberation, very much in tune with Gutiérrez's academic and pastoral work.

It is very striking that within his major works he focuses more on the experience of groups that interact with a wider social and political society rather than small parish communities asking questions about practical and localized implications of the gospel for their daily lives and their Christian pilgrimage. Thus, when considering the major breakthroughs in Christian commitment to liberation within Latin America, Míguez Bonino stressed the central role played by the movement Christians for Socialism and he almost identified that movement with the pastoral guidelines set by the Latin American bishops in Medellín (1968).[141]

Born in Rosario de Santa Fe (Argentina) in 1924, he studied at the Evangelical School of Theology in Buenos Aires (1943–48) and later at the Candlier School of Theology (Atlanta, USA) and at the Union Theological Seminary of New York (1958–60). José Míguez Bonino has been internationally recognized by the translation of his work to other languages and by the conferring of an honorary doctorate from the Free University of Amsterdam in 1980. A Methodist, Míguez Bonino has been involved in the pastoral life of the Methodist Church in Argentina while fulfilling academic duties as Professor of Dogmatic Theology at the Evangelical School of Theology in Buenos Aires, serving as president of that theological institution (1961–70) and as director of postgraduate studies at the Instituto Superior Evangélico de Estudios Teológicos in Buenos Aires. Míguez Bonino has been visiting professor at the Union Theological Seminary of New York (1967–68), at Selly Oak College (Birmingham, England, 1975), at the Seminario Bíblico Latinoamericano of San José (Costa Rica, 1977) and at the Protestant School of Theology of the University of Strasbourg (France, 1980–81).

Within one of his main interests, ecumenism, he had the privilege of being the only Protestant Latin American observer at the Second Vatican Council, executive secretary of the Asociación Sudamericana de Instituciones Teológicas (1970–76), and delegate to the World Council of Churches' conferences in New Delhi (1961), Uppsala (1968) and Nairobi (1975) as well as delegate to the faith and constitution meetings of the World Council of Churches at Lund (1952), Leuven (1971) and Ghana (1974). He served as member of the World Council of Churches' commission on faith and constitution (1961–77) and as member of its central committee (1968–75) being elected member of the World Council of Churches' Presidium in 1975.

Theological Context

The social and political context of his early work was the Cold War that was the international tension and distension between the United States and the Soviet Union and their spheres of influence. Within that distension the Latin American armies had been allied with the United States and a significant number of Latin American army officers had been trained at the military academy for Latin America, the School of the Americas located in Panama and with headquarters at Fort Benning, Georgia.[142]

However, despite those efforts to align Latin Americans with the political values of the United States, there were groups of social activists in Argentina that sided with a Marxist view and analysis of society, some of them armed groups that became part of the 'subversive' threat to Argentinean society. Those groups were encouraged by the Cuban Revolution, the example of the Argentinean medical doctor Ernesto 'Ché' Guevara and the Colombian priest Camilo Torres, who left his traditional pastoral ministry in order to fight alongside the Colombian guerrillas – both of them activists killed as guerrilla fighters.[143] The majority of Argentina's guerrillas were part of the extreme left of the *peronistas* and many of them received training in Cuba.[144] Because of the Catholic base of Argentinean society, most of those groups were formed by utopian youth who had been part of youth Christian movements but had decided that the only viable way of changing Argentinean society was a guerrilla-type armed struggle. In the case of the guerrilla group

Montoneros, for example, the group declared itself Marxist and Christian, and all guerrilla organizations found support in progressive Catholic organizations sustained by the social doctrine of the Church and the conclusions of the 1968 General Meeting of Latin American bishops in Medellín (Colombia), 1968.[145] Within those organizations there was also a constant dialogue about the possibility and impossibility of violence and revolution within the Latin American context with the progressive Argentinean movement 'Priests of the Third World'.

Twentieth-century Argentinean politics was dominated by the figure of Juan Domingo Perón, and the effort by his followers, mostly working-class based, to exclude the middle classes from the ongoing running of the nation. However, it is also possible to argue that Argentinean politics were dominated by the dichotomy Peronist/Anti-Peronist with the trade unions forming the social base for the Peronist movement (*sindicalismo peronista*) and the Argentinean Armed Forces pushing for an anti-peronism narrative for political action.[146] That political and social dichotomy, suppressed for years, came back to the political arena with the return to Argentina of Perón and his new wife María Estela Martínez de Perón (20 June 1973) after 18 years of exile. Subsequently, on 23 September 1973 Perón was elected president of Argentina but he failed to reach an understanding with the trade unions and the business organizations. The situation in Argentina became very violent after a full economic crisis unfolded. Inflation rocketed and by 1974 the European Common Market closed down meat imports from Argentina.

Moreover, the main political crisis took place within the movement that followed Perón (*peronistas*) in which some revolutionary factions were not happy with his economic practices and the subsequent alliance of Isabel Perón with private businesses that took place after Perón's death in July 1974. Within 1975 there was a full economic crisis and the displaced left-wing groups among the followers of Perón – the revolutionary wing of the Peronist Party *Montoneros* and the Marxist *Ejército Revolucionario del Pueblo* (ERP) – continued the armed struggle with attacks on military barracks, kidnappings of well-to-do people and assassinations. In response to those events, the right-wing military groups organized by the *Alianza Argentina Anti-Comunista* (AAA) targeted opponents, particularly those supporters of the left-wing organizations that, because of their positions, didn't go into hiding, for example, teachers, lawyers, university professors, medical doctors and middle-class professionals. The Minister for Social Welfare, José López Rega, had organized the AAA as a neo-fascist group in order to cleanse the Peronist Party of Marxist elements and their supporters and restore a peaceful state of affairs to Argentina.

As a result of the political chaos and political violence, and encouraged by the experience of the Chilean military, the Argentinean Armed Forces deposed Isabel Perón and took over political power. Argentinean pastoral agents suffered heavy casualties due to sustained political persecution of 'subversives', while the Argentinean bishops did not speak openly about the gross human rights violations by the military junta led by Jorge Videla, who became president of Argentina in March 1976.[147] Other civil organizations such as the mothers of the disappeared (Madres de la Plaza de Mayo) took a public stand against human rights violations and every Thursday they paraded in silence at the May Square requesting information about their loved ones who had been arrested, tortured and made to disappear by the repressive state apparatus.[148] The military regime supported an anti-communist pro-American crusade throughout Latin America and remained in power until the war for the Malvinas/Falkland Islands challenged military authority and their capabilities of leading the Argentinean nation in the future.[149] On 30 October 1983 the Radical Party won 51.75 per cent of the total vote and on 10 December Raúl Alfonsín became the newly democratically elected president of Argentina.[150]

Theological Proposals

Míguez Bonino was aware that by the mid-1970s many books on liberation theology had already been written and that the conclusions of the Latin American meeting of Latin American bishops had been either deemed as a unique moment of Christian history or had been ignored by those who decided that Marxist-oriented bishops had lost their way. Therefore, in a more systematic but concise manner he assessed the new developments in Latin American theology through his seminal work *Revolutionary Theology Comes of Age.*[151]

Míguez Bonino proposes the following actualizations of twentieth-century theology as moves forward, as unique developments and as beacons of hope for Christian practice and Christian life. First of all the context of theology has evolved from the study of religion or metaphysics. Second, there has been a closer alliance between the study of biblical research and human experience. Third, the realm of history has mediated that biblical research and human experience. Fourth, theology has used a more political language through which experience, action and history have become prime movers of an ongoing theological reflection. Further, those theological developments were radicalized by Latin American theologians who asked questions about the social, political and religious realities of a particular context – Latin America.[152]

Christians and Marxists

One of his main concerns following from that context and its related theological reflection, not an intellectual but a practical concern, was the work that Christians and Marxists were pursuing within the Latin America of the early 1970s. Indeed, he was present in Santiago, Chile during the international meeting on trade and commerce of those nations, considered part of the Third World, that were represented by the United Nations agency UNCTAD. In 1972 the international meeting of the

UNCTAD took place in Santiago, at a purposely built conference centre in Alameda Avenue, a meeting that was hosted by the socialist government of Salvador Allende.[153]

However, Míguez Bonino was not part of the trade delegation sent by the Argentinean government but he was attending an international meeting of the movement Christians for Socialism that was taking place on the same days in Santiago, without the blessings of the then Archbishop of Santiago, Cardinal Raúl Silva Henríquez.[154] Míguez Bonino saw hope in those priests, nuns and pastoral agents who were challenging the traditional view of the gospel and who were asking questions about social realities of poverty, violence and oppression, without knowing that a year later Chile was going to be dominated by the military, while another Argentinean military coup was going to follow a couple of years later.

Míguez Bonino could have been accused of leaning towards Marxism but he wasn't. He lived the action by Christians and Marxists at that particular time and thought that it had made a difference to the ongoing dialogue and understanding of Christians and Marxists within European circles. If within Europe Christianity and Marxism were understood as two different systems of thought, what united them within the Latin American experience was their common action for the poor and the marginalized that took precedence over systems of thought and intellectual debates about ontology or even theodicy. Despite further questioning of those contextual alliances Míguez Bonino stated clearly in the context of the 1974 London lectures in contemporary Christianity: 'The God of the covenant has himself designed a pattern of action which such words as justice, righteousness, the protection of the poor, active love, help us to discern.'[155]

Nevertheless, within the Latin American context in which Míguez Bonino was operating many Christians considered themselves Marxists and vice-versa. For Míguez Bonino there was a 'strategic alliance' that responded to a common concern and a common project: the social and political challenges that arose out of a situation of poverty, oppression and marginalization of a larger part of the Latin American population and that in the case of Argentina and Chile had given way to socialist utopias led by Salvador Allende and by Juan Domingo and Evita Perón within their base among the Argentinean workers. In the Argentinean case Míguez Bonino allied himself with the Christian position of the minority as the Argentinean bishops were much more conservative and traditional than those in Chile.[156]

For Míguez Bonino there could not be a person who could embrace a hybrid identity as a 'Christian-Marxist' or a 'Marxist-Christian'; however, there could be a contextual position in which a Christian could follow the Marxism paradigm in order to extend his own analysis of a social situation of injustice or oppression. On the other hand, there could be a Marxist who, having been brought up as a Christian or realizing the challenging demands of 'love of neighbour', could also find it useful and appropriate to follow those narrow parameters of Christian interpretation in order to achieve the same goal: the defence of the poor and the marginalized and the advent of a more just society. Four areas of common understanding did exist and were outlined by Míguez Bonino as follows:

(i) Knowledge is not abstract but an engagement with concrete social realities,
(ii) There is a common shared ethos of human solidarity,
(iii) There is a need for a historical mediation of any humanist intention, and,
(iv) The ultimate horizons of life, as understood by Christians and Marxists, are radically different.[157]

The 'strategic alliance' provided a contextual unity in action and within some limited theoretical understanding but separated Christians and Marxists when the aims of such alliance were achieved. At the end of the road Marxists wanted to achieve a socialist society through revolution with a base on the workers, while Christians wanted to achieve the realization of the kingdom of God with a base on the Christian communities.

Both Marxists and Christians sustained a utopian dream by the fact that neither the revolution [in Marx's understanding] nor the kingdom was to be solely achieved within a particular moment in human history.[158] If a Marxist had a structural way of perceiving the world and of reading history, a Christian had a critical way of reading God's intervention in the world called faith, which, following Gutiérrez, had to be critical and engaged with the realities of underdevelopment, oppression and sin.[159]

For Míguez Bonino this 'strategic alliance' serves the Church well because at the centre of his personal option is the moulding of a Church that has the poor at the centre and that is less involved in disappointing academic (and European) theological debates but comes out of a given individualism in order to be closer to the poor, thus to Jesus Christ, and through other groups and communities that are also looking after and learning from the poor.

His critical approach to Marxism and Marxist activists did not arise out of a critique or distrust of a 'strategic alliance' but from the fact that Míguez Bonino criticized the lack of power control within Marxist-oriented groups, usually manifested in a personality cult or the uncritical behaviour in politics due to a total allegiance to a person, a party or a system.[160] However, Míguez Bonino also recognized that the Marxist is a person fully given to a way of life, a 'militant', who gives it all and sees the selfish individual comforts and aspirations of life as secondary. Christians and Marxists do not share a common spirituality but both have one common call, understood by Marxists as 'militancy'.

For the Christian, that militancy is expressed as the revolutionary following of Jesus, symbolized by the actualization of faith, love and hope within a person's life and within the daily work in order to construct a more just society for all. For many, that realization becomes an act of self-immolation in joy, as a person gives his life and comforts so that others may have life too.[161] For the Marxist, the call to join the struggle and a militant struggle leads to the same state of self-immolation that one can see in Antonio Gramsci, dying slowly but with a purpose in one of Mussolini's jails, or the life of Ernesto 'Ché' Guevara, who left his sheltered existence and the possibility of a brilliant medical career in order to join others throughout Latin America and Africa who were struggling for a more just society.[162] Míguez Bonino prefers to call such 'militancy' a Christian spirituality because of the joy attached to a Christian life, so that 'Christian faith becomes an invitation under the conditions of responsible, joyful solidary militancy'.[163]

Christians and Atheists

Míguez Bonino engaged himself not only with groups of Marxists but also with others who didn't believe in the existence of God (atheists). In the context of a church hall attached to a Protestant congregation in Buenos Aires he gathered a group of Christians and atheists in order to open an ongoing human dialogue about the Christian faith within the context of Argentina. The format of the meeting followed Míguez Bonino's preferred style of teaching: he gave a short presentation, immediately after the participants formed small discussion groups and after the meeting he put together the initial presentation and the common thoughts shared during the meeting in a small publication available for further discussion.[164]

Míguez Bonino's exposition starts not from the point of view of asking if there is a God but from the fact that in order to show belief in a God there is the need to reject belief in others. Therefore, the Christian and the atheist have a starting common point of view in their rejection of some gods, rather than in their acceptance of a particular one. Once that initial foundation is laid, Míguez Bonino accepts that faith is a gift and therefore the possibility of believing in God requires more than a human effort. In his words, the free action of God provides the possibility of believing so that 'the Christian is like a beggar who says to another beggar "Let's go together. I know where they will give us bread"'.[165] However, he asserts that most of the further contextual disagreements between Christians and atheists come from a misunderstanding of Christianity, either by the atheists or by Christians themselves.

Those disagreements between Christians and atheists include issues of religion and science, suffering in the world, the wrong-doings of the Christian communities, the separation of religion and politics and the spiritualization of religion with a distorted concept of the goodness of humanity. Míguez Bonino's conception of religion as an expression of belief in community is very clear: human beings become Christians in community so that without an incarnated principle of humanness and human goodness, expressed in solidarity with the world and in community, there is no belief in God, who after all is an incarnate God.

The issue of suffering in the world is not a metaphysical discussion but an expression of humanness, with its frailty and its need for care and compassion. The image of God's Son dying on a cross and his incarnation as a ministry of healing and solidarity with the people of his time brings not further metaphysical or ontological questions but the belief that God exists because his Son became one with us in suffering and death.

The spiritualization of religion provides a further bridge between Christians and atheists, but the ministry of Jesus of Nazareth is not only an example of human [and divine] solidarity with others but also a lead in matters of religion and politics. Therefore, Míguez Bonino rejects the notion that they are separated only because some clerics tend to speak too soon about matters where they don't have proper technical expertise. Despite those bad examples, the immersion of Christ in the world and within the society of his time shows not only the possibility but also the mandate for Christians to get involved in the running of society and in the challenges that the creation of a more just society demands. For Míguez Bonino:

> Politics is the attempt at retrieving the world for people, at seizing power from the irrational, from the high-handedness of an inhuman system, and of then restoring it to its original proposition – to serve the enrichment and fullness of the

human community. And this is a fundamental Christian obligation. You can't be a Christian without accepting it, because you can't be a human being without doing it.[166]

Within those discussions it is possible to see the liberating and social strand that Míguez Bonino brings to discussions that could be totally philosophical and ontological. For him, there is no contradiction between religion and science because Christians as human beings, first and foremost, take part in science research and are as many others interested in knowing more about the world, which after all is the world that God created. God loved the world and so we do as well. However, he is very weary of a Christianity that dwells on too many intellectual arguments or that provides a middle-class isolation where people cannot share their faith and do not have any relation with a material and social world. Míguez Bonino provides a sharp critique of middle-class Argentinean society by asking if they actually live the Christian faith or is it that they believe in God rather than practising their faith. His sociological analysis is both devastating and realistic when he writes: 'They live for themselves, introvertedly, dreaming of their houses, their own vacations, their own privacy. And their religion has the same characteristics. Since they do not share their lives, they do not share their faith.'[167]

Returning to an ongoing dialogue with atheists, issues of human fulfilment come to the core of his engagement with other human beings. The grace of believing in a God or in Jesus Christ presupposes the development of any human potential and the possibility of being human at all times. Thus, there are very good people who do not believe and others who come to believe through two different processes: challenge and consolation. Within the first process, those involved in changing society and making it better come to like and feel part of the process of liberation, individual and social, that Jesus offers in the New Testament, either by his own ministry or by those who became his followers in the early Christian communities. His project of liberation is the final triumph of life over evil and life over

67

death, a theme that is common to all humans, believers of different faiths and non-believers as well. However, other people come to believe through a process of consolation, by realizing that the message, life and actions of Jesus of Nazareth are very clear: evil and wrong do not prevail but they are always embraced and conquered by a divine goodness manifested in the Son of God.

These two processes, these two sides of faith are interrelated so that if an individual comes to believe either because of challenge or consolation, that same person quickly discovers and becomes part of the other side of faith. Many good and honest responses to the challenges of life are found outside Christian responses and for Míguez Bonino they all come from Jesus Christ, who is at the centre of good human responses and remains the source of all goodness, even locating them outside the realm of Christianity.

Míguez Bonino's involvement with society, and particularly non-Christians, has made a different contribution to the history and development of Latin American theology in that most other Latin American theologians assumed that they were challenging and reflecting on the action of Christians within an unjust contemporary society. In doing so they didn't see the possibilities of embracing the challenges of nations that for the most part had a majority of professing Christians but actually minorities of people involved directly in processes of human and societal liberation.

This is understandable because of the violence that those Christians suffered and the development of economic systems of death that alienated basic human values in order to perpetuate social injustice and political oppression. Thus, it is interesting to explore the post-persecution theologizing by Míguez Bonino, who in the past few years has reflected extensively on the processes of military oppression and dictatorship lived by Argentineans through the period of the writing of his seminal theological works.

Contemporary Assessments

In the past few years Míguez Bonino has been involved in writing about the period of the 'dirty war', the most terrible period of atrocities and violations of human rights in Argentina (c. 1976–82). In several interviews and papers he has analysed the three political periods lived by Argentineans since the military took over the government in 1976 and the 'dirty war' started. His reflections on justice and impunity come out of his own involvement since 1975 in a forum for human rights (Asamblea Permanente de Derechos Humanos), a group that included a wide political and religious spectrum, religious and non-religious, academics and non-academics, who gathered with only one aim: to stop the brutal violence that was taking over Argentinean society.[168]

During a first period, and it must me remembered that Míguez Bonino was writing his more seminal works throughout this period, the military took over the state in 1976 and until 1982 they illegally arrested people, they used systematic torture as a state practice and they forcefully made the bodies of political opponents and those who were suspects of aiding subversive groups disappear, without trials or juridical defence or appeals. Human rights groups during this period used the Argentinean Constitution and the Universal Declaration of Human Rights as legal referents in order to alert the general public about illegal detentions and situations that were taking place in Argentina. Further, they filed information and data on the cases at human rights committees of the United Nations and the Organization of American States in order to prepare future investigations and prosecutions. Together, they filed legal appeals of *habeas corpus* at the Argentinean Courts and they organized public and pacific acts to alert public opinion of what was happening in Argentina.

During the second period from 1983 to 1989 the human rights organizations supported the national return to a democratic state of affairs and tried to find archives that would provide information about the whereabouts of the thousands who had disappeared in Argentina. Those archives were never found and therefore, because of the unstable democratic situation, the Argentinean Congress was not able to push the military to reveal the truth. However, in 1983 the Argentinean government appointed a Truth Commission, as had been the case in several other countries, named Comisión Nacional sobre la Desaparición de Personas (CONADEP).[169] The Commission's Report mentioned 9,000 cases while human rights organizations put the figure of disappeared citizens close to 30,000. Legal cases and testimonies were filed in the Argentinean courts, and the verdict was clear in assigning responsibility to the state and to the military who ran the state and the centres of detention and torture.

Despite those large steps towards truth and justice Míguez Bonino regrets the passing of two laws by the Argentinean Congress: the *ley de obediencia debida* that denied legal responsibility to those who followed superiors' orders to arrest, torture, kill and make to disappear, and the *ley de punto final* that didn't allow for an ongoing legal investigation but prevented new investigations taking place after a particular date specified by the courts. The exception to that process of legal impunity was the investigation related to foreign citizens who disappeared in Argentina, legal processes in France, Italy and Spain that triggered an Interpol red alert in the cases of several Argentineans, high-ranking military officers, who were wanted in Spain for crimes against humanity.[170]

During a third period, from 1989 onwards, the democratic governments in Argentina have struggled to provide justice while the truth of many more disappearances has come out. A sad moment for many Argentineans came when President Carlos Menem, using his legal presidential prerogative, granted freedom from prison to the leaders of the military junta that ruled Argentina.[171] This step could not be ruled as illegal, as Menem was acting within the law; however, it provided a lack of hope for justice and truth for many Argentineans, a situation of social tiredness and desperation for a nation in need of justice and truth.[172] For Míguez Bonino the current difficulties of the legal system point to the need to limit state power without preventing the state from investigating economic misuse of public money and a general legal and penal insecurity faced by all Argentineans.

It is clear that 30 years after the 1976 military coup Míguez Bonino is still critically involved in a socio-theological reading of Argentinean society, but he is also deeply concerned about the ongoing life of a Church that should be closer to the poor and the marginalized, namely those who suffer from penal insecurity and suffer hunger because of a state mismanagement of resources, human expectations and democratic stability.

Despite those social and economic sobering assessments, Míguez Bonino has always remained optimistic that the continuous involvement of Christians within those difficult social and political processes had been not only necessary but mandatory. Those Christian movements influenced the development of the Church in Latin America and provided the start of an ongoing theological method of suspicion that has made Latin American Christianity one of the strongest in the world by returning to a close gospel link between Christian life and social ethics embodied by the action, theology and writings of Míguez Bonino.

Part 2

Theological Challenges

4

Pablo Richard

In his latest work, on the ethical and spiritual strength of liberation theology, Richard has not apologized for his ongoing challenge to colonial, political, Christian and social structures that, after all, affect every human being in Latin America and throughout the world.[173] For Richard, like Hugo Assmann, has used strong language over the past 30 years to challenge the possibility of any oppression in the name of Christianity associated with unjust structures.[174]

His latest work, *Fuerza ética y espiritual de la teología de la liberación*, is probably one of the most refreshing and clear works to appear in Latin America at the start of the new millennium. So much that Richard summarizes the starting point of a theology of liberation but brings it to a head-to-head challenge of contemporary globalization. Christian ethics, according to Richard, has been for too long preoccupied with the beginning and the end of biological life but has shown less interest in what happens in the middle. Thus, the task of liberation theology continues to systematize a reflection based on praxis in relation to human beings and the human as the centre of God's creation. An ethical concern for life includes several aspects that are interlinked and interrelated, such as the planet, work, health, social participation, joy and all aspects of human life.

However, Richard argues strongly for a dichotomy between welcomed trends of theological thinking on inculturation (see the chapter on Diego Irarrázaval in this volume) as opposed to the fashionable trends of globalization. For globalization is not concerned with the human but with the market and the possibility of the exchange of goods and commodities all over the world and the unification of the planet. If a traditional Christian ethics asked questions about what is good, globalization has asserted that the market is good, leaving behind the centrality of human beings who, in turn, become consumers and are only perceived as central to the global processes if they consume. As a result, the poor and the marginalized, particularly of those countries that suffer extreme poverty and starvation, are not important for the market.[175]

In that context of inculturation and the challenge offered by Christianity, Richard argues that it is within the Third World that the future of Christianity lies because western civilized nations have failed to challenge the ever-present paradigm of colonialism by approving and sustaining the war in Iraq. There is still a strong Eurocentrism that needs to be challenged and a crisis of western civilization in which Christians in the United States have supported war and destruction in the name of order, stability and globalization.

Christians for Socialism

It could be argued that Richard is one of the most consistent Latin American theologians, and therefore is sometimes ignored among the most influential writers or activists whose works have been translated into the English language. His main theme, liberation from colonialism and the idols of death, resonated already in the young Chilean involved in the movement of Christians for Socialism in Allende's Chile. At this point it is worth dwelling on that particular moment in Latin American history simply because other theologians discussed in this volume, José Míguez Bonino and Diego Irarrázaval, were supporters of that movement and the movement drew pastoral and theological strength from the emerging theology of liberation so that Gustavo Gutiérrez was among their invited guest-speakers.

During 1968 and at the same time that Gustavo Gutiérrez had given his seminal talk to priests in Chimbote calling for the development of a theology of liberation, a group of Catholics who called themselves the 'young Church' had started their own journey. During that year Pope Paul VI was going to visit Colombia in order to open the 39th International Eucharistic Congress. The 'young Church' interpreted that visit as an institutional blessing of poverty by the Catholic Church and on 14 June 1968 they gathered at the parish of San Luis Beltrán in Santiago in order to protest. In July 1968 the group protested against the proposed building of a new Catholic National Shrine in Maipú. Following those protests a group of 200 people who had attended the evening Mass on Saturday 10 August 1968 remained within the Santiago Metropolitan Cathedral and refused to leave the premises. There were eight priests, nuns and lay people among them and their concern was that the alliance between the Church and the rich had slowed down the pastoral reforms proposed by the Second Vatican Council and the 1968 meeting of Latin American bishops in Medellín, Colombia.

It was clear that there was an ongoing growth of discontent about the established Church and that discontent became focused in a pastoral and political hope with the presidential election in Chile on 4 September 1970. On that day Salvador Allende, representing a left-wing political coalition (Popular Unity), obtained the partial majority of the vote but did not have enough votes to become the new Chilean president. On Saturday 24 October 1970 the Chilean Congress ratified Allende's election as President of Chile and he took over office on 3 November 1970. After the elections a group of progressive Catholic priests had gone to Allende's home to congratulate him. Because of their work in working-class areas, a number of priests already supported the reforms and the election of a socialist president. Base Communities, aided by Fernando Ariztía, examined Allende's Popular Unity manifesto (the 40 measures), compared its proposed aims with those of the New Testament and concluded that of all the political manifestos of 1970 Allende's was closest to the values of the gospel and the centrality of the poor within the Gospels.

This period in Chilean history needs to be described as a politically intensive period and therefore it was difficult for priests who were immersed in working-class areas not to side with the hope and the happiness of their parishioners. However, those priests who became part of the Christians for Socialism made a particular choice sustained by the condemnation of capitalism as a Christian way of life and they perceived the state-oriented and community-oriented branch of Chilean socialism as closer to the values of the New Testament and particularly to the life of the early Christians as portrayed in the Acts of the Apostles.[176]

In April 1971 80 priests, mainly from Santiago, but also from other dioceses met in the south of Chile in order to discuss their involvement in the construction of a socialist society in Chile.[177] They ended the meeting with a public declaration in which they welcomed and supported the election of a socialist president and showed their hope for the future.[178] The Chilean Cardinal Raúl Silva Henríquez expressed, on behalf of the Chilean bishops, a clear statement that reiterated that while priests could have their own personal political options, the Church could not side with a single political party or political system.[179] The Christians for Socialism were accused of clericalism and the positions of those involved hardened; however, some professors of the Faculty of Theology at the Catholic University also joined the movement.

In July 1971 the group of 80 priests became 200 when they met to discuss the role of the Catholic priest in the contemporary world in preparation for the Roman Synod on that theme that took place at the Vatican during that year. Among those who participated in the meetings was Rafael Maroto, one of the Episcopal Vicars of the Archdiocese of Santiago. The 200 pushed for a renewed ecclesiology and for the end of priestly celibacy within the Catholic Church. Despite those criticisms the Roman Synod reinforced the practice of celibacy within the Catholic Church and it was clear that at local level those discussions created confusion among lay Catholics and non-Catholic observers.

In April 1972 the groups of the 80 and the 200 priests for socialism had become officially Christians for Socialism and they organized a Latin American meeting of all those progressive forces within Latin American Christianity to coincide with the international meeting of the United Nations Conference on Trade and Development (UNCTAD) that took place in Santiago. They had invited Cardinal Silva Henríquez, Archbishop of Santiago, to sponsor the meeting but Silva Henríquez condemned the possibility of choosing one single political way of understanding society. Further, the Secretary of the Archdiocese of Santiago, Fr Sergio Valech, informed all organizations and parishes that the archdiocese did not agree with such a meeting. Delegates from all Latin American countries attended the meeting, including the Bishop of Cuernavaca, Mexico, Sergio Méndez Arceo. At that time there were already lay Christian communities that had decided to live according to the principles of the Chilean revolution, one of them led by a Spanish priest, Ignacio Pujadas. Pablo Richard commented that those communities had principles that reflected how the life of the Christians for Socialism was lived within the grassroots of Chilean society; for example, the eleventh point of Pujadas' community manifesto stated that 'only revolutionary morality can lead us to a revolutionary Christianity. Only a revolutionary Christianity can help us towards the liberation of man.'[180]

Silva Henríquez met with the members of Christians for Socialism and challenged their ideological positions; however, some members of the group had become so radicalized that they almost cancelled a meeting with President Salvador Allende, whom they labelled as just another politician. Two trends became clear during 1972: (1) Christians for Socialism lost some momentum and some of their members became immersed in left-wing political parties and within the guerrilla movement, Movimiento de Izquierda Revolucionario (MIR), and (2) in doing so, they prepared the future co-operation between the left-wing parties and the Catholic Church that until then had not been possible because of the distrust shown by the revolutionary left towards the Chilean bishops and priests.

By March 1973, a Catholic priest stood as parliamentary candidate for the left-wing movement MAPU (United Popular Action Movement) and the Christians for Socialism revived their movement with the arrival of José Comblin, the well-known theologian, who had been expelled from Brazil and was welcomed by the diocese of Talca. Consequent visits to Talca by Gustavo Gutiérrez and Hugo Assmann helped the movement, but the military coup saw its members listed for arrest and assassination and members of the Christians for Socialism, particularly foreign priests, had to leave Chile or go into hiding.

Pablo Richard was part of that political context and took part in the Christians for Socialism movement. Thus, his ongoing theological reflection was shaped by his own experience of the rise of that movement as well as the crude persecution by the military on all its members after the military coup of September 1973.[181] If others, such as Gutiérrez, were marked by pastoral work in poor areas of the urban cities, those who belonged to Christians for Socialism were theologically influenced by their own experience of state persecution, exile and a critique of the power of empires, previously Spain and, during this political period of the Cold War, an empire represented by the political and economic interests of the United States of America in Latin America. There is a very close intellectual dependency between Richard's ideas and those of Hugo Assmann and while it is not possible to prove that they influenced each other, it is possible to argue that the formative period of the Christians for Socialism and the hard language of Richard's theology regarding empire and idolatry remained ongoing tropes in his later writings and reflected the hard theological language of Assmann, who used Marxist revolutionary language within theological interpretations of social processes of change and liberating praxis.[182] Assmann provided a description of his own theological writings of 1980 in the following terms:

> It is an unpretentious putting into writing of a few of the many things that one learns in conversations with male and female comrades in the struggle, when there is a willingness

to take seriously what the Final Document from Puebla terms 'the evangelizing potential of the poor'.[183]

Theology, Liberation and Idolatry

Pablo Richard was born in Chile in 1939 and he was ordained as a Catholic priest in the Archdiocese of Santiago in 1967. Richard pursued theological and biblical studies obtaining the Licentiate in Theology (Catholic University of Chile) and the Licentiate in Sacred Scripture (Pontifical Biblical Institute, Rome), having pursued biblical archaeological studies at the Biblical School of Jerusalem and having received a doctorate in the sociology of religion from the Sorbonne, Paris.

Later, Richard became a priest of the Archdiocese of San José, Costa Rica, Professor of Exegesis at the National University of Costa Rica and at the Latin American Biblical University and Director of the Departamento Ecuménico de Investigaciones (DEI), working tirelessly in the programmes for ongoing formation for lay pastoral workers of Latin America.

As a biblical scholar, and as a theologian of liberation, Richard has explored the challenges that the Word of God brings to the ongoing socio-political processes, departing from a spiritualistic reading of the biblical text and stressing the challenge that the Bible offers to socio-political and ecclesial structures, structures of society and the contemporary world in general. His pastoral immersion as a scholar has been with those who have brought their own challenges and toils to bear within an ongoing pastoral formation of those who are working within the Latin American pastoral communities together with the poor and the marginalized of Latin American society.

In his work of the early 1980s Richard emphasized the fact that within Latin American social processes of secularization, and therefore the rise of atheism or agnosticism, had not been prominent and that at all levels religion, and particularly expressions of Christianity, had guided the socio-political conflicts of that time. Indeed, military dictatorships had fought

Communism aided by the United States of America as a crusade against atheism and the possible destruction of a Western civilization based on Christian principles and the freedom to worship privately and publicly. However, the capitalist system that in the 1980s was already growing into a larger globalized experience required and was getting, according to Richard, a theological response not against those who didn't have faith but against those who were creating fetishes, commodities and idols that were opposed to the praxis and Christian life of liberation. Richard remarked that: 'The poor can seek the visage of the real God only by working within a political praxis of liberation. Likewise, class struggle has been transformed into a struggle of the God of Jesus Christ against the Olympus of the gods of the capitalist system.'[184]

One can still hear the resonance of the challenge of capitalism by socialism and the challenge to the American empire by Ernesto Cardenal, among others, in these words, written shortly after the triumph of the Nicaraguan revolution in 1979 and after years in which Pablo Richard had been immersed in the pastoral reality of Costa Rica with Chile as part of his virtual reality of information and past. It is in that context that Richard explores the theme of idolatry within the Old and New Testaments with a sense of faith rather than historical criticism and with a common thread to his investigation: themes of idolatry are well developed within biblical texts that were written in times of persecution.

In his study Richard differentiates two meanings for the word 'idolatry': one found within worship and the cultic images of Yahweh, the other found within the possible worship of other gods, that is, false gods. Both understandings are present within the following text: 'I am Yahweh your God who brought you out of the land of Egypt, out of the house of slavery. You shall have no gods except me. You shall not make yourself a carved image or any likeness of anything in heaven or earth beneath or in the waters under the earth; you shall not bow down to them or serve them' (Exodus 20.2–4).[185] In another passage, that of the story of the golden calf (Exodus 32.1) the advancing people of Israel, out of Egypt but still needing to advance to the promised land, rebelled against Moses and built the image of a golden calf in order to be assured that God was leading them. They wanted a God that consoled them in their oppression rather than the God who would lead them through different paths unto an eventual liberation. Richard comments on this passage as follows: 'The sin against the transcendence of God, therefore, consisted in the people's refusal of its own liberation, and in the construction of a false liberation through the alienating worship of a god who would console them, but not set them free.'[186] A similar episode takes place when the northern King Jeroboam built two golden calves for the people in the north so that they would not have to go to worship in Jerusalem where the enemy king was (1 Kings 12.28). In this case, the people avoided a confrontation with the king and instead of being liberated, unified and stronger as a people they fell into idolatry. Later in the Old Testament, in order to avoid any idolatry, a whole theology of anti-idolatry was developed whereby any image of God was forbidden following from the high theology of Genesis in which only human beings are the image of God.

Richard's analysis is not only convincing but directly linked to the risks experienced within the liberation proposed by God in which idolatry is portrayed through human efforts to dilute a true religious practice and to change it into a passive attitude of compliance that becomes a hindrance to divine processes of liberation. Thus, the anti-idolatry attitude within the New Testament is absolute and stronger, centred in the dignity and centrality of human beings, and centred on the final revelation and centrality of the God of history who has sent his Son as the ultimate image of his liberation. The discussions between Paul the Apostle and the Greeks in Athens challenge the possibility of an 'unknown God' but incorporate it, not as a challenge to the God of Jesus Christ, but as a path to the ultimate worship of the true incarnate God (Acts 17.16–34). God is finally present in history, in nature, in the cosmos and any process of fetishization or idolatrization of the human represents the ultimate idolatry – the destruction of God's world and God's work in history.

The idolatry of money has a central place within the New Testament and the message is unequivocal: greed for more and therefore the love of money contradicts the life of faith, the Christian life in community and the values and attitudes associated with the kingdom of God (1 Corinthians 5.9–13, 6.9–11, 10.14–17, Galatians 5.19–21, Colossians 3.5, Ephesians 5.5, 1 Peter 4.3, Matthew 6.24). Further, the idolatry of the law that takes over all personal desire for God and his kingdom can also become an idol (Galatians 4.8–11, 4.21—5.1, Mark 2.1—3.12). Finally, Richard expands on the idea of the idolatry of oppressive political power, a clear slavery by those who worship the idol of the oppressive ruler and therefore lose their freedom and their liberation in Christ. The passages related to this kind of idolatry emerged out of the confrontation between the Lordship of Christ and the divine status of the Roman Emperor. Christians did not directly challenge the emperor but they asserted clearly that their Lord was Christ. They became enemies of the state, of an oppressive state in which the authority had not been given by the people themselves but by a decree of the same person who became ruler, idol and beast (Revelation 13.11–18, 14.9–13, 15.1–4, 16.2, 19.20). The message of liberation given by the book of Revelation was clear; however, it carried with it the risk of arrest, torture and death.

The final conclusions made by Richard bring the strength of his biblical analysis full circle to the history of the Christian communities in Latin America that suffer the temptation of idolatry around them, the presence of fetishes and commodities that replace human beings at the centre of history and the oppressive system of capitalism that arises out of the rich North and is exported particularly by a system of American capitalism. In Richard the satisfying knowledge of the biblical text becomes a challenge, a political analysis and a warning. Scripture becomes the *locus theologicus* to be explored further through a life committed to Christ and the liberating God who offers once and again the possibility of a liberating praxis to the Christian communities in Latin America and to all. Richard concludes: 'If capitalism were atheistic, it is possible that our faith would not have this subversive strength within a practice of political liberation. But capitalism is idolatrous rather than atheistic, which poses a political and theological problem at the same time, especially within the context of Latin American capitalism.'[187]

Globalization and Liberation

One of the central questions posed to theologians of liberation after the collapse of the Soviet Union and the demise of socialism in Europe, related to the parameters of Marxist hermeneutics that dominated Latin America in the 1970s and the 1980s. The response by Richard was clear. He continued using concepts associated with Marxist analysis but quickly adapted to the change in the Latin American context. That was not difficult as, unlike Assmann, he had provided a biblical analysis that could be applied to changing and diverse contexts and at the same time he had already expanded on the association capitalism–idolatry that could be expanded to globalization–consumerism–idolatry.

That insightful biblical analysis is applied in his people's commentary on the book of Revelation which unfolds many of the themes that he had previously explored.[188] One of the striking contexts of this work is that it was researched through his participation in a team, following his previously published critique to western biblical scholarship.[189] At the Ecumenical Research Department in Costa Rica the biblical team, which included Elsa Tamez, provided the framework for an ingoing discussion while Richard's lecturing to many workshops of indigenous and lay pastoral teams throughout Latin America provided the context. Finally, his engagement with two protestant seminary communities in Indiana and Virginia, USA allowed him not only to check on the bibliographical sources but also to write his commentary within the belly of the empire that he had always challenged in his writings.

Richard's work presupposes several methodological points that become quite important for his ongoing contribution to a Latin American biblical theology and to Latin American theology in general. For him: (1) the book of Revelation arises at a time of persecution, it is a liberating book, full of hope, it offers guidance for the construction of an alternative world and it is full of political utopia that unfolds in history. (2) The book of Revelation is rooted in the history of Israel and the history of the Jesus movement, it allows for a universal sense of critique and resistance later forgotten within the established monarchical Church and it brings new challenges for Christian life within an established church today. (3) The eschatological themes in Revelation are focusing on the present rather than the future because the present is already filled with the death and resurrection of Christ. (4) Revelation is about a process in a double-folded history that is continuous, that is, the empirical history of the earth and the transcendent history of heaven. (5) Revelation discloses rather than conceals and it discloses wrath for the oppressors and liberation for the oppressed. (6) Revelation operates through myths and symbols, myths create a community identity and are polysemic, the use and recreation of myth is encouraged within the Christian community. (7) Revelation provides a historical certainty that encourages visions, visions not as dreams to be interpreted but as visions of a hopeful alternative world. (8) The violence of Revelation assumes an intense persecution and a release/catharsis by those who write and read the book. (9) Revelation provides prophecy, a call to conversion and universal salvation in Christ. (10) Revelation offers a unified eschatology and politics, whereby the vision of the future history clashes with the contemporary experience of a historical Roman Empire and its idolatry. (11) Revelation should be interpreted in its historical context rather than out of context.

It is this ongoing search for biblical liberation in the reading and interpretation of the literature of the oppressed that brings Richard's polysemic theology to the forefront within the collapse of the socialist systems of governments in the Eastern

Bloc. For it is in that historical context that Richard explores the possibility of the great debacle of the Roman Empire and the possibilities of other larger structures that need to be challenged. In his complementary work, and better known in English, *Death of Christendoms, Birth of the Church*, Richard pursues the same thematic: the possibility that organized empires, be they secular or Christian, conduce to the probability of developing a Christianity allied with the powerful, while Christianity as its genesis and roots was a movement of the oppressed and the marginalized.[190] Revelation has the possibility of challenging the ongoing growing structures of Christendom and those challenges are the challenges taken by other theologians who have also questioned the possibility of a Christian bureaucratic machinery rather than a Christianity closer to the original model left by Christ, close to the poor, close to the oppressed and with a new project of life that challenged social and economic prosperity and those anti-values that betrayed the values of the kingdom of God as portrayed in the New Testament.[191]

Richard pursues the same critique in his challenge to a 'Jesus without a face', that of the creeds, of dogma, and of tradition.[192] Accepting that communities adopt and develop creeds in order to prevent heresy and to create belonging, the Church developed and accepted the Apostles' Creed and the Niceno-Constantinopolitan Creed as compromises to all different understandings that were taking place at the time. However, for Richard, the creeds do not speak about a historical Jesus and who he was. Those descriptions are found in the four Gospels and he wonders why the Christian communities cannot assume the Gospels as their creeds rather than some theological assumptions that speak of a Christ that is not really with the community but exists in philosophical and theological terms. The Jesus of the Gospels has a human face, of a carpenter, not of a Pharisee or a scribe, a face that laughs, dances, is angry, weeps and shows hope and distress. For Richard, 'the later traditions, theologies, definitions of the magisterium, and icons will erase the face of Jesus or create a new and different face'.[193]

How can we solve the question of the diversity of the Gospels and the diversity of the face of Jesus in them? There is no solution to his problem as the Gospels were canonized, included into the canon of the Church as sacred texts, and so diversity and the diversity of the face of Jesus remains with them. In reference to those Gospels, there are, according to Richard, three different approaches that need to be respected at all times: the literal meaning of the text, the historical meaning of the text and the spiritual meaning of the text.[194] In the first, the text needs to be approached as a literary text with all the richness of its genres while in the second there is a history behind the formation, composition and location of the text. However, for Richard, the third approach is the most important because contemporary readings enter into the message provided by the Word of God, their own contemporary situation and their own personal situation whereby the sacred text becomes life for them today. It is this third step that Richard explores as the source of inclusion into the life of Christ for the excluded, the oppressed and the marginalized so that 'women, young people, indigenous peoples, blacks, peasants, ecologists, and other groups come into direct contact with Jesus, and in these encounters Jesus continually take new faces'.[195] Through this encounter, as it happened in the Gospels, not only those who read the text get transformed but also Jesus transforms himself into many faces and many voices.[196]

That biblical leap of the contextual reader returns full circle to the foundations of a Latin American theology, which starts with a Christian experience within a socio-political milieu, an action that precedes theology, which becomes, as previously outlined in Gutiérrez, a second act.

The Challenges of Theology

Richard's main contribution to the development of Latin American theologies was his systematic attempt to outline the characteristics of a theology within the movement for a liberation theology and to argue for an ongoing discussion and explo-

ration of a liberating praxis.[197] For the experience of doing theology in Latin America comes out of an experience of death and
life rather than of being and non-being as it is within the dominant European theology. This way of doing theology is experienced by the poor and the marginalized and, with them, by the
theologians who share the ordinary experience of death and
insecurity in order to reflect on God's life for his people.

The place for doing theology remains a place of death in
which life is also found. In Richard's words:

> God is revealed as the life, strength, hope, gladness, and
> utopia of the very poorest and most oppressed. This is why
> the world of the poor is so disturbing. In the struggle of
> the poor for life, there are spiritual depths antecedent to all
> theological reflection, depths that surprise us, amaze us, tran-
> scend us, and fill us with joy.[198]

That God is not to be discussed in terms of his existence in the
contemporary world but assumed as the God who is present
where the poor and the marginalized are because it is not possible to assume that God is an oppressor and therefore that God
dwells where the oppressors are. Thus, the theology within a
theology of liberation is a reflection about God, but about God
in a context of liberation. It is not a systematic theology because
'abstract, a-historical and ideological theologies speak a great
deal about God, but are empty of the presence and word of
God'.[199]

Within this liberating spirituality it is clear that the kingdom
of God, the reign of God, is larger than the Church and that the
Word of God illumines the social reality of the poor beyond
those who consider themselves Christians or part of a Christian
community. Thus, sometimes the Church has been afraid of this
kind of theology, not because it does not support liberation, but
because 'it fears that God and the Reign of God will be spoken
of, and that out of this experience of God may come a judgement or questioning of the meaning of the entire church'.[200]
Within that fear the Church has supported the preferential

option for the poor but God had made that option first. Thus, the role of theology is not to guide the action of God's people but to help the denunciation of idolatry, that is, the worship of false gods that challenge the primacy of the God of life, who moves with and resides with the poor and the marginalized.

For liberation theology, and indeed for all Latin American theologies, God intervenes in history, in a single history, not in an abstract reality. God acts within a contemporary history of liberation from death for the poor, for the economically poor as well as for the marginalized and oppressed for many reasons and by many powers. Thus, 'the liberation of the poor is historical and concrete when it accepts conflict: after all, the history of the poor is always the history of the struggle of the poor for their liberation'.[201] However, for Richard the Bible is the map that allows us to decipher life and death in contemporary history and it allows us to recognize God's work and God's action within history.

Richard advocates the birth of the Church of the poor, present not only within the Base Ecclesial Communities but beyond in the popular Christian world of Latin America. Richard supports a new model of Church that challenges the models of organizational empire and returns to the first models of Christian communities present in the New Testament. Finally, Richard summarizes the great impact of a Latin American liberation by finally arguing that it 'accomplishes its function on three levels: as liberative spirituality in the very depths of the popular religious awareness, as popular theology in the base communities, and as a critical, systematic theology in the professional centres of theological production'.[202]

5

Ernesto Cardenal

Contemplative, poet and revolutionary Ernesto Cardenal will always be remembered as the priest scolded by Pope John Paul II on his arrival to Nicaragua. Cardenal represents many faces of a theology of aesthetics in which prayer, poetry and liberation intermingle. If a poetic text was ever a theological one, as in the case of St John of the Cross, Cardenal managed to write poetic lyrics that came from the heart of a revolutionary theologian. His theological texts were not systematic treatments about God but the fruit of a contemplative aesthetics immersed in a revolutionary practice. As I will suggest in the following two chapters, what unites Ernesto Cardenal and Oscar Romero is their practice of love and their subsequent reflections on a theology of love so that for Cardenal 'love is not only personal but political, planetary and even cosmic'.[203] When asked what was the essence of Christianity, Cardenal answered 'the love of neighbour'.[204]

The Nicaraguan Context

Nicaragua had been under Spanish colonial rule from 1522 to 1822 but didn't achieve independence when the Spaniards left. Instead, Nicaragua became part of the Mexican empire of Agustín de Iturbide in 1822, then a member of the Central American Federation in 1823 and an independent state only in 1838. However, civil strife continued between conservatives supported by Britain and liberals supported by the United States. In 1855 a wealthy American soldier, William Walker, sailed from California with a group of men in order to assist the liberals and he became president of Nicaragua in July 1856. Walker restored slavery and declared English as the national language, creating strife with the British, who had established a protectorate for the Miskito Indians, and soon other Central and South American armies were fighting against the American presence in Nicaragua. In 1857 the US Government intervened and Walker left Nicaragua.

Several conservative governments followed until 1893 when José Santos Zelaya took over power and kept himself in government until 1909. After renewed strife and the killing of two US mercenaries, US troops occupied Nicaragua from 1912 to 1925 and from 1926 until 1933. The reasons for the occupation were economic ones and the USA secured a treaty that allowed them to build a channel for commerce through Nicaragua. By 1933 there was a peace agreement between the USA and the rebel forces of Augusto César Sandino, with the creation of a Nicaraguan independent force that could enforce peace and therefore prosperity. The National Guard of Nicaragua, commanded by an English-speaking Nicaraguan politician, Anastasio Somoza García, took over from the US Marines and four years later the Somoza family, aided by the National Guard, took control of the country.[205]

On 21 February 1934 Somoza gave orders for the arrest and subsequent execution of Sandino, who at that time was a possible political opponent. On 1 January 1937 Somoza became president of Nicaragua until his death in 1956 when on 20 September a young poet, Rigoberto López Pérez, shot him at a party. His son Luis Somoza Debayle took over the presidency while Luis's brother Anastasio took over the headship of the National Guard. In June 1967 after a fraudulent election Anastasio Somoza Debayle took over as president of Nicaragua. After a bloody revolution, he finally departed for Miami on 17 July 1979 and two days later the revolutionary forces of the Frente Sandinista de Liberacíon Nacional (FSLN) entered Managua and declared a provisional government acclaimed by people on the streets.[206] Ernesto Cardenal became part of the new government of Nicaragua.

The Contemplative

Cardenal was born in Granada, Nicaragua on 20 January 1925 into one of the first Spanish families to arrive from Europe in the twentieth century, son of Rodolfo and Esmeralda (Martínez) Cardenal. When he was five years old they moved to the town of León, where Rubén Darío, the greatest Nicaraguan poet, had been born. Cardenal was educated in a Catholic school run by the Christian Brothers until he was ten years of age when his parents sent him to the Jesuit boarding school Centroamérica in Granada. The school had close contact with two celebrated poets, José Coronel Urtecho and Pablo Antonio Cuadra. Cardenal was related to both and his grandmother encouraged him to read poetry at all times. At the school the Spanish Jesuit and poet Angel Martínez Baigorri also guided him and encouraged him to write poetry. It is said that his love for a young lady, Carmen, triggered a vast amount of his early poems; however, the main influences on his early poetry were Pablo Neruda and César Vallejo.[207]

After completing secondary school, he studied Philosophy and Letters at the universities of Mexico (1942–46) and English Literature at Columbia University, USA (1947–49). It was in New York that Cardenal was influenced by Ezra Pound and where he read for the first time the poems of Thomas Merton.[208] It was by reading and studying American poetry and Pound's direct treatment of the subject without using any superfluous words that Cardenal discovered his vein of direct and revolutionary poetry.[209] It was by reading Merton and by his life with Merton that Cardenal made poverty a *sine qua non* for the act of poetry and the life of a poet. After a few months in Madrid and Paris, in 1950 he returned to Nicaragua and became an active member of the revolutionary group UNAP (National Union for Popular Action). In 1952 he had to go into hiding because of his political activities and he took part in the failed plot against Somoza in 1954. The UNAP had planned to surprise Somoza inside his palace and take over power. The plan collapsed because there were not enough people among the plotters and most of them were arrested after one of Cardenal's comrades gave, under torture, all the information needed by the security forces. Cardenal's hiding is mentioned in his poem 'Hora O'.[210]

In 1956 when the poet Rigoberto López Pérez assassinated Somoza, Cardenal underwent a religious conversion and applied to become a Trappist monk in the United States. On 8 May 1957 he entered the Trappist Monastery of Gethsemani in Kentucky, where Thomas Merton was at that time the novice master. Cardenal had to sign an agreement with the Abbot stating that he would not write poetry or at least would not have it published and he took a new name, Mary Lawrence. Cardenal lived in Gethsemani for two years and had to leave the novitiate because of ill-health. He suffered constant headaches and the doctor at the monastery expressed his opinion that the monastic life was not for him. For Cardenal those two years were the happiest of his whole life.[211] During those two years he discovered the creativity of Merton and Merton discovered the complexities of Latin America, including the role of the United States within the social exploitation and poverty present throughout the continent. Cardenal and Merton wrote to each other frequently and Merton remained a constant influence on Cardenal.[212]

After leaving Gethsemani, Cardenal lived at the Benedictine Monastery of Cuernavaca in Mexico as a guest. That was a very productive literary period in which Cardenal regained his poetic voice. However, in order to continue his studies for the priesthood he moved to La Ceja in Colombia, where he remained from 1961 to 1965. It was at La Ceja that Cardenal wrote his own rephrased version of the psalms, *Salmos*. Because of its revolutionary reading of the Hebrew Scriptures *Salmos* was translated into many languages and it was considered subversive by the police in several Latin American countries.[213] It was through the *Salmos* that Cardenal became a well-known Latin American poet and the work was translated into several languages.[214] Once he completed his theological studies Cardenal was ordained as a Catholic priest at the Colegio de la Asunción of Managua on 15 August 1965.

The Nicaraguan Monk

After his ordination Cardinal was not sent to a parish but started a priestly life that was to be rather different from that of other priests. Merton had talked to Cardenal about the possibility of opening a branch of Gethsemani in Nicaragua and Cardenal continued to be enchanted with the simple and contemplative life of the Trappists. As Merton could not join him, while he had the intention of doing so, Cardenal moved to the islands of Solentiname together with two former Colombian classmates, Carlos Alberto and William Agudelo.[215] Two poets, Pablo Antonio Cuadra and José Coronel Urtecho, accompanied them on their journey.[216] Three of them started their community life on 13 February 1966, but the Colombians did not last.

Carlos Alberto found that a monastic life did not suit him, while William Agudelo missed his Colombian girlfriend Teresita. They both left, but eventually Agudelo and Teresita rejoined the monastic community which, after consultation with Merton, had been expanded to married people. The monastic community followed the traditional search for God through the recognition that contemplation led to him. It is interesting that Cardenal recognized that he went to Solentiname searching for God in contemplation and he found a God who eventually led him to others, to revolution and to Marxism as a tool for social change. Thus, it was the reading of the gospel that led him to Marxism; it was contemplation that led him to revolution.[217]

Cardenal identified his community with a lay monastery under the name of Our Lady of Solentiname. William Agudelo and Teresita had two children named Irene and Juan and they were joined by some local young men, Alejandro, Elbis and Laureano. They lived on the produce of the land and while from the start they cultivated the land, they were forced to work also on objects that could be sold and indeed were later sold all over the world. That work included the making of ashtrays, candlesticks, or souvenirs in the shape of local fauna. They shared their profits in a common purse and supplied the needs of each individual community member. The utopian nature of the community was summarized by Cardenal's wish that one day there would be no money in the world and that everybody would be filled with love for each other.

Cardenal celebrated the Eucharist at Solentiname and on Sundays allowed those who took part to exchange their own thoughts about the readings of the day. Some of them were recorded and transcribed in two volumes that remain as an inscription of shared Christian life.[218] The comments by those present linked very closely the life of Jesus and that of his disciples with the social reality of Somoza's Nicaragua. Cardenal had been teaching courses on ideology and the history of ideas to the community and it is that challenging mingling of Marxism and Christianity that comes out in the dialogues *post-evangelium* that took place in Solentiname. Within those dialogues Cardenal explained the historical context of the passage while those present expressed their own understanding for their lives and those of Nicaraguan society. Because of the deep social divisions within Nicaraguan society, some of the dialogues were harsh critiques of a Church allied with the rich and carried the hope that a revolution would bring Nicaraguan society closer to the values of the gospel.

It is clear that there were many such examples of vernacular hermeneutics in Latin America after Vatican II but there are few textual transcripts of those conversations. The community of Solentiname attracted many visitors from Europe and the United States and put forward a new way of religious life committed to the world of the poor and the oppressed. For Cardenal it was the first time that the gospel and Marxism had been presented as having the same values and as identical ideologies.[219]

In 1970 Cardenal visited Cuba for three months and that visit made an enormous impression on him – it has been called his second conversion. It was not possible to be given a visa for Cuba in Nicaragua, so Cardenal journeyed to Mexico and then to Cuba responding to an invitation to be a judge at a poetry competition organized by the prestigious Cuban publishing house Casa de las Américas. If Cardenal was impressed by Cuban society, it was not because he saw it as the social triumph of Marxism but because he felt he had arrived at the social triumph of gospel values and of Christianity.

Cardenal walked the streets of La Habana together with the Uruguayan writer Mario Benedetti, who was also invited to the literary competition, and together they saw a pleasant society where Cubans were modestly well dressed but where no economic distinctions, through fashionable clothes for some and the rags of poverty for others, existed.[220] Benedetti remarked on the lack of commercial announcements and the availability of goods in the shops – a pleasant sight for Benedetti and a refreshing discovery for Cardenal who remarked that he had gone to Solentiname looking for that simplicity and social equality in daily life. In his meeting with the Archbishop of La Habana Cardenal heard that if Vatican II had been a few years earlier the Catholic Church would not have been associated with the rich and the powerful and with the regime of Batista that had been overthrown by Fidel Castro and his revolution.

On his return to Solentiname Cardenal wrote a complete narrative of his visit, dedicated to Fidel Castro and to the Cuban people. However, in order to complete *En Cuba* he made a second visit to the island so that he could have a one-to-one conversation with Castro.[221] Castro collected him from his hotel and advised him that he was preparing his visit to Chile – a secret at that time. For four hours Cardenal accompanied Fidel on his official engagements visiting youth groups and meeting a Cuban delegation that was just back from the United States. They spoke inside Castro's car about the Church in Cuba and agreed that Castro was not personally against religion or the Catholic Church but against the experience of a Church that was united with the powerful and those who oppressed other people.[222] Castro recognized that the experience of the Church all over Latin America in the early 1970s was rather different from that of 1959 Cuba and he asked Cardenal about his visit to Chile. They spoke about the experience of the priests for socialism in Chile and Castro spoke about his planned visit to the Chilean Cardinal Raúl Silva Henríquez.[223] Castro also wanted to know about the community in Solentiname and about the possibility of a revolutionary triumph in Nicaragua.

Cardenal's visit to Cuba would have meant for any other person immediate expulsion from Nicaragua, but the Nicaraguan regime didn't arrest him, probably because Cardenal was a well-known priest and his arrest would have attracted international condemnation towards Somoza's regime. Instead, Cardenal attracted many international visitors and many poets visited him. One of them, the Costa Rican poet Mayra Jiménez had been surprised at the fact that while all sorts of art, including paintings, were produced at the community of Solentiname there was no poetry coming out. She visited Solentiname in November 1976 and after Sunday Mass read poetry to children and young people. They had never heard Cardenal's poetry and they particularly liked the poetry that was coming out of China. They started writing poetry and continued doing so even after the violent occupation of Solentiname by the National Guard.[224] They followed the 'exteriorist' style used by Cardenal and spoke of things out there rather than about their own feelings.[225]

By 1976 Cardenal was already fully involved with the Frente Sandinista de Liberación Nacional (FSLN) and he attended on its behalf the meetings of the Russell Tribunal in Rome that discussed human rights violations in Nicaragua and in the whole of Latin America. On 13 October 1977 the young people who stayed at the community of Solentiname decided to join the revolutionary FSLN and they took part in the armed attack against the San Carlos barracks where Somoza's National Guard for Solentiname was stationed.[226] Immediately after that attack the National Guard of Somoza took over the island and destroyed buildings and infrastructure. Cardenal and others sought refuge in Costa Rica and in his absence Cardenal was condemned to many years in prison. Cardenal wrote a moving letter to the people of Nicaragua explaining the genesis and aims of the Solentiname community. Cardenal also explained that in Solentiname they sought contemplation and a closer union with God and that it was through contemplation that they made a political commitment to a non-violent revolution.

However, later they realized that an armed revolution was needed and they joined that process. Cardenal included himself in those community developments; however, he was always a non-violent revolutionary who admitted that reading the Gospels had made them revolutionaries. Solentiname existed for 12 years and the islands suffered intense repression and violence throughout 1978 while Cardenal remained in exile in Costa Rica. During those years in exile Cardenal represented the FSLN at international meetings and visited many countries seeking international solidarity for the cause of the FSLN.

The Minister of Cultural Freedom

During July 1979 there were national protests against the Somoza regime and the FSLN intensified armed attacks against the National Guard. In the previous six weeks Somoza had used air power in order to suppress villages and towns with an estimated 40,000 people dead, while 150,000 refugees had crossed into Honduras and Costa Rica. The diplomatic talks between a wide political spectrum and the US Department of State failed because the USA wanted the National Guard in place after a successor to Somoza gave the political power to the FSLN. The FSLN didn't accept that part of the agreement, knowing as a historical fact that the National Guard would attempt to regain power as soon as there was any peace accord for the national reconstruction of Nicaragua. Finally, on 16 July 1979 Somoza gave his office to the President of the Chamber of Deputies, Francisco Urcuyo Maliaño, and in the early morning of 17 July 1979 those congressmen who were still able to meet elected Urcuyo as President of Nicaragua. A few hours later Somoza, together with his entourage, left by plane carrying all his relatives and the coffins of his father and brother, former rulers of Nicaragua.[227] On 19 July 1979 the Sandinista forces took over Nicaragua and declared a successful revolution against the government of Somoza.[228] The Sandinista revolt had followed many years of authoritarian rule by the Somoza family who had kept close ties with the United States and great hopes were bestowed on the new revolutionary government.[229]

The triumph of the revolution included a Mass of thanksgiving led by Archbishop Miguel Obando y Bravo and the participation of priests and Christian communities in the first years of that political process of social change and religious adaptation. It is a fact that the Nicaraguan revolution was different from the Mexican and the Cuban revolutions in that it included the active participation of sectors of the Catholic Church. Since the foundation of the Sandinista movement there had been a close co-operation between the Marxist FSLN and the Christian Base Communities (CEBs) and it was puzzling to the rest of the world how Marxists and Christians had been able not only to co-operate with each other in a common cause, but how they had also influenced each other.[230] It was not surprising then that the Sandinista government would call upon some priests, as Catholic leaders, to serve within the political coalition leading the Nicaraguan revolutionary administration.

Among those called to ministerial portfolios by the Sandinista Government of Nicaragua were the priests Miguel d'Escoto as Foreign Minister, the Jesuit Fernando Cardenal as Youth Movement Co-ordinator and Ernesto Cardenal as Minister of Culture. All of them saw their political work and involvement as part of their Christian commitment to the gospel and their commitment to a revolutionary process as part of the building of the kingdom of God.[231] For them faith and revolution were part of the same embodiment of gospel values and those of the kingdom.[232] Their political commitment was questioned by John Paul II when he visited Nicaragua in 1983 but Cardenal stated clearly that as a monk and a priest he saw his role as minister as a sacrifice for love of people. It was a period in which he did not have time to write or to seek the solitude of contemplation required of a monk. Cardenal felt proud that a Marxist government had the confidence of bestowing high offices of leadership and service on several priests. Further, he saw his ministerial portfolio as a labour of service and charity for others and culture as a gift of love to the poor. In his words to Cabestrero:

As far as culture is concerned, there has been a powerful cultural rebirth since the victory of the revolution. Along with material goods, spiritual goods have priority too. We don't conceive of material welfare without spiritual welfare. And as Christ placed his Apostles in charge of distributing the loaves and fishes, I feel he's placed me in charge of spreading culture.[233]

Later, relations between the Church and the Sandinista soured and came to a standstill because of Archbishop Obando y Bravo meeting with US businessmen and the intervention of the Contra rebels sponsored by the US administration. However, relations between the Church and the Sandinista had not always been completely open, due to the divisions within the Catholic Church in which not everybody was happy with the state domination of legislation regarding Catholic practices outlined by the Sandinista government.

Already in 1981 the US-sponsored groups of members of the National Guard, who were helped by American advisers, attacked the borders of Nicaragua from Honduras. By 1984 the Reagan administration violated international law and planted mines in the Nicaraguan harbour, an act condemned by the International Court of Justice. In 1988 the FSLN signed a cease fire with the Contra rebels and agreed to call free elections. The elections took place in 1990 and the US-backed National Opposition Union won the elections. Violeta Chamorro became the first woman president of Nicaragua. In 1996 the Liberal Party defeated the FSLN and Arnoldo Alemán became president. More recently, in 2001 Enrique Bolaños of the Liberal Party defeated the FSLN candidate Daniel Ortega and became president of Nicaragua in 2002.

The Theology of Angry Beauty

The first major poetic work published by Cardenal after the 1979 Sandinista revolution was the *Canto Cósmico* in 1989.[234]

In a long poem of more than 500 pages Cardenal resumed and developed many of the themes that had interested him over the years and that, in the light of the Sandinista triumph, became more positive and more central to the understanding of Latin America and her indigenous societies. *Canto Cósmico* represents a major work on the epic-narrative poetry that links Cardenal with the universe and divine providence within a larger world.[235] Thus, the theme of 'matter is music' relates to a larger narrative of the universe in which creation, science, divine intelligence and the appearance of Latin American societies show a complementary of aesthetic beauty through cycles of rhythm, that of lunar and solar cycles, of menstrual cycles and sea tides.[236] Cardenal's interest in the cosmic and the scientific coincides with a period of post-revolutionary reflection in which he returned to a larger Latin American concern for God's action in a larger world. Through the 'encounter' that divine world was desecrated, abused and forced by the greed of human beings opposing the cosmic union of a divine creation in which the aesthetic and the poetic find a constant music of sociability and political complementarity.

The anger of Cardenal's young and middle age is focused and sublimated in an older age in which he receives the acclamation of others and through which he provides theological reflections on Christianity and Marxism by his presence rather than by his words. The revolutionary poet becomes an ambassador for humanity; the minister of the revolution becomes a cultural icon of divine intervention and divine love for all creation. The 1992 commemoration of the 'encounter' had the same impact on many Latin American theologians and intellectuals: it fostered a Pan-American sense of social identity, divine election and ongoing thanksgiving by and with the poor of the Americas.[237] However, the mystic contemplative in Cardenal did not subside because of his many international commitments and his next work *El telescopio en la noche obscura* returned to the mystic poetry of a contemplative who wishes to be in full communion with the divine after many empirical and subjective political battles.[238]

In his memoirs Cardenal summarized his theological sense of poetic beauty, a divine attribute expressed in nature and the cosmos, and given to those who seek the contemplative life.[239] However, within those reminiscences Cardenal recognizes that contemplation leads to political commitments and that a socialist system of social equality remains closer to the values of the gospel than a capitalistic one, as expressed in the daily life of a contemplative community. It could be said that the theology of Christian contemplation and of Marxist action remains the model for Cardenal, who is only just short of a direct association between a political socialist society and a contemplative community. However, Cardenal's association of the kingdom of God with a socialist society does not have a particular association with a single political model or a single experiment of socialism. Indeed, Cardenal has many times criticized the possibility of having a triumphant revolution, a mighty bang of social change, without the ethical commitment to the dead and those who gave up their lives in order to establish a most just society, a society closer to the values articulated by Christ in the gospel concerning the kingdom of God, its justice and the places of importance within the realization of that kingdom 'here and now' and at the same time 'yet to come'.[240] In 2005 he joined with Desmond Tutu, Adolfo Pérez Esquivel, Fernando Cardenal and other activists in a weekly fast (every Friday) in solidarity with the prisoners at Guantánamo Bay.[241]

In Cardenal a theology of aesthetic, politics and contemplation meet in a way that Merton had already explored within the context of pacifism, nuclear weapons and the US intervention in Indochina. Cardenal, in his Latin American context, put forward a model of intense Christian commitment within unjust societies by a sustained dialogue with believers and atheists alike, by a poetic immersion in the sources of human emotions and divine interventions. Cardenal the monk remained a Catholic priest throughout these turbulent times and he took the place left by Pablo Neruda as the most incisive poet of Latin American history and politics.

In 2005 Cardenal was nominated for the Nobel Prize for

Literature after having been recognized by emerging new democratic societies in Latin America as a committed Christian and a political poet. His international recognition included honorary doctorates from the Latin American University of Medellín (Colombia, 1986), University of Granada and Valencia (Spain, 1987), diplomatic recognitions from Italy and France and nomination to the international committee for the celebration of the centenary of Neruda's birth (Chile, 2002).

Cardenal did not attend some of the major theological meetings of the Latin American Church such as Medellín or Puebla because he lived as a monk and as a revolutionary. It was in his poetry that a systematic theologizing of the kingdom of God arose through a theological reading of history and the possibility of a divine intervention in all the messy social moments of humanity. He celebrated the Eucharist as the sign of that historical presence of the 'God with us', particularly with the poor and those who suffer. However, following the biblical tradition of the New Testament he perceived the kingdom of God as larger than any institutional church.[242]

Cardenal's theological narratives about God arose out of his poetic narratives about human struggles for building that kingdom and the realization that the Church remains part of a serving structure that acts within society and its politics rather than outside society and its contemporary events. His contribution to spirituality and contemplation as aesthetic categories of sociability ultimately associate a reflection about God's creation and God's presence in the world, including the political and the revolutionary world.

6

Oscar Romero

One of the major theological challenges to politics in Latin America was posed by the life and actions of the Archbishop of San Salvador, Oscar Arnulfo Romero. His assassination in March 1980 at the hands of a government-paid assassin opened a new theological reflection on issues of religion and politics in Latin America in general and on the theology of love in particular. If most commentators have focused on his pastoral life, it is clear that his writings, his own theological narratives about a God who loves the poor, make a creative contribution to Latin American theology and its understanding of politics and the action of the Church in the contemporary world.[243]

The Church in El Salvador

As was the case with other Latin American countries, El Salvador as a nation arose out of the colonial conquest by the Spanish Empire and over the centuries consolidated a national identity based on a group of elite families who owned the land and the economic means of production. El Salvador is a small country in Central America, bordering with the North Pacific Ocean, Guatemala and Honduras. The whole of El Salvador covers 20,720 square kilometres, an area smaller than the state of Massachusetts. The estimated population of El Salvador is 6 million people with 75 per cent of its population considering themselves Catholics with a growing number of Protestant Evangelicals reaching 20 per cent of the total population. The country is divided into 14 counties (*departamentos*) and the majority of the population lives in the rural areas.[244]

In a small country such as El Salvador the Church has enormous influence, in particular, the Archbishop of El Salvador before Romero had worked very closely with the elite families and the government. El Salvador became independent from Spain on 15 September 1821 and remained within a close network of Central American States that were heavily influenced in their economic activities by the United States. After the 1929 Great Depression there were protests and economic uncertainty in El Salvador and in 1932 thousands of peasants were shot on orders from General Maximiliano Hernández Martínez, following a direct confrontation with the trade unions inspired by the Communist Party.[245] Hernández consolidated his power and established a dictatorship that lasted from 1931 to 1944. Successive military takeovers followed massive demonstrations in 1944 and the military consolidated a strong position within the country.

Particular benefits and privileges were given to the economic elites during the governments of Major Oscar Osorio (1949–56) and President José María Lemus (1956–60). In 1960 young army officers deposed President Lemus and started a new line of army officers that ruled El Salvador.[246] It was only in 1976, during the military government of Arturo Molina, that the first proposals for an agrarian reform were prepared.[247] Before that reform there was a close alliance between 'an agro-exporting (coffee) oligarchy and a praetorian guard'.[248] Public protests and a generalized armed conflict between the Salvadorian Army and the guerrillas followed, with a peace accord signed in Mexico in January 1992.[249]

It is within that heavily militarized, centralized and socially unjust society that Romero's action and his theology have to be understood.

The Future Archbishop

Oscar Arnulfo Romero y Galdámez was born in the town of Ciudad Barrios, department of San Miguel in El Salvador, on 15 August 1917.[250] He joined the Minor Seminary at the age of 13 and at 20 he was sent to Rome in order to complete his theological studies for the priesthood. He was ordained as a Catholic priest in Rome in 1942 and in the following year he returned to El Salvador.

From 1943 to 1967 he worked as a parish priest at the cathedral parish of San Miguel diocese. His reputation was that of a great preacher, a newspaper writer and an organizer of many diocesan activities. In 1967 Romero became secretary to the Bishops' Conference of El Salvador and moved to San Salvador, the capital city. In 1970 he was ordained as auxiliary bishop for the Archdiocese of San Salvador and filled temporary vacancies such as Rector of the Major Seminary and editor of the weekly Catholic newspaper.

After the 1968 meeting of Latin American bishops in Medellín the Church in El Salvador started liturgical and ecclesial reforms in order to journey more closely with the poor, the majority of Salvadorians. Romero distanced himself from such changes and he disapproved of the new trends within the Church. As a result, Romero was moved as titular bishop of the rural diocese of Santa María, a diocese that included his hometown. He started awakening to the realities of the poor and in 1975, after the assassination of five peasants by the rural police, he visited the families, presided at the funeral Mass and wrote a letter to the President of El Salvador outlining his concerns about the situation of his flock.

Romero's awakening coincided with the first moves for a national agrarian reform, an idea pursued in 1975 by General Molina, head of the Salvadorian government. Molina created the Salvadorian Institute of Agrarian Transformation and on 29 June 1976 the legislature approved the First Project for Agrarian Transformation. However, Molina's motivation for agrarian reform was to seek popular support for a presidential re-election and after some pressure from the powerful of El Salvador he cancelled the proposed agrarian reform by a new decree of 16 October 1976.[251] The law of agrarian reform had been challenged in court cases initiated by the landlords and was doomed to fail.

After the failure of the proposed agrarian reform, peasants started protesting against the government. However, due to the fact that peasant organizations were illegal, peasants started their discussions within the Basic Christian Communities, reflection groups that had been fostered by the Church after the bishops' meeting at Medellín. By early 1977 the landlords perceived the Basic Christian Communities as subversive and several foreign priests were expelled, accused of subversive politics and interference with political life in El Salvador. The Church was already considered an enemy of the government and the economically powerful.

At the start of 1977 Archbishop Luis Chávez of El Salvador was about to retire and discussions about his successor started. The bishops of El Salvador preferred Chávez's auxiliary, Bishop Arturo Rivera Damas, who, according to them, would be able to continue Chávez's programme of ecclesial reform. The powerful families of El Salvador preferred Romero and perceived him as their ally and as somebody who would be able to stop any further idea of a possible agrarian reform. To the bishops' surprise the Vatican appointed Romero Archbishop of San Salvador on 3 February 1977.

A Theological Conversion

Romero was reluctant to accept but, in obedience to Rome, he did. As Archbishop of San Salvador he was not able to escape the political events that surrounded him and he underwent a change in perspective that was to mark the Church in El Salvador for many years to come. He took over as Archbishop of San Salvador in a private ceremony on 22 February 1977, two days after the election of General Carlos Humberto

Romero as President of El Salvador. There were serious accusations of electoral fraud and threats of a national strike; it was a turbulent political moment for a new archbishop.

Romero's first challenge took place on 28 February 1977 when security forces and military personnel opened fire on demonstrators at the Plaza Libertad in San Salvador. While six demonstrators were killed the government declared a state of siege and, as a result, a new popular movement marking that day was formed with the name of the Popular Leagues of 28 February (Ligas Populares 28 de Febrero).

On 12 March the parish priest of Aguilares, Rutilio Grande, was ambushed and shot dead when he was travelling in his jeep together with an old man and a boy. Romero and Grande were friends; Grande had prepared Romero's Episcopal ordination in 1970 and had worked with him at the Major Seminary. As Romero visited Aguilares that night he realized that difficult things were asked of him as Archbishop of San Salvador.[252] That event marked a complete change in Romero's attitudes towards the military and the ruling families and could be assumed as Romero's conversion on the road to Aguilares, a road covered with bodies and with the blood of the poor of El Salvador.[253] The passive and gentle Romero became angry and worried and after intense prayer he took an unprecedented measure: after consultation with his clergy he closed all Catholic schools for three days of mourning and reflection. Further, he cancelled all Sunday Masses across the archdiocese and invited all Catholics to join him for the Funeral Mass of Rutilio Grande and his companions at the square opposite the Metropolitan Cathedral in San Salvador. That was the largest religious demonstration in the history of El Salvador and from then onwards Romero collided with the government authorities, the military, the bishops, with the exception of Rivera Damas, and the Vatican Ambassador. Romero was accused of being a communist and a subversive and the Church was labelled as Marxist.[254]

In May 1977 the guerrillas kidnapped Mauricio Borgonovo, a prominent member of the ruling families of El Salvador.

Despite negotiations, helped by Romero, the guerrillas killed Borgonovo and his body was found on 11 May. The death squads retaliated and they killed a priest, Alfonso Navarro, and a 14–year-old boy who was at the parish house at that time.[255] Parishioners were beaten up and forbidden to carry their Bibles or any photograph of Rutilio Grande. Shortly after the three Jesuits working at the parish of Aguilares were expelled from the country, army troops entered the church without allowing Romero to take the Blessed Sacrament from the tabernacle. When Romero finally forced his way in he found that the parish church had been half-destroyed and the Blessed Sacrament profaned.

Romero started his weekly practice of addressing Salvadorians through the radio and the printed media, analysing the events of the week in his Sunday homily, and providing a Christian reading of each particular situation. He used the radio for messages and to convey greetings when he was abroad as well as for theological reflections on practical matters and political realities while in El Salvador.[256] In his radio addresses he tried to influence people towards peace in the midst of an increasing generalized violence, poverty and human degradation. He combined well the use of the spoken and printed media and at Easter 1977 he started a practice of preparing and delivering formal pastoral letters. In a first pastoral letter he offered greetings and co-operation to all and stressed the joy of a Church close to people, a demand made by Vatican II and Medellín. As well as remembering Father Rutilio Grande and his sacrifice, he reminded the powerful of El Salvador of the misunderstandings he faced in carrying 'the difficult responsibility to defend the rights of God and of humanity'. However, he stressed the need for a mutual understanding between all in El Salvador.[257]

By 1977 Romero had changed his theological position from one of order related to the majesty of God towards one of mutual relations between God and human beings in society and between all human beings in society. Thus, for Romero a just order in society came out of God's love for his Son who is raised from the dead by his Father. The great theological change, according to Sobrino, was that 'Romero broke with the model of church power as analogous to state power in a great number of ways . . . the church found its place, its home, amidst the people. And it was with the people, not with the state, that the church entered into dialogue.'[258]

Following that theological development, Romero did not attend the inauguration of the new president of El Salvador, General Romero, on 1 July 1977. The political situation was already chaotic and in June a right-wing group had threatened the Jesuits with a systematic killing of their community if they didn't leave El Salvador. The Jesuits decided to stay in El Salvador and only faced a disastrous massacre of their university community ten years later.[259]

On the Feast of the Transfiguration, 6 August 1977, Romero delivered his second pastoral letter asserting that the church in El Salvador was the body of Christ in history, within the social and political realities of El Salvador rather than somewhere else. Romero reminded people of the realities of the Body of Christ in El Salvador and read from the news published by the Archdiocese of San Salvador on 11 July, which spoke of 'priests expelled from, or prevented from entering, the country; calumnies; threats and assassinations; entire parishes deprived of their clergy; lay ministers of the word and catechists prevented from carrying on their duties; [and] the Blessed Sacrament profaned in Aguilares'.[260] If his first pastoral letter's message was of reconciliation his second pastoral letter spoke of denunciation, persecution and Christian martyrdom. His strong theological association was to affirm that if Salvadorians were being persecuted, then the Body of Christ was being persecuted, and to suggest that the Church was not going to be frightened by the powerful. Further, he suggested that the Church would be open to dialogue with the government but only in order to create a just society and to remove unjust structures existent in Salvadorian society.

The government's response was swift and on 25 November the Law of Defence and Guarantee of Public Order was promulgated, covering all abuses against political opponents, including the legalization of torture and the banning of all public meetings. Romero started sheltering people at his house and continued helping people through the Legal Aid Office located at the Jesuit primary and secondary school, the Externado San José.[261] The political violence increased dramatically following the new legislation. For example, on 17 March 1978 a group of 100 *campesinos* went to the bank, the Banco de Fomento Agropecuario, in order to request loans. The bank was closed and they staged a protest outside. The security forces machine gunned them leaving several of them wounded.

During 1978 huge military operations were mounted in the rural areas, particularly against villages where there were organized groups of peasants. By the end of 1978 1,063 people had been violently arrested for political reasons, 147 people had been murdered by the security forces and 23 people had disappeared. The Organization of American States delegation published a report that acknowledged the systematic use of torture by the security forces in El Salvador and during that year another priest, Fr Ernesto Barrera, was killed.

On 30 April 1978 Romero denounced the corruption of the judiciary that did not protect those victims of human rights abuses. The Supreme Court challenged Romero and asked him to produce the names of those corrupt judges. Romero didn't name anybody but reiterated that it was clear that there were illegal arrests, there were no possibilities of applying writs of *habeas corpus*, there were increasing cases of forced disappearances, opposition members were exiled and the rights to association and strikes were violated.

Theological Controversies

Romero was not only misunderstood by the government and most of his fellow bishops. The elite families had made several complaints to the Vatican and wanted him removed from office. As a result, the Sacred Congregation for Bishops at the Vatican sent him a letter of invitation to the Vatican to discuss pastoral matters. It arrived at his desk on 24 May 1978.[262] It was not an unusual invitation and coincided with the visit of other Salvadorian bishops to the Vatican. After consultation with his spiritual director, Fr Segundo Ascue SJ and his friend, the psychologist Dr Rodolfo Semsch, he decided to go.[263]

The controversy was clearly political on the one side as Romero had upset those who didn't want to lose any privileges or any of their land. Further, within the situation of the Cold War and under the influence of the United States they perceived those protesting for their rights as subversives and communists. From the point of view of the Salvadorian bishops and the Vatican there were different theological approaches towards the dealings with religion and politics in contemporary society. If the majority of Salvadorian bishops had reservations about Romero's attitudes it was because of theological approaches towards pastoral work. Romero had not done anything unusual for bishops in Latin America, having followed the directives of Vatican II, particularly the idea of opening to the world outlined in the Pastoral Constitution on the Church in the Modern World.[264] Romero had particularly outlined the beginning of that document when explaining his understanding of a Church in the world:

> The joys and the hopes, the griefs and the anxieties of the men of this age, especially those who are poor or in any way afflicted, these are the joys and hopes, the griefs and anxieties of the followers of Christ. Indeed, nothing genuinely human fails to raise an echo in their hearts. For theirs is a community made of men. United in Christ, they are led by the Holy Spirit in their journey to the Kingdom of their Father and they have welcomed the news of salvation which is meant for every man. That is why this community realizes that it is truly linked with mankind and its history by the deepest of bonds.[265]

Other critics were individual priests such as Father Juan León Montoya, who wrote articles questioning Romero's confrontation of the elites, a point that Romero discussed often with his diocesan curia formed by Fathers Brito, Barrera, Monsignor Urioste and Bishop Revelo.[266] Before his visit to the Vatican, Romero met with the Salvadorian Ambassador to the Vatican, Lencho Llach, who pressed him for dialogue with the government. Romero responded that he had written to the Vatican and would await further council from the Holy See.[267] Other accusations against him had been forwarded to the Vatican's Sacred Congregation for Catholic Education by Bishop Aparicio and concerned his worries about education in Catholic schools and the lack of piety and proper ecclesiastical training at the Major Seminary.[268]

On Saturday, 17 June 1978 Romero, Bishop Rivera and Monsignor Urioste travelled to Rome for their visit of two weeks.[269] They stayed at the Pensionato Romano and during their first day they prayed at St Peter's Basilica and visited the Jesuit General House where Romero had talks with Fr Pedro Arrupe SJ, the Superior General of the Jesuits, who offered his continuous help and all the resources of the Jesuits for his visit to Rome and his pastoral work in El Salvador. The Procurator of the Jesuits briefed Romero on protocols with the Vatican and other general practices that usually helped a successful outcome of ecclesiastical negotiations.[270]

During an interview with Cardinal Sebastian Baggio, Prefect of the Congregation of Bishops, Romero was able to clarify misinformation that had been sent to the Vatican regarding the work of the Salvadorian Bishops' Conference.[271] On Wednesday 21 June 1978 and after the General Audience Pope Paul VI met with Romero and Bishop Rivera. The audience was an intimate one and Paul VI spoke to him at length while holding his right hand. Romero didn't remember exactly all the many words he heard but he summarized the Pope's words in his diary as follows: 'I understand your difficult work. It is a work that can be misunderstood; it requires a great deal of patience and a great deal of strength. I already know that not everyone thinks like you do, that it is difficult in the circumstances of your country to have this unanimity of thinking. Nevertheless, proceed with courage, with patience, with strength, with hope.'[272] Paul VI wanted Romero to support any calls for unity and to preach peace not violence at all times. In his response Romero promised to do so and he expressed his 'unshakable allegiance to the magisterium'.

On the following day Romero visited Cardinal Garrone, Secretary to the Sacred Congregation for Catholic Education, in order to clarify the situation of Catholic schools and the Major Seminary, and Archbishop Maximino Romero, Secretary to the Sacred Congregation for Clergy, about relations of priests in El Salvador. Finally, on the same day Romero visited the Pontifical Justice and Peace Commission in order to brief them on recent developments in El Salvador.[273] During the following days Romero had a long meeting with the Superior General of the Jesuits and once again visited the Sacred Congregation for Bishops, where Monsignor Michele Buro advised Romero on prudence and 'purely evangelical' preaching.[274] On Thursday 29 June Romero flew back to El Salvador where on arrival he celebrated Mass at the cathedral feeling confirmed in his work, his ideals and his hopes for the Church in El Salvador.[275]

The Politics of Religion

On their return to El Salvador Romero and Bishop Rivera continued exercising their influence on religious communities and politicians in order to serve the poor. On 6 August 1978 they published a combined pastoral letter in which they argued that while not every citizen is called to an active political life, those who are called should strive to serve the poor. They reminded the popular political groups of their duty to put the concern for the poor before their own interests and to strive within the political system for a more just society, suggesting strongly that violent means can only be the last resort for change.

Romero and Rivera also requested from those in power that they serve the people with a sense of truth and justice. They made the following concrete suggestions: that those who have power pass laws that account for the fact that most

Salvadorians lived in the countryside rather than in the capital city, that they widen political discussions, that they allow those deprived of human rights to organize themselves legally, that they be made aware of the people's rejection of the Law for the Defence and Guarantee of Public Order, that they stop terrorizing the poor and organizing peasants against each other and, finally, that they create a climate of reconciliation by declaring an amnesty for political prisoners without trial and for the many Salvadorians in exile. Romero and Rivera ended their letter by stating that those changes were the will of God and that people should listen to God.[276]

If those requests could be rejected as political solutions out of place for ecclesiastical powers, Romero and Rivera's theological analysis was very clear: *opus iustitiae pax* – peace is the fruit of justice – and therefore violent conflicts do not disappear until the structures that provoke those conflicts are removed.

The division of the Salvadorian bishops was very clear and as a response to Romero and Rivera's pastoral concerns the rest of the bishops published a letter on 28 August 1978 in which they analysed the situation of El Salvador in a more pre-Vatican II style and asserted that the Church would not get involved in politics and would instead pray for all.

The Road to Resurrection

The violent situation increasingly became worse and Romero had to witness more killings and was shocked by his conversation with a supposedly 'disappeared' person who had escaped from jail in which that person told him about the tortures and the numbers of people being held against their will in secret locations. Romero wrote:

In the afternoon in the chancery, we talked with Father Moreno, with Bachiller Cuéllar, to question one of those who had disappeared who has escaped from jail. And he has told us about horrible things that happen in the mysterious realms of the jails of the security forces where, I am sure, are several peoples we mourn as disappeared. It is a very sensitive secret; some really dreadful revelations![277]

In November another priest, Fr Rafael Ernesto Barrera, was killed in a violent manner by the security forces. The priest was found shot after a house in his parish of Mejicanos was attacked by the security forces, but Romero was conscious that there were those who said that the priest had been killed before the attack and that his body was purposely placed inside the house after he was already dead.[278] There were rumours that the priest belonged to the rebel group FLP (Popular Liberation Forces) and his body was buried at the parish church in order to avoid any protests against the government at the cemetery.[279] Another priest, Fr Octavio Ortiz, together with four other young men, was killed on 20 January 1979 when the National Guard entered the area of El Despertar in the Parish of San Antonio Abad.[280] Once again, Romero gathered the Christian communities at the cathedral for an early Mass concelebrated by 100 priests with the body of Fr Ortiz present.[281] Later that day the body was taken by the Christian community back to the community of San Francisco in Mejicanos for burial at the church. Romero led the burial together with 40 priests on the same afternoon. It is difficult to imagine the strength of Romero as he travelled to Mexico two days later in order to take part in the meeting of Latin American bishops at Puebla.[282]

As Romero's involvement in daily events increased his international reputation grew. In December 1978 118 British Parliamentarians nominated him for the Nobel Peace Prize and three of them visited him in December 1978 conveying the news. He arranged for them to visit jails, peasant communities and church projects and had an opportunity to explain his work for justice and peace.[283] During that year Romero had been given an honorary doctorate by Georgetown University. The ceremony took place at the Cathedral of San Salvador due to the fact that, while accepting that honour, he didn't want to leave El Salvador in case the government didn't allow him back.[284] In January 1980 Romero journeyed to the Catholic University of Louvain where he received an honorary doctorate and in his acceptance address spoke of the political dimensions of the Christian faith.[285] In that last trip to Europe he stopped in Rome where he met John Paul II who encouraged him to continue his difficult pastoral work in El Salvador.[286]

On Sunday 23 March 1980 Romero addressed soldiers at his early morning Mass and asked them to obey a higher authority, that of God, and not to kill their brothers and sisters. That was perceived as a call to mutiny and as he celebrated a memorial Mass at the Chapel of the Divine Providence Hospital he was shot and died in the hospital emergency room.

Romero's theological outlook had managed to link very closely the work of the Church and God's divine will with the pilgrimage of his people in El Salvador. Romero did not interfere in politics but analysed daily political and social events from a Christian perspective. He journeyed with the Christian communities in daily life and in prayer. Indeed, his reflections, on returning from the bishops' meeting at Puebla, were that he had told the Latin American bishops that he led a diocese that had its strength in prayer.[287] If there is ever the danger of perceiving Romero as an activist, his theology of prayer is very clear: 'He is the God who converses with us. How can we humans live without praying? How can a person spend a whole life without thinking of God, leave empty that capacity for the divine and never fill it?'[288] His theology of divine love was a theology that in his diaries and homilies spoke of the violence of love, of the ever creative love of God for all and of the love for everyone expressed through the Eucharist in the Christian communities. The violence of love rather than the violence of armed struggle dominated his writings and his speeches.

As the peace accords of 1992 bore fruits of peace, the armed conflict ended on 1 February 1992.[289] Thousands of people gathered in San Salvador; they came in their thousands out of the countryside in order to celebrate. Their banners were not political signifiers but a very large banner displaying Romero's face dominated the scene.

Part 3

Contemporary Issues

7

Leonardo Boff

A prolific Brazilian theologian, Leonardo Boff became the face of theological controversy when he was silenced by the Vatican's Sacred Congregation for Doctrine in 1985 after the publication of *Church, Charism and Power*.[290] His wide contribution to different aspects of liberation theology makes him part of the first generation of liberation theologians who spoke about Christ as the liberator. However, in the past ten years he has opened theological discussions related to eco-theology and the human obligation to take care of the planet, God's gift entrusted to us – a new variety of liberation theology.

Franciscan and Theologian

Leonardo Boff was born in Concórdia, Santa Catarina on 14 December 1938.[291] His grandparents were Italian immigrants from Veneto to Rio Grande do Sul, who arrived in Brazil at the end of the nineteenth century. Boff went to school in Planalto, Concórdia (SC, 1944–49), Luzerna, Joaçaba (SC, 1950–51), Rio Negro (PR, Seminario S. Luis de Tolosa, 1951) and Agudos (SP, Seminario Santo Antônio 1953–58). He entered the Franciscan Novitiate at the Convento S. Francisco de Assis (1959) before studying philosophy in Curitiba (PR, Seminario Mayor de la Provincia de la Inmaculada Concepción 1960–61) and theology in Petrópolis (RJ, Facultad de Teología de los Franciscanos 1962–65). In 1970 he completed his doctorate in theology and philosophy at the University Ludwig-Maximillian of Munich (Germany, 1965–70).[292] During the academic year

1968–69 he followed postgraduate courses in linguistics and anthropology at the University of Würzburg (Germany) and the University of Oxford. In 1970 he also received a doctorate in the philosophy of religion awarded by the Institute of Philosophy and Social Sciences of the Universidad Federal del Estado de Rio de Janeiro.

For 22 years he was Professor of Systematic and Ecumenical Theology at the Franciscan Theological Institute of Petrópolis, while Professor of Theology and Spirituality at various universities of Brazil as well as the Universities of Lisboa, Salamanca, Harvard, Basil and Heidelberg. He was at the centre of a theological reflection that developed different aspects of the theology of liberation, particularly aspects of human rights and the social means to live with dignity within each Latin American society. Boff has received honorary doctorates from the University of Turin (Politics) and the University of Lund (Theology) and on 8 December 2001 he was awarded the Right Livelihood Award in Sweden, known as the alternative Nobel Prize 'for his inspiring insights into the links between human spirituality, social justice and environmental stewardship, and for his decades-long commitment to helping the poor and excluded realize these values in their lives and communities'.

In 1984 the Sacred Congregation for Doctrine of the Vatican started a process against him and in 1985 he was given a forced year of theological silence, being removed from editorial boards and from his academic functions, without being able to teach, to write or to speak in public. While during 1986 he was allowed to return to his academic activities, during 1992 he was once again threatened with suspension by the Vatican. Boff resigned his priesthood on 26 June 1993 and declared himself a lay person. Boff increased the amount of his prolific writing, continued supporting the Basic Christian Communities as well as the movement of those without land in Brazil. In 1993 he returned to an academic post at the University of the State of Rio de Janeiro where he became Professor of Ethics, Philosophy of Religion and Ecology. Boff's partner Marcia Maria Monteiro de Miranda has one daughter and five sons and they live in Jardim

Araras where they share a life close to a new ecological para-digm, the care for the planet, a cause that Monteiro de Miranda had previously followed within her own political activism.

Boff has written more than 60 books in areas as diverse as theology, spirituality, philosophy, anthropology and mysticism.

Jesus the Liberator

It is not possible to do justice to Boff's enormous academic and pastoral production, however there is no doubt that the first book that caught the attention of theological circles and cer-tainly of the Brazilian authorities was *Jesus Cristo Libertador*, published in 1972 and later translated in English as *Jesus Christ Liberator*.[293] Gutiérrez had published his work on a theology of liberation in 1971 and Boff followed with reflections on the nature and activity of Jesus of Nazareth as a liberator from oppression that embraced the poor and the marginalized and who, as a result of his actions, was arrested and killed as a political prisoner of the Roman occupying army. If Gutiérrez had set the structural analysis for the development of a theology of liberation Boff had immediately followed with a work on Christology, centred on the person of Christ, intended to bury the image of a pious Christ who didn't mingle with political or liberation movements.

If the Christ, as hermeneutically analysed by Boff, was a political prisoner who had been killed by the Roman oppres-sors, the implications for the theologians and for the Church were obvious: they were also called to see their own Christian life in the light of the historical Jesus and his martyrdom at the hands of the oppressors as part of their contemporary existence. However, Boff also suggested that the hermeneutical reading in a historical context of Jesus Christ the Liberator, then and now, had implications for contemporary Christology: 'such a Christology entails a specific socio-political commitment to break with the situation of oppression.'[294]

Boff managed to outline a two-way theological look at the

person of Christ: a past lens that incorporates Scripture and tradition and a present lens that transports a synchronic Christ into a diachronic figure in time who, following accepted elements of pastoral work and apostolate, works through his Church today, a Church immersed in a particular context, a socio-political context of poverty, injustice and repression for the Brazil of the 1970s.

The first edition of *Jesus Cristo Libertador* had to be edited, taking away 31 pages (later published in the English edition of 1978), due to the censorship and problems faced by Boff within the context of a militarized Brazil. Brazil was the first Latin American country to push the Basic Christian Communities, the reading of the Bible at all levels and the involvement of the Catholic Church within the ongoing social realities of ordinary people; however, the 1964 military coup focused most of the church's attention on a repressive situation rather than on a creative one. It is difficult to know if the Brazilian church would have grown so much after Vatican II and Medellín without that experience of a military dictatorship, but certainly Brazilian Catholics were more active in socio-political life than those of Argentina or Chile at the time of Vatican II and therefore at the time of the military coup.[295]

In March 1964 a military coup, supported by civilian conspirators, deposed President João Goulart and started an authoritarian system of government whereby the president was designated by the army and approved by the Brazilian congress.[296] The system, with periodical moves from mild liberalism to further authoritarianism, was to last until 1985 when the first attempts to pass legislation that allowed the direct election of the Brazilian president and the control of the budget were restored to the national congress.[297] Therefore the most seminal years of Boff's theological production took place while the Brazilian state was arresting and torturing dissenters and within a continuous political game of considerable violence between the police, the guerrilla and some right-wing paramilitary groups. Brazilian security and interrogation advisers were provided to other emerging military regimes such as the Chilean military in 1973 and Brazil also supported the work of the Southern Cone intelligence forces through the *Operación Cóndor.*[298]

Boff was part of a very active Catholic Church with prominent personalities such as Cardinal Evaristo Arns (São Paulo), Archbishop Helder Cámara (Recife and Olinda) and Bishop Pedro Casaldáliga (Araguáia).[299] The Brazilian Basic Christian Communities united in a large movement, known as the 'popular movement', asked questions not only about social, economic and political participation in Brazil, but also about the democratization of the Catholic Church and the creation of a 'popular Church'.[300] Within those challenges large sectors of the Brazilian church's hierarchy became active in politics and as it was to be in the Chilean case the Catholic Church in Brazil became one of the few voices of dissent towards subsequent authoritarian regimes.[301] Thus, over a period of 30 years since the formation of the National Bishops' Conference of Brazil (CNBB) in October 1952, the Catholic Church changed its view of the world and chose to be politically involved, in the name of the gospel.[302]

The Challenge of Liberation

Leonardo Boff, together with Gustavo Gutiérrez, suffered processes of theological investigation by the Vatican, suspected of having published theological works that contradicted the tradition of the Roman Catholic Church. Issues that were challenging at that time for Pope John Paul II were connected with the use of social theory, particularly Marxist analysis, within the theology of liberation; issues that worried the head of the Sacred Congregation for the Defence of Faith, Joseph Ratzinger – later Pope Benedict XVI – were connected with issues of theological authority and the teaching office (for doctrine and faith) given to the college of bishops as successors to the Apostles. Gutiérrez and Boff reacted in a slightly different way to the Vatican's scrutiny, representing the two strands of liberation theologians within Catholic theology in Latin America: Gutiérrez was deeply hurt by the inquisition on his writings but recognized that his role as parish priest and pastor of a flock had a significant drive in his writings about the poor, while Boff remained defiant during those times and continued challenging authority many years later. Both Gutiérrez and Boff remained close to the poor after the crisis; however, their personal paths and thus their personal responses to crisis were different: Gutiérrez joined the Dominicans in the late 1990s while Boff left the priesthood in the early 1990s.

The theological discussions with the Vatican and his suspension from teaching within Catholic institutions triggered Boff's unusual response. Boff received an invitation from Fidel Castro, the Cuban leader, to spend two weeks with him on the island. He decided to accept the invitation because he had enjoyed long conversations with Frei Betto, one of the few priests who had been able to engage Castro in an interview and in conversations about religion. With Boff present, Fidel Castro called the Apostolic Nuncio in Cuba and reported to him that Boff was his guest and that he personally would make sure that Boff would not talk to other people, or give interviews. In total freedom and using his own transport, Fidel Castro showed Boff the island of Cuba and allowed himself long conversations about politics, religion, Marxism, revolution and a general critique of democracy. Evening meals were particularly long and conversations went well into the night, sometimes into the early morning. Regardless of the short night, at 6.00 a.m. Fidel Castro would swim for 40 minutes and start his day's work, while Boff would write down a summary of their conversations and go to sleep for a couple of hours.

Years later, Boff wrote some of his thoughts about the visit but after his return to Brazil his car was broken into and his four notebooks taken, and so Boff never wrote the book that he wanted to write.[303] Boff had been impressed by Fidel Castro's knowledge of theology and the many books of Latin American theology that he had read and underlined. Over the years Boff and Frei Betto had given lectures on Christianity and religion in general to the Cuban government ministers as requested (or mandated) by Fidel Castro. Castro has stated that 'I am ever more convinced that no Latin American revolution will be true, popular and triumphant, if it does not incorporate the religious element.'

With the lifting of the Vatican's silence imposed on Boff there was time to reconstruct the process that had led to Boff's writings to be considered problematic. According to Robert McAfee Brown, Boff's troubles had already started with the ideas and conclusions that he forwarded in his doctoral thesis, submitted and defended in Germany under the supervision of his fellow Franciscan Boaventura Kloppenburg and with the second supervision by Joseph Ratzinger.[304] The doctoral thesis was approved with the highest academic distinctions; however, when the thesis's ideas appeared as a chapter of *Church, Charism and Power*, Kloppenburg, who had become a critic of liberation theology, wrote a review of the book suggesting that Boff was putting forward heresies.[305] Boff was disturbed about this and sent a copy of the review and a copy of the book to Ratzinger. Ratzinger suggested that Boff replied to Kloppenburg's criticisms and Boff did as he was told.

Instead of solving the matter, in May 1984 Ratzinger sent a six page letter to Boff summing the accusations against him and summoning him to Rome in order to explain himself. Ratzinger suggested that Boff had distorted old Christian doctrines by reinterpreting them using a contemporary context, that is, ideological perspectives from history, philosophy, sociology and politics, perspectives that were not fully informed by theology. Ratzinger questioned whether Boff was guided by faith or by other principles of an ideological nature and he indicated serious problems with three areas covered by Boff's book: (1) Boff seemed to suggest that Christ has not determined the specific form and structure of the Church, thus implying that other models could be as valid as the Roman Catholic one, (2) Boff seemed to suggest that doctrine and dogma could be mediated by contemporary readings 'led by the Spirit', an idea that could lead to the legitimization of fashionable trends over 'timeless truths', and (3) Boff used Marxist analysis in order to assume that few within the Church owned the means of production (forgiveness and the sacraments) and proposed a model in which theological privileges are not concentrated in the few. It is clear that the Vatican was not worried about the use of Marxist analysis but about the ownership of the Holy Spirit, which, within Boff's writings, goes out from the hierarchical Church into the Basic Christian Communities.

In other writings, Boff had already challenged the sociological use of the term 'people of God', a term very prominent within the documents of Vatican II, and had termed it 'ambiguous'. For Boff, who followed the analysis by Pedro Ribeiro de Oliveira, there were five meanings for the 'people of God' in context, and a sixth one was already in the process of being accepted: the 'Church of the Poor' or 'Popular Church' (*Igreja dos pobros ou a Igreja Popular*).[306]

Boff journeyed to Rome in September 1984 and chose a theologian to help him at his meeting with the Sacred Congregation: His Eminence Cardinal Alois Lorscheider, head of the Brazilian Episcopal Conference. While the proceedings of that meeting remain confidential, it was clear that the silencing of Boff was not the hardest punishment that the Sacred Congregation could have chosen and that the presence of Cardinal Lorscheider deterred them from further canonical punishments for Boff. However, the case was well documented by the international media and the Brazilian official media used the occasion to marginalize the Catholic Church from any power of decision related to social issues that were being discussed during 1985.[307]

When Boff's silencing was lifted in 1986, the Sacred Congregation issued a public declaration on liberation theology that clarified many aspects of its development and asserted the role of the Church within the pastoral engagement with the world as arising out of the mission of the Church rather than out of a particular social analysis, be it Marxism or otherwise.

It is difficult to know if the silencing of Boff ended because Ratzinger was actually happy with his writings or because there was significant international pressure on the Vatican to continue the policies of engagement with the world as previously stated by Vatican II and to comply with charters of human rights agreed by the Vatican State as a member of the European Union (EU). The right of freedom of expression and of academic research within the EU was at odds with the silencing of intellectuals within the Catholic Church. In other cases, such as that of Charles Curren in the United States, the Vatican questioned the possibility of imprimatur and his academic tenure within the Catholic University of America but they did not have the power (or the right) to silence a writer who operated within the democratic institutions of the United States of America. If Boff could be silenced it was because he was a theologian based within a Third World institution in a country that had challenged the centralized tenures of a European-centred Christianity, already in decline.

The ideas expressed by Boff in *Church, Charism and Power* had already been published in his *Eclesiogênese: As comunidades eclesiais de base reinventam a Igreja* (1977) and within a paper in the *Revista Eclesiástica Brasileira* (1981).[308] Within those publications the origin, development, pastoral and theological importance of the base communities are outlined. Boff expresses clearly that, in his experience, those small groups of Christians that share the Scriptures, work actively within the realities of the neighbourhood, share the Eucharist in the shantytowns in houses and open spaces and challenge the oppression of the nation/state and its injustice are closer to the ancient experience of the early Church and remain far from the hierarchical structures and ornate represented by the Vatican. If Boff's critique of structures and hierarchies were only a critique it would resemble those moments and discussions that had already taken place within the European Reformation of the sixteenth century. However, Boff's theological consistency with the framework of the New Testament and with the tenets of liberation theology makes his analysis of the base communities rich in social and theological meaning to the point that his writings must have threatened the Eurocentric perception of Ratzinger and those around him. Thus, my own assessment would suggest that his silencing was lifted because there was more harm in attracting attention to his writings than from ignoring them as those of a radical priest who was on the way out of the Church's own hierarchical structures.

Boff creates and maintains a theological fabric that permeates the possibility of a complete turnaround on God's location within the world. If for traditional ecclesiology God is first and foremost a sovereign that accepts and indeed welcomes the *doxa*, the praise of his infinite being, Boff's image of God is that of an active deity who has left his pedestal and has decided to incarnate himself within the poor and the marginalized; in the words of Marcella Althaus-Reid 'poverty and economic structures of injustice needed to become the legitimate central locus for reflection, from which all other reflections would arise'.[309]

Boff recognized that the traditional linear and vertical structure bishop–priest–laity created a sociological exclusion for lay people and a theological vacuum regarding lay charismas and spiritual gifts. The Base Christian Communities provided a different kind of relatedness whereby specialized teams of priests and consecrated agents moved around the communities supporting their tasks and recognizing the movements of the Spirit within those communities. For Boff 'the basic communities are a response to the question: How may the community experience of the apostolic faith be embodied and structured in the conditions of a people who, in Brazil as throughout Latin America, are both religious and oppressed?'[310] In asking questions about the historical Jesus' will for a Church in a particular form, Boff is clear that the whole Christological experience of Easter creates the necessary conditions for the growth and the organization of a community of believers that given particular understandings and historical developments start to become an institutionalized Church. However, that Church operates within the possibility of diverse understandings and, as shown by the development of dogma through diverse councils, changes and evolves according to common understandings. It is to note that the general understanding of the kingdom of God as central to the development of a clear relation church–world starts to appear and locates the practice of the Basic Christian Communities as places where diversity in unity can exist.

If at the time of Boff's writings those communities were plentiful, the problem arose about the lack of priests to serve them through traditional practices such as a daily celebration of the Eucharist. Thus, lay leaders started to emerge as leaders of liturgical celebrations for the Brazilian Basic Christian Communities that resembled the breaking of bread within houses of the early Church. Within this model lay participation is high and the sense of individual redemption and personal piety rests within a larger influential model of togetherness in community.

That model of ecclesiology from below was to be complemented by Boff's work on the evangelization by the poor rather than to the poor. It is the communities that evangelize rather than the priests who evangelize the community, and within that model the bishop remains a centre of unity but ceases to be an administrator of all possibilities of Christian involvement within society. However, the Basic Christian Communities operate within local 'cultures' and are also to engage with those who through Christianity have been robbed of their cultures and traditions – the indigenous populations. For it is those indigenous populations that have something to teach Christians about their own theological understandings of God, and more importantly about the relation between God's creation and human beings' stewardship of God's creation.[311]

Ecological Concerns

For the next few years Boff engaged himself in academic work related to key parts of the Christian life, such as the Our Father as prayer of liberation and the contribution of St Francis of Assisi in the ongoing process of grace and human liberation.[312] However, by the 1990s and as he left the Franciscans, it was clear that his activities with the movement of those without land and the reality of the indigenous populations of Brazil had made an impact not only on his socio-political life but also on his theological reflections. A string of writings on theology, ecology and globalization coincided with meetings of representatives of different nations concerned with conservation issues and the planet in Rio de Janeiro and with the ongoing meetings of the World Social Forum in Porto Alegre, Brazil, in 2005 (21–25 January).[313]

There is no doubt that the year 1992 is crucial in order to understand Boff in the context of a Latin American emerging diversification of theology. If women theologians such as Elsa Tamez had already managed to influence a change within a politicized male-white theology, the Latin American Christian communities were reflecting on the forthcoming 500th anniversary of the encounter between Christopher Columbus and his crew and the indigenous populations.[314] The meeting of all Latin American bishops in Santo Domingo and the visit by Pope John Paul II to Santo Domingo marked an institutional concern for the indigenous within a climate of further democratization in most Latin American nations. There was no cause for celebration as 'the encounter' had brought misery and annihilation to millions of people living in the Americas but, as they were forced to convert to the gospel, 1992 marked an anniversary with growing numbers of Christians throughout the continent and with mature Christian communities that were able to decide their ongoing as well as their new pastoral priorities.

Boff was not unique in his criticism of any ecclesiastical celebrations; however, he was under closer scrutiny than any other Latin American Catholic theologian. If Gutiérrez and others had to organize parallel sessions in Santo Domingo in order to be able to make their views heard, Boff's dissent was not going to be tolerated and Vatican pressure made him take a complete break by deciding to leave the Catholic priesthood a year after a couple of his theological monographs on the colonial conquest had been published in Brazil with the expectation of quick translations into English to follow.[315] The Santo Domingo meeting sanctioned a further preoccupation and pastoral care of indigenous populations despite the fact that a growing number of bishops, appointed since 1978 by Pope John Paul II, had very conservative views in theology and traditional outlooks regarding the role of the Catholic Church within contemporary society. Once free from theological constraints, Boff started the elaboration of an eco-theology of liberation that used much more the social and the historical without the constraint either of Scripture or tradition. Unlike others, such as Diego Irarrázaval, who stressed a Latin American theology of inculturation, Boff moved quickly into a more universal and globalized paradigm of understanding of the liberation of creation and the unity of all human beings within a single large ecosystem, a common habitat, made by God and entrusted to all human beings.

Boff attempted to define ecology 'as the science and art of relations and of related beings'.[316] Thus, within the habitat of the world all living human beings, matter, energy and forces are in permanent relation with one another. For Boff, that ecological relation of communion and dependency can be compared to the Trinity and the eternal relationship of Father, Son and Holy Spirit (*perichoresis*). Without discarding the perspectives of the poor and poverty, Boff argued that ecological issues were not only the preoccupation of the rich but of all, including the poor. Using the same theological analysis provided by liberation theology for other complex issues, Boff concluded that it was necessary to get involved in ecological movements and ecological issues due to the fact that the ecological crisis was not the result of natural disasters or changes without human control within the planet, but the ecological crisis was a direct result of human intervention, human policies and a consumerist way of life.

From that point of view Boff clearly stated that it was not sufficient to ask questions about a global crisis in which relations between living beings were being altered with threatening consequences to them, it was also necessary to take action at personal, national and international level in order to provide policies and styles of life that could respond to a more balanced relation between related beings, with the Trinity as a divine example of a perfect relation of communion. Latin America, according to Boff, has a lot to offer to discussions on ecology. On the one hand, a large part of the rainforests that regulate global climate are located within Latin America, on the other hand, 'one of the most original phenomena in Latin American society is the proliferation of social movements'.[317]

Towards a Globalized Liberation

It is clear that Leonardo Boff has managed over the years to construct his theology consistently with the methodology explored within liberation theology. The pastoral ecclesial level moves into the political realm of society where Christians ask some of the following questions: 'What are the political and social practices in which Christians engage? Does Christian militancy merely reinforce a situation that is demonstrably wicked and unjust? Or are Christians being incorporated into movements for social transformation that aim at a society of greater popular participation, a society in which the poor are heard and their needs met?'[318] As a result of years of involvement with Christian communities and popular movements, Boff is able to acquire the conviction that, following Vatican II, Christians remain immersed in the world – distinct from the world, yet in the world.

The implications of Boff's theology are extremely influential for contemporary society, be they political discussions in Brazil, France, the United States or the United Kingdom. What kind of relation with the state must Christian communities maintain? What is the role of faith communities within the state? For Boff it is clear that separation or integration are not the issues but involvement in social movements for further popular participation where the poor and the marginalized have a voice, and where social movements influence policies by the state regarding democratic participation and ecological issues. If, and only if, some thought for a moment that liberation theology was outdated and out of fashion because Marxist social analysis and socialist utopias had lost their social immediacy, Boff brings back an ethical urgency of Christian commitment, divine grace and human liberation into the religious and the political arena. When pressed by a German interviewer during the World Forum for Theology and Liberation he summarized the good news of liberation with three concepts already chosen by the World Council of Churches: 'justice, peace, and the integrity of creation'. Those three dimensions cannot be separated and they constitute for Boff the contextual embodiment of today's good news for the world.[319] Thus, for him, organized religion has a task: to awaken spirituality within human beings so that they become ever more compassionate for others and for the planet; within that particular awakening 'liberation theology is increasingly timely'.[320]

Boff's influence on a new generation of theologians is maybe less documented than his influence on a new generation of committed Christians, political activists and prophetic men and women. One of those examples is Mgr Luiz Flávio Cappio of Bahia, a Franciscan who was Boff's student of theology in Petrópolis in 1970 and 1971. One day Fray Luiz disappeared from the Franciscan house in Sao Paulo. The Franciscan superior (provincial) finally heard that Fray Luis had left dressed in his habit and with a copy of the New Testament and had taken two months to reach Barra (Bahia) because he had not taken a bus but had begged for lifts from truckers. The Franciscan superior asked Boff to come with him to Bahia in order to collect Fray Luiz, as he had gone mad. Boff quickly replied that there were other mad people in the New Testament, see for example Mark 3.21 where it says that when Jesus' relatives heard that he was preaching somewhere they decided to look for him because, according to them, he had gone mad. The same had been said about the Apostle Paul who preached a Christ crucified and of St Francis of Assisi who embraced simplicity and poverty at a time when the norm was to join a monastery and live from the land attached to monastic communities. Boff didn't go to search for Fray Luiz and years later President Lula, on a visit to Bahia, met with an ecological group that had visited all those who lived beside the river and had been inspired by the simple life of Dom Luiz, by then the local bishop of Bahia.[321]

If theological utopias still exist, Leonardo Boff has made a substantial contribution to keeping them alive.

8

Elsa Tamez

Within the theological developments arising out of the ongoing debates within the Christian communities of Latin America there was an ever increasing awareness that within the socio-political context of the poor those who suffered extreme marginalization were women. If within a European and North-American context there have been challenges to male-oriented discourses and to patriarchy through the so-called feminist theology, Elsa Tamez was part of a group of pioneering Latin American women who asked questions about the context of liberation theology vis-à-vis the life and suffering of Latin American women.[322] However, Tamez managed over a biological generation to sustain a biblical hermeneutics of liberation that sustained a theological critique towards the world and towards patriarchy by reading the biblical texts through the eyes of the poor, particularly through the prism of Latin American women. If chronologically Tamez's writings appeared much later than Gutiérrez's, her involvement with the poor and the marginalized began very early in her life.

From the Poor and the Marginalized

Born in Mexico in 1950, she grew up in Monterrey, north of Mexico City, a city of many Latin American contrasts between the poor and the rich. She remembers that she was a happy child, unaware of the possibility of being unhappy and tied to timetables or routines, while her family experienced a constant shortage of food. In a small house of three rooms there were her parents, seven brothers and sisters, an aunt and a cousin. Her father was visually impaired and constantly unemployed, while her mother distributed the small food with equity and worried about the next meal for the family. However, she was a sickly child who received special attention from her mother: she was given from time to time a glass of milk, without the knowledge of her brothers and sisters. In her words:

> If it hadn't been for the hunger of my seven brothers and sisters, perhaps I would like milk better. I guess I don't like it today because my brain, like a closet where memories are stored, associates milk with the image of a thin, sickly girl hiding under the table where she quickly drinks a glass of white liquid, hoping her brothers and sisters won't discover her. They couldn't ask for something they couldn't have. Why make mother suffer? She had done enough managing to provide a glass of milk for her daughter who was more prone to tuberculosis. Now, whenever I see the boxes, bottles and bags of milk in the grocery stores, I see myself there, under the table drinking milk, in complicity with my mother, being careful to wipe off the white moustache after the last sip.[323]

If some of the Latin American theologians embraced the poor because of a later awareness of oppression and marginalization, Tamez grew up among the poor and at the age of fifteen left Monterrey in order to live with her older sister, married to a protestant minister, in Mexico City. As a child her second home was a very traditional Presbyterian congregation, where she developed her own identity and where she felt that God was very close to her. It was the experience of self-discovery and the closeness of God that made her want to study theology when she completed her secondary schooling. However, the first obstacle for her as a woman was that the Presbyterian Church of Mexico didn't accept women for theological studies, so in 1969 she emigrated to Costa Rica in order to study at the Seminario Bíblico Latinoamericano.

The ecclesial experience of Costa Rica was that of a church

involved with the ongoing economic divisions of the people and Tamez was touched by the experience of a God who was beyond the sacred space of a church and within the streets and the daily concerns of ordinary people. The experience of Costa Rica was that of Latin America in general, where the military regimes of the Southern Cone and of Central America were being lived as experiences for ecclesial reflection by the Christian communities and by the Catholic bishops meeting in Medellín (Colombia) in 1968. Nevertheless, Costa Rica stood as a haven within that political turmoil, not a developed nation but a nation without an army. Costa Ricans had managed to enlarge old political systems through a violent crisis that led to an armed revolution in 1948.[324] After the crisis ended, the government of Costa Rica decided to disband the army and to rely on volunteers and policemen in times of trouble.[325] Throughout the years, successive Costa Rican governments managed to reject offers of armed co-operation with the United States and managed to live through international crises that affected them due to the fact that their neighbour, Nicaragua, was usually at odds with liberation armies and other guerrilla movements. Within that context it was possible for many Latin American students and intellectuals to find shelter and a good academic atmosphere within Costa Rican institutions of higher education, particularly those associated with faith communities.

The late 1960s was a time of enormous political activity in Latin America in which the documents of Medellín and the writings of Gutiérrez not only affirmed the work of the Church in Latin America but also reflected an ongoing ecclesial experience that had started before 1968.[326] As she continued her studies, Tamez was integrated in 1976 into the newly formed Departamento Ecuménico de Investigaciones (DEI), a research community that discussed theological knowledge from the point of view of involvement with the world. The first book published by DEI was Franz Hinkelammert's *Las armas ideólogicas de la muerte*, a book that influenced Tamez's theological thought then and still influences her writings today.[327]

She graduated from the Universidad Nacional, Heredia,

Costa Rica, in 1973 and after marrying José Duque in 1975 she continued her theological studies and graduated with a licentiate in theology in 1979. Her initial period of theological reflection centred on reflections on life itself and in 1978 she wrote one of her first books, *La hora de la vida*. In 1985 she completed further studies in literature and linguistics with a thesis on the *Song of Songs* in which she explored the biblical text as a literary text and dwelt upon the meaning of pleasure and joy in the midst of a context marked by suffering and death. By then she had completed a book with a selection of interviews of theologians of liberation that she had carried out in an informal way during theological conferences and meetings.[328] She had asked them about the role and place of women within the newly emerging phenomenon of liberation theology, thus combining her two major theological interests: the God of the poor and the role of women within the biblical text.

It is at this stage in her life that the Presbyterian Church offered her a scholarship in order to write her doctorate at the University of Lausanne, where she studied and resided with her husband from 1987 to 1990. In her doctoral work Tamez returns to a central theme within the ecumenical movement, justification by faith, but she asked fresh questions about the context, understanding and interpretation of justification within Latin America. Her doctoral thesis with the title *Contra toda condena: La justificación por la fe desde los excluídos* was later published by DEI in Costa Rica and triggered several other works that established her as one of the leading women protestant theologians of Latin America.

Changing Theological Phases

There is no doubt that there was a continuous progression and change within Tamez's theological thinking. Her methodological presuppositions and theological method has been consistent in order to achieve the changing awareness needed for a contextual theology: she has read the biblical text asking questions about hermeneutical readings that have reproduced former understandings, which on the one hand have excluded the poor and on the other hand have excluded women from the centrality of God's work.

If from the beginning of her studies she took part in a re-reading of the biblical text from the point of view of the poor and the marginalized of Latin America in the context of the Cold War, of economic and political oppression, of revolution and socialist utopias, she was able to accept the criticism thrown at her by Ivonne Gebara, who argued that Tamez had created a 'patriarchal feminist theology'. Within that early hermeneutical work the orthodoxy of Christianity was kept without much questioning and the liberating God of Gutiérrez continued, showing traces of a God immersed in the *orthodoxy* of the Catholic Church while encouraging an *orthopraxis* outside the protection of the sacred space and of the patriarchal Church. That theological hermeneutics was eventually corrected as women liberation theologians pointed to the fact that women were oppressed in two ways: by the capitalist state and by the patriarchal system that impeded their development and voice, not only within society but also within the churches. The hermeneutics of theological epistemology continued being patriarchal through understandings of the Trinity, Christology and ecclesiology, while the hermeneutics of the social evolved into an inclusive questioning that ceased to be open to women when new social and political systems replaced the totalitarian state enforced by capitalism and the Cold War.[329]

Tamez's theological development coincides with the socio-theological moments led by women theologians and women activists in Latin America. The first theological questioning by women on liberation theology coincided with the first congress of women theologians in Mexico in 1979, which took place while the general meeting of Latin American Catholic bishops in Puebla de los Angeles was in progress. At that congress women were assumed as historical subjects, agents of liberation and of theological production, nevertheless oppressed by narratives and contexts related to gender and class. The tools for a development of theologies by Latin American women arose out of Tamez's hermeneutical tools provided in her 1979 work *La Biblia de los oprimidos* and her 1980 seminal paper 'La mujer que complicó la historia de la salvación' in which she re-read the story of Hagar as a woman who suffered three kinds of oppression under Abraham and Sara: oppression due to class, race and gender.[330] That paper became a focal point for women theologians at the Fifth International Conference and First General Assembly of EATWOT in New Delhi, India (17–29 August 1981), where Tamez told participants:

> Hagar is a woman who suffers a threefold oppression, like many women in the Third World. Hagar is thrice oppressed: because of her class (she is a slave); because of her race (she is an Egyptian, an impure race according to the Hebrews); and because of her sex (she is a woman).[331]

The second congress of Latin American feminist theologians took place in Buenos Aires in 1985 and it was at that meeting that, by then, a larger number of women problematized the androcentric theological discourse of the first generation of male liberation theologians and proposed the development of a liberation theology from the perspective of women. The collected papers, edited by Elsa Tamez, opened a series of methodological considerations for an ongoing theological project by women and a year later Tamez published a further epistemological tool through the essay 'The Power of the Naked', a full critique of machismo inside the Church and within the theological discourse of liberation theology.[332] This seminal essay ends with a utopian assertion and an agenda for future theological explorations:

> Latin American women, along with their partners, want to recreate cultural, ecclesial, and theological history, cultivating it with new hands, new seeds, new care, and new weapons in order to produce new fruit, new everyday relations, new ways of practising our faith within the church, and new theological discourse.[333]

Within that utopian perspective there was also a critical approach towards the Church, perceived as predominantly masculine, and to theology as a hermeneutical tool of the Church, as monopolized by men. It was not only a challenge to male liberation theologians but a call to them and to the churches to recognize the role of women and the contribution by women theologians within Latin American theology.

During the third congress of women theologians in Rio de Janeiro in 1993 there was a further development in their thought and their theology by the fact that gender theory was incorporated as a hermeneutical tool in order to continue the development of a Latin American theology that would include women's perspectives and women theologians as agents of, by then, a well-established theological movement for liberation. Within that development, gender theory was recognized as a tool in order to read the Bible and to rephrase many of the male-oriented paradigms given to liberation theology. For Elsa Tamez those developments are no more than a full realization of a theological understanding: women are made as image and likeness of God and therefore should occupy the same place within creation that a man has. Already in Buenos Aires women theologians had started the development of a male–female study of God, following North American theologians who already years before had spoken of the feminine side of God and the importance of male–female stable energies and social relations within most symbolic and cultural systems in the world.[334]

Ethics and Liberation

Tamez's energies have a lot to do with such developments because while it is possible to argue, with her, that the context of Latin American history after Vatican II and the traditional numerical presence of women within the Basic Christian Communities triggered a context of female involvement in theological developments, one must also recognize that most of the first generation of liberation theologians of the twentieth century were men – priests or ministers, who had had the opportunity to study in Europe and who were able to become pastoral catalysts of evangelical action and theological thinking. As a result, Tamez's work always faces the scrutiny of more traditional biblical scholarship, centred more in linguistic and historical analysis rather than in contextual analysis of God's action in an ever-changing world, be it that of the Old Testament or that of the Christian communities today.

Tamez's work and ethical commitment to liberation in Latin America falls within the classificatory heuristic devise of the first generation of liberation theologians because her own response to society's crisis of oppression of the 1970s was to think theologically the place of religion as an ethical divine commitment to justice systematized in a narrative labelled as theology – a narrative about God. Her contribution, however, built upon the parameters of theological praxis provided a more universalistic reading of the sacred texts of Christianity. Therefore, unlike Assmann and his contextual interpretation of Christianity vis-à-vis Marxism, Tamez provided a critical analysis and an interpretive model that could be used in a later period even when Marxism and the use of the social sciences had lost their fashionable appeal sustained by the Cold War syndrome.

If *Bible of the Oppressed* challenges a reading of the Bible outside the perspective of the poor and the marginalized, and women as doubly marginalized, Tamez moved her own ethical agenda of solidarity with the poor from the social structures of pastoral communities to her own development as university professor, biblical scholar and, lately, head of the Universidad Bíblica Latinoamericana in Costa Rica.

After the shocking events of 9/11 in the USA the syndrome of the Cold War was raised by the American administration and her allies, with one proviso: those on the other side were no longer revolutionary powers triggered by the Soviet Union but extremists within Islam who were creating the international conditions for a Cold War applied to the world religions. If for most commentators religion had nothing to do with the Cold

War, religion and discourses about religion had a lot to do with the creation, development and management of international crises within the early years of the twenty-first century. The response by the American administration, labelled as 'a war on terror', created colonial structures of force imposed upon other countries such as Iraq and Afghanistan and subsequently made the possibility of intellectual exchanges of ideas between non-US scholars and those within the United States more difficult. In fact, the response to national security by the United States proved ever more difficult for those visiting the United States, and particularly citizens of Latin America and Africa, the first theological base for theologians of liberation. The invasion of Iraq that followed once again divided the world between those who were for the aims of the Bush administration and those who were against them.

It is in that context that Elsa Tamez issued a public letter to fellow theologians and those who regularly invited her to the United States for lectures and conferences stating her own ethical position regarding war and international violence. Tamez is not a pacifist, or at least has not declared herself to be one; however, she felt strongly about her embargo on travelling to the United States due to the fact that in a press conference justifying the invasion of Iraq in 2003 President Bush 'declared that during the war with Iraq there should be prayers for his soldiers and for the people of Iraq'. Tamez expands on Bush's words by stating the following: 'This for honest Christians is a complete inversion of all Christian values in which we see in Jesus Christ, the Prince of Peace, and in God, the fullness of love and mercy. How can one bomb a people with weapons of mass destruction and at the same time pray for them!'[335] Within the same letter she invited other theologians, church leaders and all Christians of Latin America 'to abstain from travel to the United States in protest against the war, and to unite themselves in the already existing struggle against the possession of chemical weapons and weapons of mass destruction'.

The response to the letter was of respect given to a theologian who guided her actions by her own reading of the Bible and of solidarity with a person who could think about the world from a faith perspective rather than through the fashionable political trends of politics or religion. Rosemary Radford Ruether, Carpenter Professor of Feminist Theology at Graduate Theological Union/Pacific School of Religion, Berkeley, California, wrote a public letter to Elsa Tamez assuring her that in some Christian quarters the letter had been understood as a Christian challenge to violence and to the ill-conceived violent policy of 'pre-emptive strikes' against any nation in the world. She wrote: 'I want you to know that I and many others here greeted your letter with great appreciation and thanksgiving. I regard this letter as an expression of high regard for how the United States should (and is not) relating to the rest of the world.'[336] Ruether's further thoughts were of a boycott of all international meetings of the World Council of Churches in the United States and the 'further building of a global coalition of those who really believe that a different world is possible'.

Tamez's use of the literary genre of letters shows the identification with her scholarship on ancient letters, such as the pastoral letters of the New Testament. However, it also illustrates her ability to communicate ethics and liberation through means that are pastoral and grounded in praxis rather than solely on academic discourse. For example, in an address to a meeting of theologians of Latin America in Sao Paulo, Brazil in July 2003 she decided not to read the paper she had written for the volume of conference proceedings but to read a letter she had written to all participants. In doing so, she reminded her audience of the importance of letters within antiquity and within the canonical books of the New Testament. The letter titled 'Epistle to Priscilla and all brothers and sisters gathered in Sao Paulo, Brazil' aimed at encouraging the following of Christ by the delegates but also made a provoking critique of the role of the churches and some of their members within a climate of consumerism and hedonism or within the contemporary scandals of child abuse that also touched the social and pastoral realities of Latin American countries.[337] Even when she seemed to have made a tremendous impact in those meetings of theologians she herself has intimated that her identity as a biblical scholar remains at the centre and that she is not too sure that her contribution to big theological meetings leaves her with the same satisfaction as her biblical work among Christian communities and women's groups.

Biblical Hermeneutics

Her influence on others stems from a solid biblical hermeneutics that explores themes of exploitation and social oppression but relies on a solid biblical formation and the examination of ongoing historic and literary approximations on the biblical text by European and North American scholars. This methodology, in which she is able to serve the oppressed through her scholarship but at the same time engage with the semantics of biblical words in Hebrew or Greek, marks a departure from the more socio-historical reading of Gutiérrez and his own very successful re-reading of the book of Job.[338] The variety of approaches to the same historical solution can be seen in Tamez's interpretation of the conflicts within the early Christian communities and their leaders' solutions to conflicts regarding the increasing numbers of wealthy members, the leadership of women, theological questions and the different ways of life of the Christian communities and Graeco-Roman society. The comparative method used in order to assess the different responses to conflict provided by 1 Timothy and James showed different responses were offered by them to issues of community organization. Later bodies of tradition decided to keep the authority principle stated by Timothy and Titus and chose to ignore the larger discussions on justification and works of mercy emphasized by James in his letter.[339]

Despite all her many other works in biblical hermeneutics Tamez's agenda remains set by the hermeneutical principles proposed within her seminal work *Bible of the Oppressed*.[340] In her work Tamez studied the theme of oppression in the Old Testament not as yet another study of a biblical theme but with the conviction that the themes of oppression and liberation always go together.[341] For Tamez, the history of oppression [and of liberation] in the context of Latin America is a continuation of God's revelation within the Bible so that 'oppression and liberation are the very substance of the entire historical context within which divine revelation unfolds, and only by reference to this central fact can we understand the meaning of faith, grace, love, peace, sin, and salvation'.[342] However, unlike discourses and analyses that associate salvation solely with an individual acceptance of redemption, Tamez reinforces the fact that a close reading of the Old Testament emphasizes and reiterates the idea that the God of the Old Testament sides with the oppressed rather than with the victors, or the oppressors.

The experience of oppression (*'anah*) within the Old Testament does not relate to oppressed souls but it is a real experience, a human experience through which God communicates with real human beings and acts on their behalf showing a process and action of liberation.[343] Oppression comes from other human beings and the process of oppression creates poverty and powerlessness due to the fact that in an economic system that relates to a social system, a very agrarian system of production, the enrichment of some creates an immediate process of poverty in others. In summary, for Tamez 'the oppressed and the poor suffer exploitation and death, both physical and psychological; they suffer discrimination and degradation. To speak of liberation, therefore, is to speak of the struggle of an oppressed people in quest for their rights and spurred on by the hope that the victory will be real because their God is at their side in the struggle.'[344]

Within that general exploration of oppression, Tamez combines sub-themes such as oppression at the international level, oppression at the national level, agents and objects of oppression, oppressors and oppressed, forms and methods of oppression. Her conclusion is very clear, God does not act with military might in order to support the oppressed, but the experience of liberation becomes a divine experience by which faith is sustained and enriched, it becomes a spiritual experience of bonding with the God who upholds the basic rights of all, and particularly of those who suffer injustice. Tamez writes:

> Yahweh concretizes in himself the justice and love that are experienced in the course of history. And since justice and love cannot become concrete realities except in a society where there is no oppression, Yahweh comes on the scene at every moment in solidarity with the oppressed, for the purpose of assuring the concrete realization of love and the removal of oppressors.[345]

For Tamez the Bible is a book of testimonies, personal and social, of particular moments in which people in their daily toils and within ordinary political processes have recognized the deliverance and liberation provided by their faith in God. That theme extends from the Old Testament to the New Testament through the metaphor of 'good news'. Jesus of Nazareth proclaims good news to the poor and the marginalized and extends the care of a liberating God for his people, at difficult times due to the Roman occupation and the isolation of the periphery from Jerusalem. The liberating God, once again, exercises a support mechanism through his Son in order to remind those who had the possibility of supporting change that justice was at the heart of a peaceful society and that justice was not being offered to large sectors of the population of Israel, Judea and Samaria. The biblical term 'poor', those who are to receive the Good News, are 'the helpless, the indigent, the hungry, the oppressed, the needy, the humiliated. And it is not nature that has put them in this situation; they have been unjustly impoverished and despoiled by the powerful.'[346]

Hermeneutics of Justification

In order to be part of the justice and mercy of God, Tamez concludes, Christians must undergo a process of conversion, understood as 'a gift from God because it shows us the way and invites us to enter the world of freedom, the world of life. But at the same time conversion is a human task, because it demands of us an individual and collective commitment to the building of that world.'[347]

Within that commitment Christians of all denominations became divided through historical processes and theological disagreements. One of those disagreements, the whole debate regarding justification, dominated the period of the Reformation and Counter Reformation in Europe. Tamez returns not to the theological debate but to the Latin American context in order to re-work justification as good news to the excluded.[348] Further, she explores the meaning of works within the construction of a just society in Latin America by a detailed exploration of the biblical text of James in order to apply some of the hermeneutical concepts outlined in *Bible of the Oppressed*, to provide a contextual reading of James for Latin America.[349] This twofold project by Tamez cannot be ignored as separate, but is a theologically connected pioneering work that opens new avenues of exploration for years to come. This project reflects the theological engagement by a reformed Christian working within a majority non-reformed Latin American Christian population with issues that most theologians would like to avoid. Tamez does not ignore them but confronts the reality of Latin American theology, with the poor at the centre of the discourse, free from doctrinal discrimination and narratives of exclusion, be they social or theological.

In *The Amnesty of Grace* Tamez asks critical questions about the understanding and oral use of 'justification by faith' in a Latin American context. She argues that within the common use of the phrase there has been a proper reflection on its meaning so that the term alludes to an action by God that seems purely individualistic and closely related to the single sacrifice of Christ, so an individual Christian is justified by the blood of Christ. Tamez challenges the ongoing use of an individual perspective, reminding readers that the discussions that triggered the Reformation in Europe had a different context than the Latin American one. Thus, she explores the biblical texts in the context of Latin America rather than the oral tradition of evangelists that brought an oral tradition that corresponds to other lands and other contexts. She writes:

> From this analysis it is clear that the doctrine of justification has been invested with meaning both explicitly and implicitly, with or without people's awareness of doing so. The need to reformulate the doctrine of justification is equally evident now that individualism, subjectivism, universalism, passivity, and general misinterpretation (whether explicit or implicit, conscious or unconscious) have contributed to the confusion of its meaning.[350]

Tamez re-explores the use of 'justification' within the writings of Paul and concludes that the aspect of justice, as social redistribution, has been taken out and ignored by commentators that have related 'justification' solely with belief and acceptance of the redemptive sacrifice of Christ. It is not possible to underestimate the importance of this particular study. By reassessing the context of Paul's words of justification in the letter to the Romans, Tamez rediscovers the close connection of justification and liberation whereby not only the individual becomes justified by belief but also society becomes God's world by the actions of those justified within God's world. She concludes that 'by considering the solidarity of God as the root of justification, the excluded person is aware that God is present in solidarity in Jesus Christ, the excluded person par excellence, and also in others who are excluded'.[351]

The realization that involvement with the excluded by particular actions by the justified is part of God's salvific work relates to Tamez's previous biblical exploration of the letter of James. In the introduction she once again recognizes the difficulties posed by traditional followers of 'justification by faith' alone due to the clear message of James towards the help of widows and orphans and the letter's critique to landowners and oppressors in general. The letter was not fully accepted into the biblical canon until the fourth century and reformers such as Erasmus and Luther had problems with its inclusion within the canon. Luther could not accept the canonical inclusion of James, Hebrews, Jude or Revelation and in his German translation of the New Testament he included those books at the end but without a number in the general index.

Tamez's contribution relates to the fact that she accepts justification by faith but, as in the case of her work on justification, she assumes that justification requires justice and that any challenges to social oppression reinforce the justification of those who exercise the mercy of God and challenge injustice. The main oppressors within the letter of James are the rich because they oppress others and fail to build a just society where God's work of justification could take place. Thus, Tamez argues that: 'For James, the link between the experience of oppression and eschatological hope is the practice of faith' summarized by the help to widows and orphans (James 1.27).[352] Within that experience of oppression dialogue with God through prayer is crucial, but through a genuine prayer that conduces to actions that alleviate suffering but also challenge structures of oppression within society.

In conclusion, Tamez's sense of a widely possible diversification of liberation theology and the critique of first-generation male-oriented theologians in Latin America led to her own realization of a Latin American diversity, socially and theologically. She expressed that important challenge within the second general assembly of Third World theologians in Oaxtepec, Mexico in 1986 (7–14 December). She spoke of the creative cross-fertilization between the theologies of Africa, Asia and Latin America; however, she also pointed to the fact that there was the need to focus more closely on the richness of Latin American 'cultures' and particularly on the vitality of indigenous religions, without of course forgetting the location of women within that exploration.[353] Efforts for a new evangelization of Latin America are emphasized by Tamez in the following words: 'This continent has been baptised but not evangelised ... We are working on the evangelisation of our culture in the midst of social conflicts and poverty. There are many challenges coming from this work, and we are very attentive to the experience of other continents.'[354]

That realization was to create a third wave of theological discourse related to the indigenous populations of Latin America (*pueblos originarios*) taken seriously by the Fourth General Conference of Latin American bishops in Santo Domingo in 1992 (12–28 October).[355] Thus, after a second wave had raised issues of oppression to the poor as women, gendered beings made in God's image, Latin American theologies diversified even more, recognizing that if a poor woman was oppressed twice, a poor indigenous woman was oppressed thrice. In the next chapter I focus on the theological efforts by Diego Irarrázaval and his theology of inculturation for Latin America and his engagement with the values, symbols and contribution by the indigenous populations of Latin America.

9

Diego Irarrázaval

In the past few years Diego Irarrázaval has opened a new area in Latin American theology by consolidating many efforts already in existence and by taking to heart the conclusions of the General Meeting of the Latin American bishops in Santo Domingo in 1992. In doing so Irarrázaval has explored the complexity of elements that create a context for a Latin American theology and has consolidated the efforts of many of those theologians explored in the previous chapters. For him,

> This key of inculturation opens many doors to our situation. We of course have other keys: socio-political; ecological; gender and generational; emotional and sexual; racial-indigenous, black, and mestizo; economic; and ethical. These are various ways of understanding and building an everyday reality. Each of these keys can be complementary to the others, and they make us more alert to a complex universe.[356]

Missionary in Peru

Diego Irarrázaval, a Catholic priest of the Congregation of the Holy Cross, was born in Chile in 1942 and at the early age of 16 took part in summer missions in rural Talca, southern Chile. Through that experience he discovered the possibility of becoming a priest. Later he was involved with the Christians for Socialism movement, an organization of priests and lay people who wanted to support the option for socialism made by a number of priests in Chile at the time of the socialist government of Salvador Allende. Among those who started the movement in 1971 were a number of foreign priests ministering in working-class areas of Santiago and several Chileans, such as Gonzalo Arroyo, Pablo Richard, Sergio Torres and Diego Irarrázaval. Others, including Pablo Fontaine, Ronaldo Muñoz and Esteban Gumucio, participated within the movement as 'critical observers'.[357]

Irarrázaval continued working through the Christian communities after the military coup of 1973 but eventually had to leave Chile in 1975. He moved to Chimbote, on the Peruvian coast, and in 1981 he arrived in Chucuito, a location 3,880 metres above sea level with a majority population of Aymara-speaking peoples.[358] Irarrázaval was ordained as a priest in that locality in 1984 and stayed there for 20 years.[359] The pastoral and theological outlook of the Peruvian church was very progressive after the Second Vatican Council, and theologians such as Gustavo Gutiérrez found a good patron and a supporter in the Cardinal of Lima Juan Landázuri Ricketts (1955–90).[360] Indeed, Peru became a focal point for the development of liberation theology and the Catholic University in Lima a first-class academic institution that provided courses on pastoral formation for large numbers of lay people and a focal point for the development of an ongoing dialogue between theology and the social sciences. Particularly in Chimbote, Bishop Luis Bambarén, formerly auxiliary bishop of Lima, led a pastoral renewal that influenced the Peruvian church in general following on the work of the American Dominican James Burke. The exception remained the Archdiocese of Ayacucho, located in the mountains where the Shining Path movement was very prominent and where an ageing clergy, depleted in numbers, failed to address the lay Catholic involvement within contemporary social life. When John Paul II visited Ayacucho in 1985 he consoled a population that for five years had already suffered shootings and violence and the Jesuit provincial addressed the possibility of dialogue between the factions involved in terrorism and state violence. Those efforts failed and Shining Path spread from Ayacucho to other parts of Peru; however, throughout the violence it was very clear that the main enemy of the terrorist movement was the progressive clergy within the Peruvian Church who, through pastoral reflections and the praxis of liberation, were able to provide a different path for the youth and those who challenged poverty and violence in rural Peru.

Irarrázaval lived within that progressive Church through most of his priestly life; however, in 2004 he moved to the Parish of San Roque in Peñalolén, Santiago, where he continued his pastoral work as assistant priest, together with his academic work and his lectures to many groups throughout South America. Irarrázaval served as President of the Ecumenical Association of Third World Theologians (EATWOT) from 2001 to 2006.

His experience with indigenous peoples in Peru is the backbone of his theology, so that his major works only appeared after many years of pastoral work among the Aymaras. For the Aymaras there is a close connection between human beings and Mother Earth and the Marian celebrations of the year are important feasts in which communities dance and sing. Irarrázaval recognized that the major problems within those communities were the lack of economic opportunities, the peripheral existence they live within a modern state, domestic violence and the excess of alcohol consumption. There is no doubt that his ministry must have been difficult because of two social realities: (1) the challenges of developing an indigenous or inculturated Christianity within a territory that suffered a violent imposition of Christianity by the conquistadors and the foreign missionaries within colonial times, and (2) the suspicion by Peruvians of all Chileans and things Chilean since the Pacific War of 1879 when the Chilean armies appropriated territories belonging to Peru and Bolivia and occupied by force Peruvian territories including Lima, the Peruvian capital city. Despite those difficulties, Irarrázaval learned from those indigenous communities hope and happiness, values that he has explored through a contextual theology in his latest writings.[361]

A Theology of Inculturation

Until the end of the twentieth century there was less awareness of any process of inculturation in Latin America, in comparison to other continents such as Africa or Asia. A process of inculturation, of using symbols, languages and indigenous customs within the life and celebration of Christianity was a phenomenon that started centuries ago with the arrival of the Jesuits in China and Japan. However, the debate within Third World theology was led by the growth and lively liturgies celebrated by Christian communities in Africa.[362] Thus, after the approval of the use of vernacular languages within the liturgy at the time of the Second Vatican Council, the Zairian Rite and other African approved liturgical rites led an ongoing vernacular hermeneutics of a European and Roman rite. It was clear that those changes in liturgical rites within Africa were not cosmetic, as the emerging Christianity, large in numbers and in creativity, was endorsed by the visit of Pope Paul VI to Kampala in July 1969, where he not only assumed that a process of change from a Latin liturgy to the vernacular was complex but also encouraged all African bishops gathered there to have an African Christianity.[363]

If one compares the developments in Christianity and local theologies after the Second Vatican Council, it could be argued that Africa centred its reflections and practices on a theology of inculturation, while Asia stressed inter-faith dialogue and a Christian dialogue with the world religions and Latin America centred most pastoral and theological developments on Christian challenges to poverty, oppression, under-developments and socio-political inequality.

If at a localized level missionaries in Latin America integrated some symbols and examples of inculturated symbolic and liturgical realities, Africa received an institutional boost by the fact that Pope Paul VI in his visit to Kampala in 1969 stressed the value and need of an African Christianity, while Latin Americans struggled to face European challenges when speaking of a Latin American Christianity and a Latin American theology. It is in this context that Irarrázaval's contribution systematizes the possibility of an inculturated Latin American theology, 30 years after African theologians had received their seal of approval and the encouragement to continue their own liturgical explorations, a process that was re-affirmed by the 1994 African Synod of Bishops.

The Fourth General Conference of the Latin American bishops met in Santo Domingo from 12 to 28 October 1992, exactly 500 years after the arrival of Columbus's expedition to the island.[364] There had already been many writings by Latin American theologians highlighting the plight of the indigenous populations and appealing for a new evangelization that would include them in their own right and would allow the indigenous peoples of Latin America to dictate their own path within the Church. Was this a movement towards inculturation that came too late? Maybe. However, it coincided with the natural development of socio-political processes in Latin America during the 1990s. The climate of Latin American political movements changed from the centrality of the military governments to the local and indigenous movements for land, ecology and indigenous rights.

Irarrázaval, who had already been involved in the daily task of supporting Christian communities in Peru, among indigenous populations, relied for his Latin American theology of inculturation on the strong and multiple statements given by the Latin American bishops at Santo Domingo. John Paul II, in his inaugural speech, put emphasis on the attention needed by 'indigenous cultures and afro-Americans' taking into account all that those cultures have to offer and particularly cultural traits that are deeply human and humanizing.[365] Together with those traits, John Paul II highlighted the signs of liberating movements deeply rooted in Christianity that united the indigenous and the Christian, such as the ecological movements.[366] The great symbol of that inculturation, for John Paul II, was the mestizo Virgin of Guadalupe, which expressed the transformation of authentic cultural values through the gospel and the rooting of Christianity within indigenous cultures.[367]

If the inaugural speech did not go far enough, the conclusions of the Santo Domingo conference placed a heavy emphasis on the inculturation of the gospel and offered a central role for the indigenous populations in the evangelization of twenty-first-century Latin America. The three main themes implemented by the Latin American bishops on return to their own local diocese were: (1) a new evangelization, (2) the human promotion of people, particularly the poor, providing continuity with Medellín, and (3) an inculturated evangelization. Within that inculturation process, the Latin American bishops wished to become closer to the indigenous populations and the Afro-Americans in order to foster a full life in Christ already present in their communities and cultures, and also to strengthen an ongoing dialogue between indigenous communities and Christian communities in order to enrich the latter.[368] In summary, the Catholic Church committed itself to support the requests by indigenous populations to be recognized in law, to own their land, to speak their language, to live according to their traditions and to communicate and share their values with other indigenous populations nationally and internationally.[369]

It is important to remark that documents do not provide immediate social or pastoral action but act as catalysts of social and pastoral realities already in existence. Thus, the documents of Santo Domingo outlined an ecclesial and theological practice that was already taking place, as we have already outlined in the ecological theology and practice of Leonardo Boff (see Chapter 7 in this volume). If before Santo Domingo inculturation was a foreign term to Latin Americans, after Santo Domingo it became the new term for pastoral action and political alliances within many sectors of a larger civil society. Irarrázaval in his work outlines some important systematic paradigms in order to reflect on a contextualized evangelization.

Inculturation and Liberation

Aylward Shorter, in his work on a theology of inculturation within the African context, had acknowledged the relation between inculturation and liberation; however, it had understood the two theologies as different from each other.[370] Irarrázaval, in his work, advances the complexity of liberation theology and therefore assumes that inculturation and liberation go together hand in hand so that a theology of inculturation is a process of liberation and that all processes of liberation require processes of inculturation.

Those processes of inculturation occur and are necessary within a Latin America that has seen the arrival of modernity. In Irarrázaval's words:

> The continent of South America is a mosaic of various kinds of sensitivities, groups, and processes. We belong to modernity with its values and impasses. There are indications that we stand at a change of epoch. It is within this complex and thrilling situation that inculturation takes place. It is not about nostalgia for customs, nor does it mean that the cultural is separated from other aspects of the human condition.[371]

Indeed, the source of all inculturation in theology is the incarnation of the Son of God and his life in Nazareth, while this is not the whole story. Thus, without the incarnation there would be no inculturation and no need to link communal inculturation with developments within the Church, the Christian communities in relation to the social context in which those communities operate.

Irarrázaval departs from the focus of inculturation in liturgical or aesthetic forms and argues strongly that there are groups and processes that trigger manifestations of inculturation and that have been ignored as agents within religious practice. The poor, for example, have been portrayed as dependent on the educated, and a symbolic dichotomy, a false dualism, has been created between the established Church and the popular church, between the educated sectors and the popular sectors of society and Church. This argument resonates with the past projects of a 'popular church' as opposed to an institutional or established Church or the portrayal of popular religiosity as a phenomenon for uneducated or older generations.

Thus, it is challenging that the first movers for an ongoing inculturation in Latin America, according to Irarrázaval, are the young, not surprisingly the main recipients of the Church's attention at the meeting of Latin American bishops in Puebla (Mexico, 1979). The life of all Latin Americans is full of a mestizo modernity in which goods are available at all times and they are pushed in front of all Latin American customers, but not all Latin Americans have access to them, not all trust them and not all trust them at all times. Therefore, Latin Americans devise a certain social and religious strategy that deals with ongoing changes and the possibility that their means not always achieve happiness or fulfilment or closeness with divine realities. Irarrázaval's social analysis is poignant in that one is reminded that among the people he lived with in Peru there have been many changes since the encounter between their ancient civilizations and the conquistadors, and they have managed to keep some of their ancient traditions while operating within the religious and ritual systems of the oppressors, be they the conquistadors or the economic oligarchic powers of any contemporary modern state.

Plurality is the dominant process present in all. It is through plurality that people can function within a private sphere of the family, the public sphere of the market and within the different symbolic systems that create and recreate sociability. It is through plurality that people inculturate all symbolic systems and systemic messages so that, by using symbols and sacralizing reality, humans can also manipulate social reality to their own advantage. It is at this point that Irarrázaval departs from a naive inculturation that predicates all human goodness and implements all divine realities. If all human life is an ongoing inculturation there must be elements that do not conform to the gospel and there is always the need of a critical inculturation in which some elements could be part of a human inculturation but not of a Christian inculturation. These are deep issues that require focused attention because, as was the case with challenges to dictatorial political systems in the 1970s and 1980s, they could create a rift between different groups within society and within the churches. Thus, Irarrázaval is aware that 'male power is sacralized in the form of keeping women from advancing. Likewise, many attributes of the white elite surround Christian symbols (saints, the Virgin, images of Christ); this is all imbibed uncritically by the Latin American population.'[372]

In the context of a Latin American modernity there are several ways of dealing with spiritual realities and the less preferred is a secular one, even when there are numbers of atheists and agnostics within the Latin American population. There are two characteristics that unite Christians in Latin America: a happy and emotional celebration of Christianity and a deep sense of the spiritual world expressed and lived in many different forms. For Irarrázaval there are three types of spirituality: (1) a devotional alliance, (2) a militant spirituality, and (3) an occasional spirituality.

Within a devotional alliance a person has a direct relation with a male or female saint, the Virgin Mary or Christ at a very personal and individual level. This spirituality is commonly expressed and observed in the urban centres where at any time of the day there are several individuals performing devotions at a church or a shrine, usually associated with a particular saint. Within a militant spirituality the social is emphasized and a person who belongs to a particular Christian group expresses its own inculturated Christianity in a preoccupation with community with either spiritual and ritualistic aims or socio-political involvement within the contemporary nation/state. The most common is the occasional spirituality where Latin Americans do not choose (1) or (2) but take part in baptisms, weddings and funerals or other moments of symbolic connection with the divine, usually related to inculturated moments of socio-religious life, without professing a particular spirituality but being happy to take part in social moments that include religious expressions of faith, devotion, covenant or commitment.

Within those three expressions of a spiritual or religious life, Latin Americans have also been influenced by the rules of the globalized market and they have learned how to choose their individual type of religion. This type of inculturated rephrasing of the market has, in my opinion, been the main factor for the growth of Pentecostal churches, which offer a particular and very clear way to salvation with a practice that departs from the organized relations of class, race, and social status attached to the locality and the colonial and post-colonial parish in Latin America. This has been one of the main challenges to liberation theology because the basis of liberation theology is not the individual per se but the community, the Christian community that deals with socio-economic and political realities from the point of view of the faith.

Within that individual response and appropriation of the values of the globalized market, the youth of Latin America remain the source for a social critique and a sense of community. Unlike European youth, they do not have access to education, economic prosperity or the goods of the market and therefore are less likely to find their group cohesion or individual fulfilment outside a group. However, young people sometimes find a way of protesting against secularism and the consumer society by taking part in fundamentalist movements, groups that assure them of a clear rule and a clear path in life that challenges others to the point that all diversity and social plurality becomes wrongdoing and must be excluded from a unified society. Just as some extreme forms of nationalism during the period of the military regimes created social conditions for aggression and violence, some groups of Christians that reject processes of inculturation, plurality and diversity could create the social conditions for cultural or social exclusion during the twenty-first century.

The main contribution by Irarrázaval to Latin American theology has been a new deep sociological and historical analysis

of the challenges posed by Christian communities in construct-
ing local theologies. His sense of a theology of inculturation
as part of diversity in theologies provides a methodology of
complexity, diversity and plurality that returns full circle to
Gutiérrez's seminal work, *A Theology of Liberation*, and relo-
cates issues of development and history from the 1960s into the
twenty-first century. For it is clear for him that, 'Inculturation is
not the property of specialists; rather, it has to do with everything done, believed, and celebrated by God's people.'[373]

Cultural Identities and Meanings

In his latest work in Spanish, still not translated into other
languages, Irarrázaval has made a significant contribution to
the connections between very complex spectrums of liberation
theologies in Latin America. His personal context has changed
from Peru to Chile but his wide reflections continue making an
impact on a wider Latin American theological and pastoral
praxis.

For Irarrázaval, if liberation is part of a process of inculturation and liturgical adaptation, such inculturation is only part of
a more diversified typology of themes and contexts that require
social liberation and a theological praxis. This theme, already
expanded by Tamez and Richard, presumes a surprising
presupposition: processes of globalization have created semantic fields that are terribly unified and through which notions of
identity have been labelled in practice as monogenic. Thus,
according to Irarrázaval, the universal process of globalization
has not conduced to the joys of semantic freedom but has
actualized an authoritarian model of mimetic identity.[374]

Latin America, as a multifaceted continent of many peoples,
languages, histories and theologies seems resigned to comply
with the unification of the world, and to challenge such a
unification seems to be a task of the theologian in daily life as
much as the task of contra-imperialism outlined by Pablo
Richard or the gendering of society and of theology proposed

by Elsa Tamez. If Leonardo Boff has argued for an ecological theology of world and land, Irarrázaval has managed to provide a complex critique that has finally moved Latin American theology into the concerns of the poor and the marginalized of the twenty-first century.

Irarrázaval highlights three contextual presuppositions that have guided his own socio-pastoral practice and his own writings about identity in Latin America in the context of a contextualized theological reflection: (1) The theological production in Latin America has devalued the complexity of identities and there has been very little interaction and dialogue between those who have lived and produced a Latin American theology. (2) There is still a vacuum between the theological knowledge of the academic and the hopes and lives of the people of God – there is an urgent need for dialogue between a reflexive faith, the human sciences and the wisdom of the poor. (3) Theology is required to search deeper for 'the signs of the times' as located in the unfolding of identities within a Latin American reality that is oppressed, multifaceted and with new life projects in the making.[375]

Irarrázaval is clear in arguing that identity is a polysemic concept developed by various academic disciplines and it is not an easy, simple and one-dimensional concept or social reality.[376] For many years and in many writings arising out of Latin America identity has been closely linked to cultural issues and cultural lives; however, within that theoretical association it is necessary to include the complexity of economic, psycho-social, biological, technical and aesthetic aspects of identity.[377] The social sciences' approach, so much present within Latin American theology, and particularly within theologies of liberation, has a complexity of identities within the ecclesial realities of the Church and the Christian communities, with the roles assigned to people within that ecclesial community and the diversity and complexity of the different Christian churches within Latin America. Theological identities are also present, and contradictory and opposed ones: the neo-conservative one that argues that any Latin American identity is primordially a

Catholic one and the servant theology that argues that any theological identity arises out of the service towards others and the immersion of the pastoral agents vis-à-vis theologians within the social realities of poverty, oppression and cultural diversity. Thus, for Irarrázaval, the theologian's identity that comes from God's truth manifests itself in diversity, finitude, complexity and pluralism, whereby God assumes a human finitude and acts within the complexities of an incarnated Latin American reality.[378]

Irarrázaval argues that identity has several dimensions in its complexity and that those dimensions need to be outlined as parts of a totality and as factors of an ongoing examination. Those diverse aspects of any identity are the biological, the gendered, the social, the economic, the mediated, and the spiritual realm of every human being and social group within society.

The biological side of identity is a category that surprisingly appears within Irarrázaval's work; however, it makes sense in that Irarrázaval argues that every human being is directly connected with the land, with the planet and with the cosmos in general. His reflections have clear implications towards an ecological sense of identity and an ecological theology but they also imply an ongoing need to relate issues of faith with issues of science, a theological dimension so far mostly ignored by Latin American theologies. Reflections on biology rather than technology provide a contemporary challenge to an anthropocentrism in which the markets seem to have located the final initiative on human beings and their own creativity while a close dialogue between faith and biology/science challenges us to return to the centrality of God as creator of all and of his world rather than ours by right.[379]

The mediated side of identity relates to a new aspect that is so much part of the contemporary Latin American context: communications and the Internet. The whole issue of mass media provides challenges for individual and social identities in that the images are not only aesthetic categories or selling means for the market but provide ultimately expressions of individual and common identity that take place in the everyday life of

Christians within Latin America. What does the Word of God say about these new phenomena? How does this new mode of virtual identity inform the writings and the reflections of contemporary theologians? Those are poignant and original questions that reflect the enormous complexities of identity in Latin America but also the new challenges for Christian communities and the complexity of contemporary Latin American theologies.

Irarrázaval concludes that discussions on identity are crucial in order to understand not theories of identity but in order to problematize how human beings act in globalized, pluricultural, conflictive, and historical contexts.

Inculturation and Identity: A Generational Postscript

There is no doubt that the context, socio-political and religious, in Latin America has changed over the past decade and that among all the themes of theological praxis and liberation outlined in previous chapters those of inculturation and identity remain crucial in order to understand the work of God and his Church in Latin America. Themes that come together as contextual realities remain central to the awareness and building up of the kingdom of God within Latin American societies that on the one hand appear globalized, and thus monothetic, while in practice they are very complex and polythetic. It is within that societal complexity that indigenous populations and secularized agents have taken part in critical social initiatives and have allied themselves with the ongoing challenges towards capitalism and globalization.

If inculturation and liberation are to take place at any time and in any context, those processes and theologies are also to challenge the socio-political structure of the churches, as has been the case in the work and challenge provided by the thousands of Christian communities of Brazil and indeed throughout Latin America. Thus, the comments of Hugo Hinfelaar, a seasoned missionary in Zambia, are pertinent to understand the challenges posed by the theologians examined within this volume. Hinfelaar writes:

> Is inculturation not primarily a liberation from the accumu-
> lated burdens of history, an invitation by the new-comers to
> the old members of the Christian community to free them-
> selves from human structures and accept a new form of being
> church? It is never a 'going back' always a 'step forward' by
> the entire and universal Church because a new way of being
> church is born every time a new culture is accepted into the
> warmth of the Christian community.[380]

The challenge of a Latin American theology that accepts the indigenous populations' view of the world is to change the path of history and to incorporate new ways of being church while keeping the continuity of communion with centuries of history. For some this is impossible, for others such as Irarrázaval there is always the possibility of advancing towards different models of church and models of society.

If further pastoral work is needed in the context of changing social realities in Latin America, it is also possible to argue that if Latin American theologies have come of age, and in my opinion they have, those involved in the liberation movement should involve themselves at all times with a changing civil society. The pastoral agents and Christians of Latin America in their action constitute the prime movers of these theologies while much more needs to be done in classifying, organizing and reflecting upon the academic contribution of these Latin American theologies. The two fronts, the socio-religious and the academic, are not contradictory but one follows the other through a methodology of ongoing suspicion about the inten-tions and values provided by a consumerist and secularized society that wants God out of society and would prefer not to have Christian communities, indeed all kinds of faith com-munities, challenging the economic oppression of the poor and the devaluation of human beings in general for the sake of the market, of profit, and of greed.

If one were to be consistent with the action-reflection-action theological model then those who were not academic theologians in Latin America but systematized a pastoral practice of liberation should also be part of the history and the politics of a rainbow of Latin American theologies for the twenty-first century. I am thinking here of Oscar Romero, Pedro Casaldáliga, Sheila Cassidy, and many other Christians, men and women, who gave their lives and their comforts to a pastoral action for the poor and the marginalized, for the oppressed in society and within the churches in Latin America. It is through such ongoing understanding that we can continue speaking of 'generations' of theologians and we could include also those of a new generation that have applied Latin American theologies to other contexts and others realms of political engagement such as those explored by Marcella Althaus-Reid, Ivan Petrella or Pedro Trigo.[381]

The first generation of Latin American theologians set a unified theme of liberation, socio-political and religious, that marked profoundly the history of theology and the history of the Church. However, the proof of their enormous contribution to theology lies in the fact that they triggered a complexity and diversity of themes and actions within Latin American theology that has challenged other theologies, other political worlds and other ways of being church. A second generation generated further complexities and discussions within a pastoral realm of changes in the Latin American context while a third, and a current generation has used the standard methodologies of liberation theology in order to expand the complexity of liberation theology outside the constraints of tradition or ecclesiastical practice while maintaining the orthopraxis and the freedom of spirit of the first generation.[382] I am afraid that those who thought that Latin American theologies in general or liberation theology in particular had had their day were not aware of the ongoing praxis and reflection that has provided theology and the churches with a stronger and ever dynamic theology of praxis for the twenty-first century.

Notes

Introduction

1 Enrique Dussel, 'Preface to the Second Spanish-language Printing', in *History and the Theology of Liberation: A Latin American Perspective*, Maryknoll, NY: Orbis, 1976, p. xvi.

2 Hannah W. Stewart-Gambino and Everett Wilson, 'Latin American Pentecostals: Old Stereotypes and New Challenges', in Edward L. Cleary and Hannah W. Stewart-Gambino (eds), *Power, Politics, and Pentecostals in Latin America*, Boulder, Colorado: Westview Press, 1998, pp. 227–46; Harvey Cox, *Fire from Heaven: The Rise of Pentecostal Spirituality and the Reshaping of Religion in the Twenty-first Century*, Reading, Massachusetts: Addison-Wesley, 1995.

3 Edward L. Cleary and Juan Sepúlveda, 'Chilean Pentecostalism: Coming of Age', in Edward L. Cleary and Hannah W. Stewart-Gambino (eds), *Power, Politics, and Pentecostals in Latin America*, pp. 97–121.

4 Rowan Ireland, 'Pentecostalism, Conversions, and Politics in Brazil', in Edward L. Cleary and Hannah W. Stewart-Gambino (eds), *Power, Politics, and Pentecostals in Latin America*, pp. 123–37, and Cristián Parker, *Popular Religion and Modernization in Latin America: A Different Logic*, Maryknoll, NY: Orbis, 1996, pp. 154–60.

5 Ivan Vallier, *Catholicism, Social Control and Modernization in Latin America*, Englewood-Cliffs, NJ: Prentice-Hall, 1970.

6 For a current analysis of those ecclesial models see Nigel W. Oakley, 'Base Ecclesial Communities and Community Ministry: Some Freirean Points of Comparison and Difference', *Political Theology*, 5 (2004), 447–65.

7 Mario I. Aguilar, *A Social History of the Catholic Church in Chile vol. I: The First Period of the Pinochet Government 1973–1980*, Lewiston, N.Y., Queenston, Ontario, and Lampeter, Wales: Edwin Mellen Press, 2004; Daniel H. Levine (ed.), *Church and Politics in Latin America*, Beverly Hills, California: Sage, 1980; Daniel H. Levine (ed.), *Religion and Political Conflict in Latin America*, Chapel Hill: University of North Carolina Press, 1986; Scott Mainwaring and Alexander Wilde

Notes

(eds), *The Progressive Church in Latin America*, Notre Dame, Indiana: University of Notre Dame Press, 1989, and Brian Smith, *The Church and Politics in Chile*, Princeton, NJ: Princeton University Press, 1982.

8 It is clear that Ríos Montt did not use his political power in favour of any spread of Pentecostalism. He was a professional soldier, however his example encouraged the possibility of considering Pentecostalism as an official way of being religious within a politically troubled Guatemala. See Everett Wilson, 'Guatemalan Pentecostals: Something of their Own', in Edward L. Cleary and Hannah W. Stewart-Gambino (eds), *Power, Politics, and Pentecostals in Latin America*, pp. 139–62.

9 Edward L. Cleary, 'Introduction: Pentecostals, Prominence and Politics', in Edward L. Cleary and Hannah W. Stewart-Gambino (eds), *Power, Politics, and Pentecostals in Latin America*, pp. 1–24, at p. 7; Andrea Damacena Marlins and Lucia Pedrosa de Padua, 'The Option for the Poor and Pentecostalism in Brazil', *Voices from the Third World*, 25 (2002), pp. 205–38.

10 However, despite their large power of mobilization, the Catholic *comunidades eclesiais de base* (CEBs) never had an impact in the electoral ballots; see Carol Ann Drogus, 'Popular Movements and the Limits of Political Mobilization at the Grassroots in Brazil', in Edward L. Cleary and Hannah Stewart-Gambino (eds), *Conflict and Competition: The Latin American Church in a Changing Environment*, Boulder, Colorado and London: Lynne Rienner, 1992, pp. 63–86.

11 Marcela López Levy, *We Are Millions: Neo-Liberalism and New Forms of Political Action in Argentina*, London: Latin America Bureau, 2004.

12 The mothers of the Argentinean disappeared, known as the Madres de la Plaza de Mayo, kept a weekly silent walk around that square in Buenos Aires in order to direct public opinion towards the lack of effort by subsequent Argentinean administrations to provide information on the 25,000 people who disappeared during the military regime, '30 years on, mothers continue to march for missing children', *The Times* 10 December 2005, p. 54 and Jo Fisher, *Mothers of the Disappeared*, London: Zed and Boston: South End Press, 1989.

13 Gregory Baum, 'The Impact of Marxist Ideas on Christian Theology', in Gregory Baum (ed.), *The Twentieth Century: A Theological Overview*, Maryknoll, NY: Orbis, London: Geoffrey Chapman, Ottawa: Novalis, 1999, pp. 173–85 at p. 184.

14 Enrique Dussel, *Hacia un Marx desconocido: Un comentario a los Manuscritos del 61–63*, Mexico: Siglo XXI/UAM-I, 1998; *Towards an Unknown Marx: Commentary on the Manuscripts of 1861–1863*, London: Routledge, 2001; *El Marx definitivo (1863–1882) y la liberación latinoamericana: Un comentario a la tercera y cuarta redacción*

de 'El Capital', Mexico: Siglo XXI, 1990, *Las metáforas teológicas de Marx*, Estella, Navarra: Editorial Verbo Divino, 1993, and *Un Marx Sconosciuto*, Rome: Manifestolibri SRL, 1999.

15 See his lectures 'Modernity, Coloniality, and Capitalism in the World-System', Center for Latin American Studies, University of California at Berkeley 5 April 2002, 'Will to Power, Will to Live: Towards a Politics of Liberation' and 'Planetary Politics', Center for Cultural Studies, University of California at Santa Cruz, 18–19 April 2005.

16 Jon Sobrino, 'El cristianismo ante el siglo XXI en América Latina: Una reflección desde las víctimas', in *Teología de la liberación: Cruce de miradas*, Lima: Instituto Bartolóme de Las Casas-Rímac and Centro de Estudios y Publicaciones, 2000, pp. 207–38 at p. 214.

17 Gregory Baum, 'The Impact of Marxist Ideas on Christian Theology', in Gregory Baum (ed.), *The Twentieth Century: A Theological Overview*, pp. 173–85 at p. 184.

18 Mario I. Aguilar, *Being Oromo in Kenya*, Lawrenceville, NJ: Africa World Press, 1998. Karl Mannheim (1893–1947) was born in Budapest and held academic posts at Heidelberg and Frankfurt. In 1933 he was suspended from his post for being a Jew following the first National Socialist enactments. Mannheim was invited to take the post of lecturer at the London School of Economics and was appointed to the Chair of the Sociology of Education at the University of London. He was the last and the least appreciated of the founding fathers of classical sociology.

19 Karl Mannheim, 'The Problem of Generations', in Paul Kecskemeti (ed.), *Essays on the Sociology of Knowledge*, London: Routledge & Kegan Paul, 1952, pp. 276–320 at p. 301.

20 Ernest K. Bramstedt and Hans Gerth, 'A Note on the Work of Karl Mannheim', in Karl Mannheim, *Freedom, Power and Democratic Planning*, London: Routledge & Kegan Paul, 1951, pp. vii–xv, and Karl Mannheim, *Man and Society in an Age of Reconstruction*, London: Kegan Paul, Trench, Trubner and Co., 1940.

21 Paul Kecskemeti, 'Introduction', in Karl Mannheim, *Essays on Sociology and Social Psychology*, New York: OUP, 1953, pp. 1–11 at p. 1.

22 Gustavo Gutiérrez, *Teología de la liberación: Perspectivas*, Salamanca: Ediciones Sígueme, 1999 [1971].

23 For a good history of this first period see David Tombs, *Latin American Liberation Theology*, Boston and Leiden: Brill, 2002.

24 Elsa Tamez, *Bible of the Oppressed*, Maryknoll, NY: Orbis, 1982; Pablo Richard, *Apocalypse*, Maryknoll, NY: Orbis, 1995.

25 Marcella Althaus-Reid, *Indecent Theology: Theological Perversions in Sex, Gender and Politics*, London and New York: Routledge,

Notes

2000; *The Queer God*, London and New York: Routledge, 2003.

26 This critique has been dealt with by José M. Vigil, 'The option for the poor is an option for justice, and not preferential: A new theological-systematic framework for the preferential option', *Voices from the Third World*, 27 (2004), pp. 7–21.

27 Elsa Tamez, *Contra toda condena: La justificación por la fe desde los excluídos*, San José, Costa Rica: DEI-SBL, 1991.

28 Ignacio Ellacuría SJ and Jon Sobrino SJ (eds), *Mysterium Liberationis: Conceptos Fundamentales de la Teología de la Liberación*, 2 vols, Madrid: Editorial Trotta, 1990 and the abridged editions, Ignacio Ellacuría SJ and Jon Sobrino SJ (eds), *Mysterium Liberationis: Fundamental Concepts of Liberation Theology*, Maryknoll, NY: Orbis, 1993 and Ignacio Ellacuría SJ and Jon Sobrino SJ (eds), *Systematic Theology: Perspectives from Liberation Theology*, Maryknoll, NY: Orbis, 1996.

29 Marcella Althaus-Reid, *Indecent Theology: Theological Perversions in Sex, Gender and Politics*, p. 6.

30 Diego Irarrázaval, *Inculturation: New Dawn of the Church in Latin America*, Maryknoll, NY: Orbis, 2000, and *Rito y pensar cristiano*, Lima: Centro de Estudios y Publicaciones, 1993.

31 Robert J. Schreiter CPPS, 'Foreword', in Diego Irarrázaval, *Inculturation: New Dawn of the Church in Latin America*, pp. vii–viii.

32 Leonardo Boff, *Cry of the Earth, Cry of the Poor*, Maryknoll, NY: Orbis, 1997.

33 Gustavo Gutiérrez, 'Speaking about God', in Claude Geffré, Gustavo Gutiérrez, and Virgil Elizondo (eds), *Different Theologies, Common Responsibility: Babel or Pentecost?*, *Concilium* 171, Edinburgh: T&T Clark, 1984, pp. 27–31 at p. 27.

34 Julio de Santa Ana, 'Globalization and Some of Its Problems', *Voices from the Third World* 26 (2003), pp. 36–48, and *La práctica económica como religión: Crítica teológica a la economía política*, San José, Costa Rica: DEI, 1991.

35 For theological critiques of this model see Jung Mo Sung, *La idolatría del capital y la muerte de los pobres*, San José, Costa Rica: DEI, 1991, and *Neoliberalismo y pobreza: Una economía sin corazón*, San José, Costa Rica: DEI, 1993.

36 Hannah Stewart-Gambino, 'Introduction: New Game, New Rules', in Edward L. Cleary and Hannah Stewart-Gambino (eds), *Conflict and Competition: The Latin American Church in a Changing Environment*, pp. 1–19 at p. 13.

37 Within the first generation of liberation theologians there was the central issue of a liberation from idolatry, i.e. 'a worship of the false gods of the system of oppression', so that, 'all systems of oppression are

characterized by the creation of gods and of idols that sanction oppression and anti-life forces', in 'Introduction', Departamento Ecuménico de Investigaciones, San José, Costa Rica, *The Idols of Death and the God of Life*, Maryknoll, NY: Orbis, 1983, p. 1.

38 Enrique Dussel, *1492 El encubrimiento del otro: Hacia el origen del mito de la Modernidad*, Madrid: Nueva Utopía, 1992, *1492 l'occultation de l'autre*, Paris: Les Éditions Ouvrières, 1992; *Von der Erfindung Amerikas Zur Entdeckung des Anderen: Ein Projekt der Transmoderne*, Düsseldorf: Patmos Verlag, 1993; *The Invention of the Americas: Eclipse of 'the Other' and the Myth of Modernity*, New York: Continuum, 1995 and 'Eurocentrism and Modernity (Introduction to the Frankfurt Lectures)', in John Beverley, José Oviedo and Michael Aronna (eds), *The Postmodernism Debate in Latin America*, Durham and London: Duke University Press, 1995, pp. 65–76; V.Y. Mudimbe, *The Invention of Africa: Gnosis, Philosophy, and the Order of Knowledge*, Bloomington and Indianapolis: Indiana University Press and London: James Currey, 1988 and *The Idea of Africa*, Bloomington and Indianapolis: Indiana University Press and London: James Currey, 1994; and Tzvetan Todorov, *La conquête d l'Amérique*, Paris: Éditions du Seuil, 1982.

39 G. W. F. Hegel, *Sämtliche Werke*, J. Hoffmeister (ed.), Hamburg: F. Meiner, 1955, pp. 231–4.

40 Mario I. Aguilar, 'Postcolonial African Theology in Kabasele Lumbala', *Theological Studies*, 63 (2002), pp. 302–23.

41 Gustavo Gutiérrez, 'Speaking about God', in Claude Geffré, Gustavo Gutiérrez, and Virgil Elizondo (eds), *Different Theologies, Common Responsibility: Babel or Pentecost?*, *Concilium* 171, Edinburgh: T&T Clark, 1984, pp. 27–31 at p. 31.

42 Some American theologians interpreted 9/11 and other natural disasters within the United States as divine punishment; see Andrew R. Murphy, 'One Nation under God, September 11 and the Chosen Nation: Moral decline and divine punishment in American public discourse', *Political Theology*, 6 (2005), pp. 9–30.

43 Some theologians asked about the possibility of loving one's enemies and emphasized Jesus' commandment to love one's enemies, see Laurie Johnston, '"Love your enemies" – even in the age of terrorism?', *Political Theology*, 6 (2005), pp. 87–106.

44 President Bush speaks of a 'compassionate conservatism', see Ira Chermus, 'George W. Bush's War on Terrorism and Sin', *Political Theology*, 5 (2004), pp. 411–30.

45 Michael Northcott has insightfully analysed President Bush's discourses, particularly his Inaugural Address (20 January 2001) and his State of the Union Address (29 January 2002); see Michael Northcott, '"An angel directs the storm": The Religious Politics of Neo-Conserva-

tism', *Political Theology*, 5 (2004), 137–58, and *An Angel Directs the Storm: Apocalyptic Religion and American Empire*, London: I. B. Tauris, 2004.

46 See, for example, Enrique Dussel, *1492 El encubrimiento del otro: Hacia el origen del mito de la Modernidad*, Madrid: Nueva Utopía, 1992, *1492 l'occultation de l'autre*, Paris: Les Éditions Ouvrières, 1992, *Von der Erfindung Amerikas Zur Entdeckung des Anderen: Ein Projekt der Transmoderne*, Düsseldorf: Patmos Verlag, 1993, *The Invention of the Americas: Eclipse of 'the Other' and the Myth of Modernity*, New York: Continuum, 1995, *Apel, Ricouer, Rorty y la Filosofía de la Liberación*, Guadalajara, Mexico: Universidad de Guadalajara, 1994, and *The Underside of Modernity: Ricouer, Apel, Taylor and the Philosophy of Liberation*, New York: Humanities Press, 1996.

47 'Response to the war', Letter from Elsa Tamez to the Christians of Latin America 14 March 2003, *Voices from the Third World*, 26 (2003), pp. 22–5.

48 Tissa Balasuriya, 'Crucifying Christ in 2003', *Voices from the Third World*, 26 (2003), pp. 11–21.

49 Thirty years ago Dussel had already warned of that responsibility of empire and the exercise of worldwide domination by the United States, see Enrique Dussel, 'Preface to the English Edition', Mendoza, Argentina 1975, in *History and The Theology of Liberation: A Latin American Perspective*, Maryknoll, NY: Orbis, 1976, p. x.

50 Walter Wink, 'Globalization and Empire: We have met the evil empire and it is us', *Political Theology*, 5 (2004), pp. 295–306 at p. 303.

Chapter 1

51 Gustavo Gutiérrez, 'Speaking about God', *Concilium* 171 (1984), p. 31 in Claude Geffré, Gustavo Gutiérrez and Virgil Elizondo (eds), *Different theologies, common responsibility: Babel or Pentecost?*, Edinburgh: T&T Clark, 1984.

52 Gustavo Gutiérrez, *We Drink from Our Own Wells: The Spiritual Journey of a People*, Twentieth Anniversary Edition, Maryknoll, NY: Orbis, 2003, p. 35.

53 For historical data on his life see Sergio Torres, 'Gustavo Gutiérrez: A historical sketch', in Marc H. Ellis and Otto Maduro (eds), *The Future of Liberation Theology: Essays in Honor of Gustavo Gutiérrez*, Maryknoll, NY: Orbis, 1989, pp. 95–101.

54 Gustavo Gutiérrez, *Teología de la liberación: Perspectivas*, Salamanca: Ediciones Sígueme, 16th edition 1999 [Lima: Centro de Estudios y Publicaciones 1971].

55 For a collection of the major documents see Austin Flannery OP,

Vatican Council II: The Conciliar and Post Conciliar Documents, Northport, NY: Costello and Grand Rapids, Michigan: William B. Eerdmans, 1992 revised edition; for the history of the Council see Giuseppe Alberigo (ed.), *History of Vatican II*, vol. I *Announcing and Preparing Vatican Council II: Toward a new Era in Catholicism*, Maryknoll, NY: Orbis and Leuven: Peeters, 1995, vol. II *The Formation of the Council's Identity: First Period and Intercession October 1962 – September 1963*, Maryknoll, NY: Orbis and Leuven: Peeters, 1997, vol. III *The Mature Council: Second Period and Intercession September 1963 – September 1964*, Maryknoll, NY: Orbis and Leuven: Peeters, 2000.

56 Gustavo Gutiérrez, 'Theological Language: Fullness of Silence', in Gustavo Gutiérrez, *The Density of the Present: Selected Writings*, Maryknoll, NY: Orbis, 1999), p. 186; from 'Address on the occasion of his induction to the Peruvian Academy of Spanish Language 1995', full original in *Páginas*, 137 (1996), pp. 66–87.

57 Gustavo Gutiérrez, 'Mirar lejos: Introducción a la decimocuarta edición', in *Teología de la liberación: Perspectivas*, p. 38.

58 Theology as a poetic narrative on God's presence and action in the world presupposes a changing paradigm, thus it is no longer possible to write about Gutiérrez's theological work by just focusing on his major initial work *Teología de la liberación*.

59 The theological periods within the original Spanish texts are clearly chronological and they follow theological reflections that arise out of preparations for the meeting of Latin American Bishops at Medellín, Puebla, and Santo Domingo. These periods are more difficult to isolate within the published works in English due to the fact that Gutiérrez has not published everything he has ever written and that not everything published in other languages has been translated into the English language. Frei Betto has suggested that, 'It is quite likely that he is the author of more unpublished texts, known only to a small circle of readers, than of published works. Usually he does not even sign the mimeographed texts, which include an excellent introduction to the ideas of Marx and Engels and their relationship to Christianity', Frei Betto, 'Gustavo Gutiérrez – A friendly profile', in Marc H. Ellis and Otto Maduro (eds), *The Future of Liberation Theology: Essays in Honor of Gustavo Gutiérrez*, pp. 31–7, at p. 35.

60 See, for example, Marcel Mauss, *The Gift: The Form and Reason for Exchange in Archaic Societies*, London: Routledge, 1990, and Wendy James and N.J. Allen (eds), *Marcel Mauss: A Centenary Tribute*, New York and Oxford: Berghahn, 1998.

61 M.-D. Chenu, *La théologie est-elle une science?*, Paris, 1957, and *Le Saulchior: Una scuola di teologia*, Casale Monferrato: Marietti, 1982 [French original, 1937].

Notes

62 This theological schema is posed by Johann Baptist Metz, 'Theology in the struggle for history and society', in Marc H. Ellis and Otto Maduro (eds), *The Future of Liberation Theology: Essays in Honor of Gustavo Gutiérrez*, pp. 165–6.

63 Nicholas Lash compared the unification of cultural theology with classicism, where one enters that particular time and discourse as the only one through the study of Latin and Greek authors, 'Theologies at the service of a common tradition', *Concilium*, 171 (1984/1), p. 75, Claude Geffré, Gustavo Gutiérrez and Virgil Elizondo (eds), *Different theologies, common responsibility: Babel or Pentecost?*, Edinburgh: T&T Clark, 1984.

64 Gutiérrez provides an evaluation of modern Protestant Theology, for example, in an essay in which he examines Dietrich Bonhoeffer's criticism of Karl Barth, 'The limitations of modern theology: On a letter of Dietrich Bonhoeffer', in *The Power of the Poor in History*, London: SCM Press, 1983, pp. 222–34.

65 This situation affected not only Catholic theology but also theologies influenced by the Reformation, 'since the Reformation took place within the framework of an all-embracing Christian understanding of the world', see Johann-Baptist Metz, 'Theology in the Modern Age, and before its end', *Concilium*, 171 (1984), p. 14, Claude Geffré, Gustavo Gutiérrez and Virgil Elizondo (eds), *Different theologies, common responsibility: Babel or Pentecost?*, Edinburgh: T&T Clark, 1984.

66 For an excellent overview see Rosemary Radford Ruether, 'The Holocaust: Theological and Ethical Reflections', in Gregory Baum (ed.), *The Twentieth Century: A Theological Overview*, Maryknoll, NY: Orbis, 1999, pp. 76–90.

67 Gutiérrez has been criticized for having been influenced by modernity and its romantic idealism, however it is clear that the thought of Gutiérrez was in the 1960s and 1970s influenced by the Latin American context in which the Pauline vision of the 'new man' was also used by socialist discourses associated with the Cuban revolution and with a socialist conception of revolution led by the icon of Ché Guevara, see Mariano Delgado, '"Esperanza plañe entre algodones": Cuando Gustavo Gutiérrez habla de Dios', in *Teología de la liberación: Cruce de miradas*, Coloquio de Friburgo, April 1999, Lima: Instituto Bartolomé de Las Casas-Rímac and Centro de Estudios y Publicaciones, 2000, pp. 101–32, at pp. 102–3, cf. Michael Sievernich, 'Von der Utopie zur Ethik. Zur Theologie von Gustavo Gutiérrez', *Theologie und Philosophie*, 71 (1996), pp. 33–46.

68 Gutiérrez gave the name to an ecclesial reflection that had already taken place, thus 'liberation theology is not a new growth of Christian theological reflection, but rather an outgrowth of long years of such

reflection', William Boteler MM, 'Greetings', in Marc H. Ellis and Otto Maduro (eds), *The Future of Liberation Theology: Essays in Honor of Gustavo Gutiérrez*, Maryknoll, NY: Orbis, 1989, pp. 13–15, at p. 13.

69 It is clear that 'the influence of Gustavo [Gutiérrez] on theological method and praxis began in Peru long before the concretization of that influence took place in books and at high-level church conferences. Taking time to work with groups of persons – delegates of the word, pastoral agents, local religious, students groups, missionaries – became the modus operandi of these young Peruvian priests', see Luise Ahrens MM and Barbara Hendricks MM in Marc H. Ellis and Otto Maduro (eds), *The Future of Liberation Theology: Essays in Honor of Gustavo Gutiérrez*, pp. 3–4.

70 Langdon Gilkey, 'The political dimensions of theology', in Brian Mahan and L. Dale Richesin (eds), *The Challenge of Liberation Theology: A First World Response*, Maryknoll, NY: Orbis, 1981, p. 117; Inaugural Lecture as the Shailer Mathews Professor in the Divinity School of the University of Chicago, pp. 113–26.

71 Chimbote is described as 'a coastal fishing port to the north of Lima noted for his astounding stench and pollution produced by local fishmeal factories and steel mills. A small version of Lima, Chimbote harbors masses of exploited, impoverished workers who have come from the Peruvian sierra in search of work, only to find themselves unemployed and living in hellish, concentric circles of mat houses that surround the city', see Curt Cadorette, 'Peru and the mystery of liberation: The nexus and logic of Gustavo Gutiérrez' theology', in Marc H. Ellis and Otto Maduro (eds), *The Future of Liberation Theology: Essays in Honor of Gustavo Gutiérrez*, pp. 49–58, at p. 53.

72 Gutiérrez, *A Theology of Liberation* is dedicated to Arguedas, Gutiérrez's close friend and fellow writer, both influenced by Peru's socialist thinker José Carlos Mariátegui (1895–1930), and to the Brazilian priest Henrique Pereira Neto, assassinated in Recife on 26 May 1969, see Frei Betto, 'Gustavo Gutiérrez – A friendly profile', in Marc H. Ellis and Otto Maduro (eds), *The Future of Liberation Theology*, pp. 31–7, pp. 32 and 37, and Stephen Judd MM, 'Gustavo Gutiérrez and the originality of the Peruvian experience', in Marc H. Ellis and Otto Maduro (eds), *The Future of Liberation Theology*, pp. 65–76 at pp. 66–7.

73 Since 2001 Gutiérrez held the John Cardinal O'Hara Chair in Theology at the University of Notre Dame. Otherwise he lived in Rimac, 'a gray, dirty, noisy slum where residents are frantically trying to survive, to find or keep a job, to feed and clothe their children. It is a place where struggle is a common denominator and hope, however tenuous, is a thin thread that holds human lives together', Curt

Notes

Cadorette, 'Peru and the mystery of liberation: The nexus and logic of Gustavo Gutiérrez' theology', in Marc H. Ellis and Otto Maduro (eds), *The Future of Liberation Theology*, pp. 49–58 at p. 49.

74 Gustavo Gutiérrez, *La fuerza histórica de los pobres*, Lima: Centro de Estudios y Publicaciones, 1979, English translation *The Power of the Poor in History*, Maryknoll, NY: Orbis, and London: SCM Press, 1983.

75 *Gaudium et Spes* 45.

76 Gustavo Gutiérrez, 'Toward a Theology of Liberation', in James B. Nickoloff (ed.), *Gustavo Gutiérrez: Essential Writings*, London: SCM Press, 1996, p. 27.

77 Juan Alfaro, 'God protects and liberates the poor – OT', *Concilium*, 187 (1986), pp. 27–35; Leonardo Boff and Virgil Elizondo (eds), *Option for the Poor: Challenge to the Rich Countries*, Edinburgh: T&T Clark, 1986.

78 Gustavo Gutiérrez, 'God's revelation and proclamation in history', in *The Power of the Poor in History: Selected Writings*, p. 6.

79 Gutiérrez prefers the term 'encounter' or 'collision' while those reading history from a European viewpoint term it 'discovery' or 'conquest' and others even term it 'invasion' or 'covering', Gustavo Gutiérrez, *Las Casas: In Search of the Poor of Jesus Christ*, Maryknoll, NY: Orbis, 1993, p. 2.

80 It was in that context that the Jesuits developed safe places around the borders of current Argentina, Paraguay and Brazil, for indigenous peoples to live in well-bounded territories where they learned about Christianity, toiled the land, lived communally, and escaped the enslaving mechanisms of the Portuguese slavers. The Jesuits were expelled from the Portuguese colonies in 1759, from France in 1762, and from the Spanish colonies in 1767. On the 21 July 1773 Pope Clement XIV suspended the mere existence of the Society of Jesus, Michel Clévenot, 'The Kingdom of God on Earth? The Jesuit Reductions of Paraguay', *Concilium*, 187 (1986), pp. 70–7; Leonardo Boff and Virgil Elizondo (eds), *Option for the Poor: Challenge to the Rich Countries*, Edinburgh: T&T Clark, 1986.

81 Gustavo Gutiérrez, *En busca de los pobres de Jesucristo*, Lima: Instituto Bartolomé de las Casas-Rimac and Centro de Estudios y Publicaciones, 1992.

82 However, Las Casas was not, according to Gutiérrez, an isolated prophetic voice but was part of a minority group that included missionaries, bishops, civil servants and even members of the royal court who expressed their concern about the fate of the Indians under the conquistadors, Gustavo Gutiérrez, *Las Casas: In Search of the Poor of Jesus Christ*, Maryknoll, NY: Orbis, 1993, p. 5.

83 Lewis Hanke, *Aristotle and the American Indians: A Study in Race Prejudice in the Modern World*, London: Hollis & Carter, Chicago: Henry Regnery, 1959, *All the Peoples of the World Are Men: The Disputation between Bartolomé de Las Casas and Juan Ginés de Sepúlveda in 1550 on the Intellectual and Religious Capacity of the American Indians*, Minneapolis: University of Minnesota Press, 1970, *All Mankind is One: A Study of the Disputation between Bartolomé de Las Casas and Juan Ginés de Sepúlveda in 1550 on the Intellectual and Religious Capacity of the American Indians*, Dekalb: Northern Illinois University Press, 1974.

84 Gustavo Gutiérrez, *On Job: God-Talk and the Suffering of the Innocent*, Maryknoll, NY: Orbis, 1987.

85 Gustavo Gutiérrez, *Las Casas: In Search of the Poor of Jesus Christ*, pp. 6–7. Gutiérrez refers to Las Casas' account of the atrocities done by the conquistadors, *A Short Account of the Destruction of the Indies*, London: Penguin, with chronology and further reading 2004 [1992].

86 Virgil Elizondo and Leonardo Boff, 'Editorial: Theology from the viewpoint of the poor', *Concilium*, 187 (1986), p. ix, Leonardo Boff and Virgil Elizondo (eds), *Option for the Poor: Challenge to the Rich Countries*, Edinburgh: T&T Clark, 1986.

87 Virgilio Elizondo has argued, for example, that 'the transformative impact of the Medellín Conference on the Church's pastoral practice and theology was far greater than that exercised by any other council of the Church. No dogmas or confessions of faith were questioned or challenged – Protestant or Catholic. Instead, the whole edifice of Constantinian Christian thought, imagery, and symbolism was radically challenged in the name of Christianity itself. What was initiated was not a new academic or philosophical theology, but rather the transformation of the very structures and methods of doing theology. To be faithful and authentic, Christian theology will have to emerge out of the spiritual experience of the believing community grappling with its history and responding to its contemporary situation, see 'Emergence of a World Church and the irruption of the poor', in Gregory Baum (ed.), *The Twentieth Century: A Theological Overview*, Maryknoll, NY: Orbis, 1999, p. 108.

88 See Mario I. Aguilar, *A Social History of the Catholic Church in Chile*, vol. I *The First Period of the Pinochet Government 1973–1980*, Lewiston, Queenston, and Lampeter: Edwin Mellen Press, 2004.

89 Gustavo Gutiérrez, *Beber en su propio pozo: En el itinerario de un pueblo*, Lima: Centro de Estudios y Publicaciones, 1983, English translation *We Drink from Our Own Wells: The Spiritual Journey of a People*, Maryknoll, NY: Orbis, 1984, 20th Anniversary Edition 2003.

Notes

90 Gustavo Gutiérrez, *The God of Life*, London: SCM Press, 1991, p. 2. Spanish original *El Dios de la vida*, Lima: Centro de Estudios y Publicaciones, 1982, shorter version, Lima: Instituto Bartolomé de Las Casas-Rimac and Centro de Estudios y Publicaciones, 1989 longer version.

91 Gutiérrez does not dwell on issues of contemplation but those who did, for example Ernesto Cardenal and Pedro Casaldáliga, associated mysticism, aesthetics and poetics with a political commitment to social change inspired by their Christian commitment to the poor and the marginalized, see Ernesto Cardenal, *El Evangelio en Solentiname*, Salamanca: Ediciones Sígueme, 1976, and *El Evangelio en Solentiname: Volumen Segundo*, Salamanca: Ediciones Sígueme, 1978.

92 Paper presented at the first Hugo Echegaray University Seminar, organized by UNEC, in G. Gutiérrez, R. Ames, J. Iguiñez, and C. Chipoco, *Sobre el trabajo humano: Comentarios a la Encíclica Laborem Exercens*, Lima: Centro de Estudios y Publicaciones, 1982.

93 Gustavo Gutiérrez, 'The Gospel of Work: Reflections on *Laborem Exercens*', in Gustavo Gutiérrez, *The Density of the Present: Selected Writings*, Maryknoll, NY: Orbis, 1999, p. 37.

94 Gregory the Great, Pastoral Rule, 3, 21, in Gustavo Gutiérrez, 'New Things Today: A Rereading of Rerum Novarum', in Gustavo Gutiérrez, *The Density of the Present*, p. 51, note 14. Most of these ideas were given by Gutiérrez at the Catholic University of Lima during the 'Jornadas de Teología' in February 1991.

95 Jon Sobrino SJ, 'El Cristianismo ante el siglo XXI en América Latina: Una reflexión desde las víctimas' in *Teología de la liberación: Cruce de miradas*, Coloquio de Friburgo, April 1999, Lima: Instituto Bartolomé de Las Casas-Rímac and Centro de Estudios y Publicaciones, 2000, pp. 207–38.

96 In 1999 Gutiérrez argued that 'Estamos ante una estimulante y prometedora tarea en la que la teología de la liberación tiene mucho que hacer, y sobre todo por aprender', in 'Situaciones y tareas de la teología de la liberación', *Teología de la liberación: Cruce de miradas*, Coloquio de Friburgo, April 1999, Lima: Instituto Bartolomé de Las Casas-Rímac and Centro de Estudios y Publicaciones, 2000, pp. 239–64 at p. 264.

97 'Theologies at the service of a common tradition', *Concilium*, 171 (1984), p. 74, Claude Geffré, Gustavo Gutiérrez and Virgil Elizondo (eds), *Different theologies, common responsibility: Babel or Pentecost?*, Edinburgh: T&T Clark, 1984.

98 Gustavo Gutiérrez, 'Liberation praxis and Christian Faith', in *The Power of the Poor in History*, p. 36.

99 'The vanguard of Protestant theology would become the great Christian theology of modernity, for it was a current that would lend

an attentive ear to the questions asked by critical reason and individual liberty in this society forged by the bourgeoisie. For a number of historical reasons, this theology would centre in Germany, the land of the Reformation', Gustavo Gutiérrez, 'Theology from the underside of history', in *The Power of the Poor in History*, p. 178.

100 On Bonhoeffer see Gustavo Gutiérrez, 'Theology from the underside of history', in *The Power of the Poor in History*, pp. 179–81.

101 'It [the revolutionary struggle] insists on a society in which private ownership of the means of production is eliminated, because private ownership of the means of production allows a few to appropriate the fruits of the labour of many, and generates the division of society into classes, whereupon one class exploits another', Gustavo Gutiérrez, 'Liberation praxis and Christian Faith', in *The Power of the Poor in History*, pp. 37–8.

102 Gustavo Gutiérrez, 'Liberation praxis and Christian Faith', in *The Power of the Poor in History*, p. 65.

103 Frei Betto, 'Gustavo Gutiérrez – A friendly profile', in Marc H. Ellis and Otto Maduro (eds), *The Future of Liberation Theology: Essays in Honor of Gustavo Gutiérrez*, Maryknoll, NY: Orbis, 1989, pp. 31–7 at p. 36.

Chapter 2

104 Enrique Dussel, *Introducción a la Filosofía de la Liberación Latinoamericana*, Mexico: Extemporáneos, 1977, *Filosofía de la Liberación*, Mexico, DF: Edicol, 1977, *Introducción a la Filosofía de la Liberación*, Bogotá: Nueva América, 1979, and *Philosophy of Liberation*, Maryknoll, NY: Orbis, 1985.

105 See his lectures 'Modernity, Coloniality, and Capitalism in the World-System', Center for Latin American Studies, University of California at Berkeley 5 April 2002, and 'Will to Power, Will to Live: Towards a Politics of Liberation' and 'Planetary Politics', Center for Cultural Studies, University of California at Santa Cruz, 18–19 April 2005.

106 Enrique Dussel, *1492 El encubrimiento del otro: Hacia el origen del mito de la Modernidad*, Madrid: Nueva Utopía, 1992, *1492 l'occultation de l'autre*, Paris: Les Éditions Ouvrières, 1992, *Von der Erfindung Amerikas Zur Entdeckung des Anderen: Ein Projekt der Transmoderne*, Düsseldorf: Patmos Verlag, 1993, *The Invention of the Americas: Eclipse of 'the Other' and the Myth of Modernity*, New York: Continuum, 1995, *Apel, Ricouer, Rorty y la Filosofía de la Liberación*, Guadalajara, Mexico: Universidad de Guadalajara, 1994, and *The*

Notes

Underside of Modernity: Ricouer, Apel, Taylor and the Philosophy of Liberation, New York: Humanities Press, 1996.

107 Enrique Dussel, *Hacia un Marx desconocido: Un comentario a los Manuscritos del 61–63*, Mexico: Siglo XXI/UAM–I, 1998, *Towards an Unknown Marx: Commentary of the Manuscripts of 1861–1863*, London: Routledge, 2001, *El Marx definitivo (1863–1882) y la liberación latinoamericana: Un comentario a la tercera y cuarta redacción de 'El Capital'*, Mexico: Siglo XXI, 1990, *Las metáforas teológicas de Marx*, Estella, Navarra: Editorial Verbo Divino, 1993, and *Un Marx Sconosciuto*, Rome: Manifestolibri SRL, 1999.

108 Dussel remembered the hospitality granted by Argentina to his great grandfather while delivering the Frankfurt Lectures only a few kilometres away from Schweinfurt am Main where J.K. Dussel came from and he challenged the racist attitudes against immigrants to Germany during the late twentieth century, see Enrique Dussel, 'Eurocentrism and Modernity (Introduction to the Frankfurt Lectures)', in John Beverley, José Oviedo and Michael Aronna (eds), *The Postmodernism Debate in Latin America*, Durham and London: Duke University Press, 1995, pp. 66–7.

109 Dussel also received honorary doctorates from the University of Freiburg (Switzerland, 1981) and the Universidad Mayor de San Andrés (La Paz, Bolivia, 1995).

110 Married to Joanna Dussel, they had two children, Enrique and Susanne.

111 A special issue of the journal *Anthropos* used that classificatory systematization for Dussel's wide range of writings that comprises more than 50 books, see *Anthropos*, 180 (September–October 1998).

112 Jo Fisher, Mothers of the Disappeared, London: Zed and Boston: South End Press, 1989, Daniel Poneman, *Argentina: Democracy on Trial*, New York: Paragon, 1987, Luis Alberto Romero, *A History of Argentina in the Twentieth Century*, Pennsylvania: Pennsylvania State University Press, 2002 and Laura Tedesco, *Democracy in Argentina: Hope and Disillusion*, London and Portland, OR: Frank Cass, 1999, pp. 23–61.

113 Enrique Dussel and E. D. Guillot, *Liberación Latinoamericana y Emmanuel Levinas*, Buenos Aires: Bonum, 1975.

114 Enrique Dussel, 'Preface to the Third Spanish Edition', in *A History of the Church in Latin America: Colonialism to Liberation*, Grand Rapids, Michigan: William B. Eerdmans, 1981, p. xx.

115 The Military Junta was made by the commanders-in-chief of the Argentinean Armed Forces: Lt General Jorge R. Videla, Brigadier Orlando E. Agosti and Admiral Emilio E. Massera. Following a previous agreement Videla took over as president.

116 *History and the Theology of Liberation: A Latin American Perspective*, Maryknoll, NY: Orbis, 1976 and *Ethics and the Theology of Liberation*, Maryknoll, NY: Orbis, 1978.

117 Enrique Dussel, 'Preface to the First Spanish-language Printing', in *History and the Theology of Liberation*, p. xi.

118 Enrique Dussel, *History and the Theology of Liberation*, p. 75. Dussel became president of the Comisión de Estudios de Historia de la Iglesia en Latinoamérica (CEHILA, 1973–93) and wrote a full history of the Church in Latin America, see *History of the Church in Latin America*, Grand Rapids: Eerdmans, 1981.

119 Enrique Dussel, *History and the Theology of Liberation*, p. 133.

120 Within this whole discussion socialism does not equate Marxism, see Enrique Dussel, *History and the Theology of Liberation*, pp. 134 and 137 and 'Ethical Problems of Contemporary Socialism' in Enrique Dussel, *Ethics and Community*, Liberation and Theology 3, Maryknoll, NY: Orbis and Tunbridge Wells: Burns & Oates, 1988, pp. 181–93.

121 *Second General Conference of Latin American Bishops 1968: The Church in the Present-Day Transformation of Latin America in the Light of the Council II – Conclusions*, Washington, DC: United States Catholic Conference, Division for Latin America, 1973.

122 Enrique Dussel, *El Humanismo Semita: Estructuras Intencionales Radicales del Pueblo de Israel y Otros Semitas*, Buenos Aires: Eudeba, 1969, *El Humanismo Helénico*, Buenos Aires: Eudeba, 1975 and *Filosofía de la Producción*, Bogotá: Nueva América, 1984.

123 Enrique Dussel, *Ethics and Community*, Liberation and Theology 3, Maryknoll, NY: Orbis and Tunbridge Wells: Burns & Oates, 1988. This work is part of a larger attempt to address a number of theological areas from the point of view of liberation, published originally in Spanish and Portuguese with a translation under the title 'Liberation and Theology' – 'Its proponents have insisted that liberation theology is not a subtopic of theology but really a new way of doing theology. The Liberation and Theology Series is an effort to test that claim by addressing the full spectrum of Christian faith from the perspective of the poor.'

124 Enrique Dussel, *Ethics and Community*, p. 2.

125 Enrique Dussel, *Ethics and Community*, p. 28.

126 Enrique Dussel, *Ethics and the Theology of Liberation*, p. 141.

127 This is precisely the mistake made by Lenin who after the 1917 Bolshevik Revolution re-reads Marx within another context and misinterprets the fact that Marx never wrote a political treatment and therefore never equated the workers (the people) with a particular state, a mistake over-emphasized later by Stalin with disastrous consequences; see for example Tomás Moulian, *Socialismo del siglo XXI: La quinta vía*, Santiago: LOM, 2000, pp. 43–89.

128 Enrique Dussel, *Ethics and the Theology of Liberation*, p. 142.

129 Enrique Dussel, *Ethics and the Theology of Liberation*, p. 143.

130 Enrique Dussel, *Philosophy of Liberation*, Eugene, Oregon: Wipf & Stock, 2003, p. 190.

131 Enrique Dussel, *Philosophy of Liberation*, p. 196.

132 Enrique Dussel, 'Eurocentrism and Modernity (Introduction to the Frankfurt Lectures)', in John Beverley, José Oviedo and Michael Aronna (eds), *The Postmodernism Debate in Latin America*, Durham and London: Duke University Press, 1995, pp. 65–76.

133 Enrique Dussel, 'Modernity, Coloniality, and Capitalism in the World-System', Center for Latin American Studies, University of California at Berkeley 5 April 2002, and 'Will to Power, Will to Live: Towards a Politics of Liberation' and 'Planetary Politics', Center for Cultural Studies, University of California at Santa Cruz, 18–19 April 2005.

134 Enrique Dussel, *History and the Theology of Liberation*, pp. 75–109.

135 Enrique Dussel, *1492: El encubrimiento del otro – Hacia el origin del mito de la modernidad*, Madrid: Nueva Utopía, 1992, translated in English as *The Invention of the Americas: Eclipse of 'the Other' and the Myth of Modernity*, New York: Continuum, 1995.

136 Enrique Dussel, *La producción teórica de Marx: Un comentario a los Grundrisse*, Madrid: Siglo XXI, 1985, *Hacia un Marx desconocido: Un comentario a los manuscritos del 61–63*, Mexico: Siglo XXI/UAM–I, 1988 and *El Marx definitivo 1863–1882 y la liberación latinoamericana: Un comentario a la tercera y cuarta redacción de El Capital*, Mexico: Siglo XXI, 1990.

137 Enrique Dussel, *Las metáforas teológicas de Marx*, Estella, Navarra: Editorial Verbo Divino, 1993.

138 Enrique Dussel, 'The Four Drafts of *Capital*: Towards a New Interpretation of the Dialectical Thought of Marx', Department of Philosophy, Universidad Autónoma Metropolitana – Iztapalapa, Mexico, 14 September 2000.

139 Enrique Dussel, 'The Four Drafts of *Capital*', Introduction.

Chapter 3

140 Guillermo Hansen (ed.), *El silbo ecuménico del espíritu: Homenaje a José Míguez Bonino en sus 80 años*, Buenos Aires: Instituto Universitario ISEDET, 2004.

141 José Míguez Bonino, *Revolutionary Theology Comes of Age*, London: SPCK, 1975, pp. xix–xx.

142 Jack Nelson-Pallmeyer, *School of Assassins: The case for closing*

the School of the Americas and for fundamentally changing US policy, Maryknoll, NY: Orbis, 1997.

143 Germán Guzmán Campos, *El Padre Camilo Torres*, Madrid: Siglo XXI, 1968.

144 Between January and April 1970 the FAP (Peronist Armed Forces) attacked police stations, army and naval installations in order to secure weapons and ammunition; on 30 May 1970 the former Argentinean president Pedro Eugenio Armburu was kidnapped by the *Montoneros* and subsequently shot dead by this guerrilla group, which declared itself Marxist and Christian; other groups such as the Ejército Revolucionario del Pueblo (ERP), Fuerzas Argentinas de Liberación (FAL), and the Movimiento Revolucionario Argentino (MRA) also appeared, Alphonse Max, *Guerrillas in Latin America*, The Hague: International Documentation and Information Centre, 1971, pp. 67–81.

145 United States Catholic Conference, *Second General Conference of Latin American Bishops: The Church in the Present-Day Transformation of Latin America in the Light of the Council, II – Conclusions*, Washington, DC: Division for Latin America, USCC.

146 This dichotomy is elegantly explained by Laura Tedesco, *Democracy in Argentina: Hope and Disillusion*, London: Frank Cass, 1999, pp. xix–xx; see also D. James, *Resistance and Integration: Peronism and the Argentine Working Class 1946–1976*, Cambridge: Cambridge University Press, 1988.

147 The Military Junta was made by the commanders-in-chief of the Argentinean Armed Forces: Lt. General Jorge R. Videla, Brigadier Orlando E. Agosti and Admiral Emilio E. Massera. Following a previous agreement Videla took over as president.

148 Jo Fisher, *Mothers of the Disappeared*, London: Zed and Boston: South End, 1989.

149 Ariel C. Armony, *Argentina, the United States, and the Anti-Communist Crusade in Central America 1977–1984*, Athens, Ohio: Ohio University Center for International Studies, 1997.

150 The Peronist Party got only 40.16 per cent of the total vote.

151 José Míguez Bonino, *Revolutionary Theology Comes of Age*, London: SPCK, 1975, published in the United States as *Doing Theology in a Revolutionary Situation*, Philadelphia: Fortress Press, 1975.

152 José Míguez Bonino, *Revolutionary Theology*, pp. 78–9.

153 After the 1973 military coup and because of the destruction of the presidential palace (La Moneda), the military junta used it as their headquarters and legally it was owned by the Ministry of Defence. With the return to democracy in the 1990s the building became a conference centre until it was completely destroyed by a fire in March 2006 and the government of President Bachellet decided to sell it; David Maulen,

'Chile: Se vende edificio de la Unctad III (1972)', *Política en el Cono Sur Latinoamericano*, 1715, 24 November 2006.

154 Fernando Castillo, 'Christians for Socialism in Chile', *Concilium*, 105 (1977), pp. 106–12 and John Eagleson (ed.), *Christians and Socialism: Documentation of the Christians for Socialism Movement in Latin America*, Maryknoll, NY: Orbis, 1975. For a right-wing critique of Christians for Socialism, see Teresa Donoso Loero, *Los cristianos por el socialismo en Chile*, Santiago: Editorial Vaitea, 1975.

155 José Míguez Bonino, *Christians and Marxists: The Mutual Challenge to Revolution*, London: Hodder & Stoughton, 1976, p. 41.

156 The response of the Chilean and Argentinean bishops to human rights abuses by the military was very different: the Chilean bishops, led by Cardinal Silva Henríquez, challenged the military regime for the most part, while the Argentinean bishops mostly remained passive and kept silent within a political situation in which 25 times more Argentinean than Chilean citizens were arrested and made forcefully to disappear. For the Chilean bishops' actions that questioned the Chilean military, see Mario I. Aguilar, *A Social History of the Catholic Church in Chile* volumes I–IV, Lewiston, NY, Queenston, Ontario and Lampeter, Wales: Edwin Mellen Press, 2004, 2006, 2007.

157 José Míguez Bonino, *Christians and Marxists*, pp. 118–19.

158 With the collapse of the Soviet Union it was impossible to see how Christians and Marxists would have interacted in a democratic system as Marxism lost its momentum and Christians who allied themselves with them joined new political coalitions that departed from a contextual Marxist-Christian dialogue.

159 Gustavo Gutiérrez, *A Theology of Liberation*, Maryknoll, NY: Orbis, 1973, II.3 'Faith, utopia and political action'.

160 A contemporary example of this criticism can be found in the life of the Chilean poet Pablo Neruda, who as a member of the Chilean Communist Party always refused to condemn the persecution of intellectuals, writers and poets exercised by the Soviet regime and seemed to be enchanted by those who were in control of the Soviet Union during the period of the Cold War; see Adam Feinstein, *Pablo Neruda: A Passion for Life*, London: Bloomsbury, 2005, pp. 318–19.

161 José Míguez Bonino, *Christians and Marxists*, p. 136–42.

162 José Míguez Bonino, *Christians and Marxists*, p. 135.

163 José Míguez Bonino, *Christians and Marxists*, p. 141.

164 José Míguez Bonino, *Espacio para ser hombres*, Buenos Aires: Tierra Nueva, 1975, English translation published as *Room To Be People: An Interpretation of the Message of the Bible for Today's World*, Philadelphia: Fortress Press, 1979.

165 José Míguez Bonino, *Room To Be People*, p. 8.

166 José Míguez Bonino, *Room To Be People*, p. 42.

167 José Míguez Bonino, *Room To Be People*, p. 78.

168 José Míguez Bonino, 'Cómo limitar el poder del Estado? – Justicia e impunidad, *Revista Memoria*, February 1998.

169 For a review of other Truth Commissions see Iain Maclean (ed.), *Reconciliation, Nations and Churches in Latin America*, Aldershot, Hampshire, UK: Ashgate, 2006.

170 Baltazar Garzón, *La acusación del juez Baltazar Garzón contra el General (R) Augusto Pinochet – Auto de procesamiento contra Augusto Pinochet Ugarte (10.12.98). Procedimiento: Sumario 19/97 Terrorismo y Genocidio 'Operativo Cóndor', Juzgado Central de Instrucción Número Cinco Audiencia Nacional, Madrid*, Santiago: Ediciones Chile-América CESOC, 1999 and *Un mundo sin miedo*, Barcelona: Plaza Janés, 2005.

171 In September 2006 the Argentinean courts declared the constitutional pardon of General Videla unconstitutional, giving way to new trials for the kidnap and extortion of two businessmen, Federico and Miguel Ernesto Gutheim, between November 1976 and April 1977, 'Argentine junta pardons revoked', *BBC News* 6 September 2006.

172 Míguez Bonino's paper appeared before the economic and social crisis that Argentina lived in 2001, when people lost their savings, there was general chaos, violence at barricades, and the churches had once again to shelter and to feed those who lacked everything, this time middle-class Argentineans who had lost everything.

Chapter 4

173 Pablo Richard, *Fuerza ética y espiritual de la teología de la liberación*, La Habana: Editorial Caminos del Centro Memorial Martin Luther King, 2005.

174 Hugo Assmann, Brazilian, theologian and sociologist, previously professor at the University of Costa Rica and the National University of Costa Rica, member of staff at the Departamento Ecuménico de Investigaciones (DEI) and author of *Theology for a Nomad Church*, Maryknoll, NY: Orbis, 1976, an English translation of part I of *Teología desde la praxis de la liberación*, Salamanca: Sígueme, 2nd edition, 1976.

175 In all these discussions theologians failed to address the challenge of contemporary China, one of the major consumers and producers in the world that has not changed many of the autocratic systems of governance but because it offers markets and economic exchange, has been welcomed within the powerful nations of the contemporary world.

176 The most important documents of Christians for Socialism have been published in an edited collection prepared by John Eagleson (ed.),

Notes

Christians and Socialism: Documentation of the Christians for Socialism Movement in Latin America, Maryknoll, NY: Orbis, 1975.

177 The event designed as a communal workshop had the title 'La participación de los cristianos en la construcción del socialismo en Chile'. Among the priests taking part were the Jesuit Gonzalo Arroyo, Alfonso Baeza, Martín Gárate, Juan Martín, Ignacio Pujadas, Esteban Gumucio, Sergio Torres, Pierre Dubois and Santiago Thijssen.

178 *Declaración de los 80*, 16 April 1971.

179 *Declaración de los obispos de Chile*, Temuco 22 April 1971, and Conferencia Episcopal de Chile, *Evangelio, política y socialismos* 27 May 1971.

180 Ignacio Pujadas, 'Comunidades de cristianos revolucionarios: Declaración de principios', *Pastoral Popular*, 128 (March, April 1972), p. 50 in David Fernández Fernández, 'Oral History of the Chilean Movement Christians for Socialism', *Journal of Contemporary History*, 34 (1999), pp. 283–94 at p. 290.

181 Pablo Richard, *Cristianos por el socialismo: Historia y documentación*, Salamanca, 1976.

182 Hugo Assmann *et alia*, *Cristianos por el socialismo: Exigencias de una opción*, Montevideo, 1973.

183 Hugo Assmann, 'The Faith of the Poor in Their Struggle with Idols', in Pablo Richard et al., *The Idols of Death and the God of Life: A Theology*, Maryknoll, NY: Orbis, 1983, pp. 194–224 at p. 194.

184 Pablo Richard, 'Biblical Theology of Confrontation with Idols', in Pablo Richard et al., *The Idols of Death and the God of Life*, pp. 3–25 at p. 4. Originally published as *La lucha de los dioses: los ídolos de la opresión y la búsqueda del Dios Liberador*, San José, Costa Rica: DEI, 1980.

185 All biblical citations in this chapter are taken from *The Jerusalem Bible* © Darton, Longman & Todd and Doubleday and Company Inc., 1966.

186 Pablo Richard, 'Biblical Theology of Confrontation with Idols', p. 7.

187 Pablo Richard, 'Biblical Theology of Confrontation with Idols', p. 24.

188 Pablo Richard, *Apocalypse: A People's Commentary on the Book of Revelation*, Maryknoll, NY: Orbis, 1995, originally published as *Apocalipsis: Reconstrucción de la esperanza*, San José, Costa Rica: DEI, 1994.

189 Pablo Richard, 'Lectura popular de la Biblia en América Latina: Hermenéutica de la liberación', *Revista de Interpretación Bíblica Latinoamericana* (1988/1), pp. 30–48.

190 Pablo Richard, *Death of Christendoms, Birth of the Church*,

Maryknoll, NY: Orbis, 1987, previously published as *Morte das cristandades e nascimento da igreja*, São Paulo: Paulinas, 2nd edition, 1984.

191 Elisabeth Schüssler Fiorenza, *The Book of Revelation: Justice and Judgement*, Philadelphia: Fortress Press, 1985.

192 Pablo Richard, 'Different Faces of Jesus in the Synoptic Gospels', in Sean Freyne and Ellen van Wolde (eds), *The Many Voices of the Bible* (*Concilium* 2002/1), pp. 41–8.

193 Pablo Richard, 'Different Faces of Jesus in the Synoptic Gospels', p. 43.

194 Pablo Richard, 'Different Faces of Jesus in the Synoptic Gospels', p. 47.

195 Pablo Richard, 'Different Faces of Jesus in the Synoptic Gospels', p. 47.

196 Cf. José Míguez Bonino (ed.), *Faces of Jesus: Latin American Christologies*, Maryknoll, NY: Orbis, 1984, and Eugene, OR: Wipf & Stock, 1998.

197 Pablo Richard, 'Theology in the Theology of Liberation', in Ignacio Ellacuría SJ and Jon Sobrino SJ (eds), *Mysterium Liberationis: Fundamental Concepts of Liberation Theology*, Maryknoll, NY: Orbis and North Blackburn, Australia: CollinsDove, 1993, pp. 150–68. The English edition is an abridged edition of the larger original Spanish edition published as *Mysterium Liberationis: Conceptos fundamentales de la teología de la liberación*, 2 volumes, Madrid: Editorial Trotta, 1990.

198 Pablo Richard, 'Theology in the Theology of Liberation', p. 151.

199 Pablo Richard, 'Theology in the Theology of Liberation', p. 153.

200 Pablo Richard, 'Theology in the Theology of Liberation', p. 153.

201 Pablo Richard, 'Theology in the Theology of Liberation', p. 160.

202 Pablo Richard, 'Theology in the Theology of Liberation', p. 168.

Chapter 5

203 Dinah Livingstone, 'Introduction' in Ernesto Cardenal, *The Music of the Spheres*, London: Katabasis, 1990, p. 9.

204 José Luis González-Balado, *Ernesto Cardenal: Poeta Revolucionario Monje*, Salamanca: Ediciones Sígueme, 1978, p. 28.

205 Richard Millett, *The Guardians of the Dynasty: A History of the US-Created Guardia Nacional de Nicaragua and the Somoza Family*, Maryknoll, NY: Orbis, 1977.

206 Somoza was later killed with a bazooka in Asunción, Paraguay, where he lived under the protection of General Stroessner, the authoritarian ruler of Paraguay.

207 Nicaragua has always been a very literate society and the influence of poets has been central to any national developments, see

Notes

Thomas W. Walker, *Nicaragua: The Land of Sandino*, 2nd edition, Boulder and London: Westview Press, 1986, pp. 76–7. The same can be said of the influence of left-wing poets within the different periods of possible liberation from oppression, see Bridget Albaraca, Edward Baker, Ileana Rodríguez and Marc Zimmerman (eds), *Nicaragua in Revolution: The Poets Speak/Nicaragua en Revolución: Los Poetas Hablan*, Minneapolis: Marxist Educational Press, 1980.

208 Cardenal asserted: 'Mi principal influencia y mi principal maestro ha sido Ezra Pound', in José Luis González Balado, *Ernesto Cardenal: Poeta Revolucionario Monje*, p. 58. Ezra Pound (1885–1972) wrote particular aesthetic constructions that included historical assertions in his *Cantos* and also campaigned for the non-intervention of the USA in Italy during World War II, see Ira B. Nadel, *Ezra Pound: A Literary Life*, Houndmills and New York: Palgrave Macmillan, 2004.

209 For a comparative textual analysis of Pound and Cardenal, see Eduardo Urdanivia Bertarelli, *La Poesía de Ernesto Cardenal: Cristianismo y Revolución*, Lima: Latinoamericana Editores, 1984, pp. 29–50.

210 Ernesto Cardenal, *Poesía y Revolución: Antología Poética*, Mexico City: Editorial Edicol, 1979, pp. 11–25.

211 José Luis González-Balado, *Ernesto Cardenal: Poeta Revolucionario Monje*, p. 98.

212 *Del Monasterio al Mundo: Correspondencia entre Ernesto Cardenal y Thomas Merton*, Santiago, Chile: Editorial Cuarto Propio, 1998. Merton was surrounded by a group involved in the struggle against war and for civil rights. However, he also involved himself in trying to understand relations between the USA and Latin America and at one point wanted to visit Latin America, a request denied by his Abbot; see Monica Furlong, *Merton: A Biography*, London: Collins, 1980, pp. 245, 261–3. Merton showed a particular interest in Latin American poets, see Victor A. Kramer, *Thomas Merton: Monk and Artist*, Kalamazoo, Michigan: Cistercian Publications, 1984, pp. 122, 156, 165, 186.

213 In Brazil, for example, Bishop Pedro Casaldáliga when arrested was questioned about his possession of a Portuguese translation of *Salmos* and the book was declared forbidden in Nicaragua; see Ernesto Cardenal, 'Epístola a Monseñor Casaldáliga', in Ernesto Cardenal, *Poesía y Revolución: Antología Poética*, Mexico City: Editorial Edicol, 1979, p. 133.

214 For analyses of Cardenal's psalms see José Promis Ojeda, 'Espíritu y Materia: Los "salmos" de Ernesto Cardenal' and Lidia Dapaz Strout, 'Nuevos cantos de vida y esperanza: Los Salmos de Cardenal y la nueva etica', in *Ernesto Cardenal: Poeta de la Liberación Latinoamericana*, Buenos Aires: Fernando García Cambeiro, 1975, pp. 15–38, 107–31.

215 The archipelago of Solentiname has 30 islands and at that time there were around 1,000 people or near 90 families. Cardenal's lay monastery was located on the largest island, the island of Mancarrón.

216 Claribel Alegría and D. J. Flakoll, *Nicaragua: La Revolución Sandinista – Una crónica política 1855–1979*, Mexico, DF: Ediciones Era, 1982, p. 274.

217 'Yo vine a Solentiname huyendo de lo que tradicionalmente se llama en lenguaje cristiano *el mundo* y que ahora es el capitalismo y la sociedad de consumo. Vine a esta isla buscando la soledad, el silencio, la meditación y, en último término, buscando a Dios. Dios me llevó a los demás hombres. La contemplación me llevó a la revolución. He dicho otras veces que no fue la lectura de Marx la que me llevó al Marxismo, sino la lectura del evangelio . . .' in José Luis González-Balado, *Ernesto Cardenal: Poeta Revolucionario Monje*, p. 152.

218 Ernesto Cardenal, *El Evangelio en Solentiname*, Salamanca: Ediciones Sígueme, 1976 and *El Evangelio en Solentiname: Volumen Segundo*, Salamanca: Ediciones Sígueme, 1978.

219 José Luis González-Balado, *Ernesto Cardenal: Poeta Revolucionario Monje*, p. 158.

220 Mario Benedetti was born in Uruguay on 14 September 1920 and had to live in exile from 1973 to 1985 in Argentina, Peru, Cuba and Spain. His main works are *Gracias por el Fuego* (1965), *La Muerte y Otras Sorpresas* (1968), *Con y Sin Nostalgia* (1977), *Geografías* (1978) and *Primavera con una Esquina Rota* (1987).

221 Ernesto Cardenal, *En Cuba*, Buenos Aires: Ediciones Carlos Lohlé, 1972 and Barcelona: Editorial Pomaire, 1977.

222 Cardenal wrote: 'Volvemos al caso de Cuba, y me dice: "Mire yo conozco al cristianismo como lo conoce usted. Y yo sé que el auténtico cristianismo es revolucionario. Si fue la religión de los pobres y de los esclavos en el Imperio Romano. Pero aquí no todos lo conocen así, y hay ciertos prejuicios contra él con los cuales hay que contar. Que se explican además, por la forma en que se comportó aquí la Iglesia de Cuba"', Ernesto Cardenal, *En Cuba*, p. 372.

223 Fidel Castro and Raúl Silva Henríquez met at Archbishop's House in Santiago on 23 November 1971, Cardenal Raúl Silva Henríquez, *Memorias* II, Santiago, Chile: Ediciones Copygraph, 1991, p. 213. For the experience of Christians for Socialism in Chile in particular and in Latin America in general see John Eagleson (ed.), *Christians and Socialism: Documentation of the Christians for Socialism Movement in Latin America*, Maryknoll, NY: Orbis, 1975.

224 Peter Wright translator, *The Peasant Poets of Solentiname*, London: Katabasis, 1991.

225 Alfredo Veiravé, 'Ernesto Cardenal: El Exteriorismo Poesía del

Notes

Nuevo Mundo', in *Ernesto Cardenal: Poeta de la Liberación Latinoamericana*, Buenos Aires: Fernando García Cambeiro, 1975, pp. 61–106.

226 'El ataque a San Carlos', in Claribel Alegría and D. J. Flakoll, *Nicaragua: La Revolución Sandinista – Una crónica política 1855–1979*, Mexico, DF: Ediciones Era, 1982, pp. 274–91. Some of the young poets were also involved in the attack on the San Carlos barracks.

227 'Las últimas 40 horas: 15–17 de Julio de 1979', in Claribel Alegría and D. J. Flakoll, *Nicaragua: La Revolución Sandinista – Una crónica política 1855–1979*, Mexico, DF: Ediciones Era, 1982, pp. 15–25.

228 Important works on this period include Thomas W. Walker (ed.), *Nicaragua in Revolution*, New York: Praeger, 1982 and Walker (ed.), *Nicaragua: The First Five Years*, New York: Praeger, 1985.

229 For a concise and clear history of Nicaragua during the twentieth century, see Thomas W. Walker, *Nicaragua: The Land of Sandino*, 2nd edition, Boulder and London: Westview Press, 1986.

230 The Frente Sandinista de Liberación Nacional (FSLN) was founded in July 1961 by Carlos Fonseca, Silvio Mayorga and Tomás Borge, former members of the Nicaraguan Socialist Party (PSN).

231 For Luis Serra, a Nicaraguan social scientist, there was no problem between the radical clergy and the open-minded revolutionary. However, the problems between Revolution and Church occur because of the medieval structure of the Catholic Church where decisions are finally taken solely by the hierarchy. Serra wrote: 'The hypothesis of incompatibility between Marxism and Christianity is, paradoxically, the position of the bourgeoisie and of dogmatic factions of the Revolution – even though their subjective intentions might be different, the results are objectively the same', Luis H. Serra, Part 2: 'Religious Institutions and Bourgeois Ideology in the Nicaraguan Revolution', in Laura Nuzzi O'Shaughnessy and Luis H. Serra, *The Church and Revolution in Nicaragua*, Athens, Ohio: Ohio University Center for International Studies, Latin America Studies Program, Monographs in International Studies, Latin America Series 11, 1986, p. 94.

232 Teófilo Cabestrero, *Ministers of God, Ministers of the People: Testimonies of Faith from Nicaragua*, Maryknoll, NY: Orbis and London: Zed, 1983.

233 Teófilo Cabestrero, *Ministers of God, Ministers of the People*, p. 19.

234 Ernesto Cardenal, *Canto Cósmico*, Managua: Ediciones Nueva Nicaragua, 1989 and *Cosmic Canticle*, Willimantic, CT: Curbstone Press, 1993.

235 De Giorgis has argued for the division of Cardenal's literary

works in three types: the socio-political poetry of denunciation, the mystic and religious poetry and the epic-narrative poetry, see Jaime de Giorgis, 'Tres Poemas de Ernesto Cardenal: Hora o, Economía de Tahuantinsuyu and Oración por Marilyn Monroe', in *Ernesto Cardenal: Poeta de la Liberación Latinoamericana*, Buenos Aires: Fernando García Cambeiro, 1975, p. 41.

236 A single poem from the *Canto Cósmico* has been published in a bi-lingual edition as Ernesto Cardenal, *The Music of the Spheres*, London: Katabasis, 1990.

237 The Church in Latin America gathered in reflection on the 500th anniversary of the arrival of Christopher Columbus in the Americas. If in the past that moment was associated with a discovery, later writings spoke of an encounter between civilizations, those of the indigenous peoples of Latin America (*pueblos originarios*) and the conquistadors, mainly Spaniards and Portuguese. The Latin American Bishops met at Santo Domingo and John Paul II opened their fourth general meeting.

238 Ernesto Cardenal, *Telescopio en la noche oscura*, Madrid: Editorial Trotta, 1993.

239 Ernesto Cardenal, *Vida Perdida*, Managua: Anama Ediciones and Barcelona: Editorial Seix Barral, 1999 and *Las Insulas Extrañas*, Madrid: Editorial Trotta, 2002.

240 The following line is very poignant: 'You represent them, they delegated you, the ones who died', in the poem 'For Those Dead Our Dead', in *Nicaraguan New Time: Poems by Ernesto Cardenal*, London and New York: Journeyman Press, 1988.

241 'A Fast for Guantánamo', *The Peace People*, 18 October 2005.

242 This point has been systematized by Leonardo Boff in *Ecclesiogenesis: The Base Communities Reinvent the Church*, Maryknoll, NY: Orbis, 1986.

Chapter 6

243 Over the years, many of his homilies and writings have been collated in selections and collections. The most important writings translated into English are his own diary (Friday 31 March 1978 to Thursday 20 March 1980) translated by Irene B. Hodgson and published as Archbishop Oscar Romero, *A Shepherd's Diary*, London: Catholic Fund for Overseas Development (CAFOD) and Catholic Institute for International Relations (CIIR), 1993; his main pastoral letters translated by Michael J. Walsh and published as Archbishop Oscar Romero, *Voice of the Voiceless: The Four Pastoral Letters and Other Statements*, Maryknoll, NY: Orbis, 1985 and some abstracts from his homilies

Notes

translated by James R. Brockman SJ and published as *Oscar Romero: The Violence of Love*, San Francisco: Harper Collins, 1988.

244 *Departamentos* in El Salvador: Ahuachapán, Cabañas, Chalatenango, Cuscatlan, La Libertad, La Paz, La Unión, Morazán, San Miguel, San Salvador, Santa Ana, San Vicente, Sonsonate and Usulután.

245 Thomas P. Anderson, *Matanza: El Salvador's Communist Revolt of 1932*, Lincoln, Nebraska: University of Nebraska Press, 1971.

246 For a fuller history of the Church in El Salvador see 'The Emergence of the Poor and the Shifting of Context in El Salvador', in Mario I. Aguilar, *Current Issues on Theology and Religion in Latin America and Africa*, Lewiston, Queenston and Lampeter: Edwin Mellen Press, 2002, pp. 59–85. For a political history see Thomas P. Anderson, *The War of the Dispossessed: Honduras and El Salvador 1969*, Lincoln, Nebraska: University of Nebraska Press, 1981 and *Politics in Central America*, New York: Praeger, 1988.

247 Alain De Janvry, *The Agrarian Question and Reformism in Latin America*, Baltimore: Johns Hopkins University Press, 1986.

248 Tricia Juhn, *Negotiating Peace in El Salvador: Civil-Military Relations and the Conspiracy to End the War*, London: Macmillan, 1998, p. 1. See also Victor Bulmer-Thomas, *The Political Economy of Central America since 1920*, New York: Cambridge University Press, 1987 and Jeffrey Paige, 'Coffee and Power in El Salvador', *Latin American Research Review*, 28 (1993), pp. 7–40.

249 James Dunkerley, *The Long War: Dictatorship and Revolution in El Salvador*, London: Junction Books, 1982; *Power in the Isthmus*, London: Verso, 1988 and *The Pacification of Central America*, London: Verso, 1994; and Tricia Juhn, *Negotiating Peace in El Salvador: Civil-Military Relations and the Conspiracy to End the War*, London: Macmillan, 1998.

250 The most authoritative biography of Romero was written by James Brockman SJ, *Romero: A Life*, Maryknoll, NY: Orbis, 1990; other biographical summaries can be found in James Brockman SJ, 'Introduction', in *Archbishop Oscar Romero: A Shepherd's Diary*, Cincinatti, Ohio: St Anthony Messenger Press and London: Catholic Fund for Overseas Development and Catholic Institute for International Relations, 1993, Ignacio Martín-Baró SJ, 'Oscar Romero: Voice of the Downtrodden', in *Oscar Romero: Voice of the Voiceless: The Four Pastoral Letters and Other Statements*, Maryknoll, NY: Orbis, 1985 and Jon Sobrino SJ, *Archbishop Romero: Memories and Reflections*, Maryknoll, NY: Orbis, 1990.

251 Ignacio Martín-Baró SJ, 'Oscar Romero: Voice of the Downtrodden', in *Oscar Romero: Voice of the Voiceless*, p. 3.

252 It was that night at Aguilares that he met Jon Sobrino SJ for the

first time, Jon Sobrino, 'A Theologian's View of Oscar Romero', in *Oscar Romero: Voice of the Voiceless*, p. 22.

253 Ignacio Martín-Baró, 'Oscar Romero', p. 6.

254 Romero cleared those accusations in his Second Pastoral Letter when he asserted that 'insofar as Marxism is an atheistic ideology it is incompatible with the Christian faith', in 'The Church, the Body of Christ in History', Second Pastoral Letter of Archbishop Romero, Feast of the Transfiguration, 6 August 1977.

255 Romero would remember Fr Navarro's enthusiasm in his pastoral work many times and in a particular Easter homily he linked Navarro's tomb with the continuous struggle until all tombs are like that of Christ – empty; see *Diary*, Sunday 2 April 1978.

256 For example, on his visit to the Vatican in 1978 Romero spoke via the phone to Father Pedraza who recorded Romero's impressions of Rome and his meeting with the Pope. The tape was then broadcast on the same day via YSAX in El Salvador, *Diary*, Wednesday, 21 June 1978.

257 'The Easter Church', First Pastoral Letter of Archbishop Romero, Easter Sunday, 10 April 1977.

258 Jon Sobrino, 'A Theologian's View of Oscar Romero', in *Oscar Romero: Voice of the Voiceless*, p. 38.

259 On 16 November 1989, six Jesuit priests, their cook and her daughter were machine-gunned at the José Simeón Cañas University of Central America (UCA) in San Salvador at 1.00 a.m. by personnel of the US-trained military force, the Atlacatl Batallion. Jon Sobrino SJ was the only Jesuit left alive as he was abroad at that time.

260 'The Church, the Body of Christ in History', Second Pastoral Letter of Archbishop Romero, Feast of the Transfiguration, 6 August 1977.

261 *Diary*, Friday, 31 March 1978.

262 *Diary*, Wednesday, 24 May 1978.

263 Romero was not a patient of Dr Semsch; however, it is clear from his diary that he consulted with medical psychologists about his ideas for pastoral work and other personal initiatives, for example, Dr Dárdano, *Diary*, Thursday, 8 June 1978.

264 *Gaudium et Spes*, 7 December 1965.

265 GS 1 in 'The Church, the Body of Christ in History', Second Pastoral Letter of Archbishop Romero, Feast of the Transfiguration, August 6, 1977.

266 *Diary*, Saturday, 27 May 1978.

267 *Diary*, Sunday, 28 May 1978.

268 *Diary*, Saturday, 3 June 1978.

269 *Diary*, Saturday, 17 June 1978.

270 *Diary*, Sunday, 18 June 1978.

271 *Diary*, Tuesday, 20 June 1978.

272 *Diary*, Wednesday, 21 June 1978.

273 *Diary*, Thursday, 22 June 1978.

274 *Diary*, Sunday, 25 June 1978 and Monday 26 June 1978.

275 *Diary*, Friday, 30 June 1978.

276 'The Church and Popular Political Organizations', Third Pastoral Letter of Archbishop Romero, Co-authored by Bishop Arturo Rivera y Damas, Bishop of Santiago de María, Feast of the Transfiguration, 6 August 1978.

277 *Diary*, Sunday, 1 October 1978.

278 *Diary*, Tuesday, 28 November 1978.

279 *Diary*, Wednesday, 29 November 1978.

280 *Diary*, Saturday, 20 January 1979.

281 *Diary*, Sunday, 21 January 1979.

282 *Diary*, Monday, 22 January 1979.

283 *Diary*, Sunday, 3 December 1978.

284 'Georgetown Address', Address of Archbishop Romero on the Occasion of His Academic Investiture as a Doctor of Humanities, *Honoris Causa*, in the Cathedral of San Salvador, 14 February 1978.

285 'The Political Dimension of the Faith from the Perspective of the Option for the Poor', Address by Archbishop Romero on the Occasion of the Conferral of a Doctorate, Honoris Causa, by the University of Louvain, Belgium, 2 February 1980 and *Diary*, Saturday, 2 February 1980.

286 *Diary*, Wednesday, 30 January 1980.

287 *Diary*, Friday, 16 February 1979

288 Homily, 13 August 1978.

289 Tricia Juhn, *Negotiating Peace in El Salvador: Civil-Military Relations and the Conspiracy to End the War*, London: Macmillan, 1998.

Chapter 7

290 Leonardo Boff, *Igreja – carisma e poder: Ensayos de eclesiologia militante*, Petrópolis: Vozes, 1981; English translation, *Church, Charism and Power: Liberation Theology and Institutional Church*, New York: Crossroad, 1985.

291 Leonardo Boff is his literary and religious name; his civil name is Genezio Darci Boff. Boff's parents were Mansueto Boff and Regina Fontana Boff.

292 Thesis: 'La Iglesia como sacramento en el horizonte de la experi-

encia del mundo: Ensayo de una fundamentación estructural-funcional de la eclesiología'.

293 Leonardo Boff, *Jesus Cristo Libertador: Ensaio de cristologia crítica para o nosso tempo*, Petrópolis: Editora Vozes, 1972; Spanish translation published as *Jesucristo el liberador*, Buenos Aires, 1974; English translation published as *Jesus Christ Liberator: A Critical Christology of Our Time*, Maryknoll, NY: Orbis, London: SPCK, 1980.

294 Leonardo Boff, *Jesus Christ Liberator*, p. 264.

295 For a historical overview see Luis Alberto Gómez de Souza, 'The Origins of Medellín: From Catholic Action to the Base Church Communities and Social Pastoral Strategy (1950–68)', in José Oscar Beozzo and Luiz Carlos Susin (eds), *Brazil: People and Church(es)* (*Concilium* 2002), pp. 31–7.

296 Peter Flynn, *Brazil: A Political Analysis*, London and Boulder: Ernest Benn and Westview Press, 1978, pp. 308–65 and Alfred Stepan, *Rethinking Military Politics: Brazil and the Southern Cone*, Princeton: Princeton University Press, 1988.

297 Thomas E. Skidmore, 'Brazil's Slow Road to Democratization: 1974–1985', in Alfred Stepan (ed.), *Democratizing Brazil: Problems of Transition and Consolidation*, New York and Oxford: Oxford University Press, 1989, pp. 5–42.

298 The Operación Cóndor comprised a network of intelligence services from the Southern Cone, most of them associated with the military regimes of the 1970s that started after a meeting of delegates in Santiago in 1974. The general co-ordinator of the whole operation was General (R) Manuel Contreras, head of the Chilean state intelligence services – DINA, known as Cóndor number 1; see Samuel Blixen, *El vientre del Cóndor: Del archivo del terror al caso Berríos*, Montevideo: Brecha, 1994; Alfredo Boccia Paz, Miguel H. López, Antonio V. Pecci and Gloria Giménez Guanes, *En los sótanos de los generales: Los documentos ocultos del Operativo Cóndor*, Asunción: Expolibro/Servilibro, 2002, Stella Calloni, *Los años del lobo: Operación Cóndor*, Buenos Aires: Ediciones Continente, 1999, John Dinges, *Operación Cóndor: Una década de terrorismo internacional en el Cono Sur*, Santiago: Ediciones B, 2004, Nilson Cézar Mariano, *Operación Cóndor: Terrorismo de estado en el Cono Sur*, Buenos Aires: Lohlé-Lumen, 1998, and Francisco Martorell, *Operación Cóndor: El vuelo de la muerte – La coordinación represiva en el Cono Sur*, Santiago: LOM, 1999.

299 Scott Mainwaring's *The Catholic Church and Politics in Brazil 1916–1985*, Stanford: Stanford University Press, 1986.

300 Ralph Della Cava, 'The 'People's Church', the Vatican and Abertura', in Alfred Stepan (ed.), *Democratizing Brazil: Problems of Transition and Consolidation*, New York and Oxford: Oxford

University Press, 1989, pp. 143–67, at pp. 152–3.

301 W. E. Hewitt, *Base Christian Communities and Social Change in Brazil*, Lincoln and London: University of Nebraska Press, 1991 and Maria Helena Moreira Alves, *Estado e oposição no Brasil 1964–1984*, Petrópolis: Editora Vozes, 1984.

302 Thomas C. Bruneau, *The Political Transformation of the Brazilian Catholic Church*, New York: Cambridge University Press, 1974 and *The Church in Brazil*, Austin: University of Texas Press, 1982; Cardinal Aloísio Lorscheider, 'Fifty Years of the CNBB: A Bishop's Conference Based on the Council – Evangelization Projects, Political and Ecclesiastical Tensions and Challenges', in José Oscar Beozzo and Luiz Carlos Susin (eds), *Brazil: People and Church(es)* (*Concilium* 2002), pp. 25–30.

303 Leonardo Boff, 'Fidel at 80: Confidential Memories 13 August 2006'.

304 Robert McAfee Brown, 'Leonardo Boff: Theologian for all Christians', *Christian Century*, 2–9 July 1986, p. 615.

305 Kloppenburg was editor of the *Revista Eclesiástica Brasileira* and an advocate of ecumenism after Vatican II; however, he was responsible for a report on liberation theology for the military that alerted them to the fact that there were Marxists and subversives within the Catholic Church. He served at the Latin American Episcopal Conference (CELAM) and was ordained as a bishop in 1982, see Ralph Della Cava, 'The "People's Church", the Vatican and Abertura', p. 160.

306 Leonardo Boff, 'A Theological Examination of the Terms "People of God" and "Popular Church"', in Leonardo Boff and Virgil Elizondo (eds), *La Iglesia Popular: Between Fear and Hope* (Concilium 176 1984/6), pp. 89–97 at p. 89.

307 Maria do Carmo Campello de Souza, 'The Brazilian "New Republic": Under the Sword of Damocles', in Alfred Stepan (ed.), *Democratizing Brazil*, pp. 351–94 at pp. 365–6.

308 Leonardo Boff, *Eclesiogênese: As comunidades eclesiais de base reinventam a Igreja*, Petrópolis: Editora Vozes, 1977 and 'Comunidades eclesiais de base: povo oprimido que se organiza para a libertaçao', *Revista Eclesiástica Brasileira*, 41 (June 1981), 312–30. English translation of both Portuguese works published as Leonardo Boff, *Ecclesiogenesis: The Base Communities Reinvent the Church*, Maryknoll, NY: Orbis, 1986.

309 Marcella Althaus-Reid, 'Who Framed Clodovis Boff? Revisiting the Controversy of "Theologies of the Genitive" in the Twenty-First Century', in Erick Borgman and Felix Wilfred (eds), *Theology in a World of Specialization* (*Concilium* 2006), p. 102.

310 Leonardo Boff, *Ecclesiogenesis*, p. 37.

311 Leonardo Boff, *Nova evangelização: Perspectiva dos oprimidos*, Petrópolis: Editora Vozes, 1990; English translation *Good News to the Poor: A New Evangelization*, Tunbridge Wells, Kent and Maryknoll, NY: Burns & Oates and Orbis, 1992.

312 Leonardo Boff, *Francisco de Assis: Ternura e vigor – Uma leitura a partir dos pobres*, Petrópolis: Editora Vozes, 1981 and *Francisco de Assis: Homem do paraíso*, Petrópolis: Editora Vozes, 1985.

313 At that meeting Boff suggested that due to pressures from the Vatican since the 1980s theologians of liberation from Africa, Asia and Latin America had found it ever more difficult to be hosted by Catholic bishops and Catholic dioceses, thus they had chosen to meet one another while participating within larger international meetings such as the World Social Forum.

314 The term 'discovery' is no longer in use and while theologians speak about 'the encounter', the indigenous populations have also developed a revised name for themselves as 'pueblos originarios'.

315 Leonardo Boff, *America Latina: da conquista à nova evangelização*, Sao Paulo: Editora Atica, 1992, *Dimensão política e teológica da ecologia*, Sao Paulo: SEPIS, 1992, *500 anos de evangelização na América Latina*, Petrópolis: CEFEPAL, 1992, and *Cómo celebrar el quinto centenario*, Barcelona: Cristianisme i Justícia, 1992.

316 Leonardo Boff, *Ecology and Liberation: A New Paradigm*, Maryknoll, NY: Orbis, 1995, p. 11.

317 Leonardo Boff, *Ecology and Liberation*, p. 139.

318 Leonardo Boff, *When Theology Listens to the Poor*, San Francisco: Harper & Row, 1988, p. 13.

319 Henrike Müller, 'Spiritual Rebellion: Interview with Leonardo Boff', *SpiritHit News*, 27 January 2005.

320 Inara Claro, 'Interview with Leonardo Boff: Liberation theology is increasingly timely', *Terraviva Online*, 26 January 2005.

321 Leonardo Boff, 'Elogio de la locura de Dom Luiz', *Koinonia*, 14 October 2005. Boff writes a weekly column for the Christian network *Koinonia*.

Chapter 8

322 Elsa Tamez (ed.), *El rostro femenino de la teología*, Costa Rica: Departamento Ecuménico de Investigaciones [DEI], 1986; published in English as *Through Her Eyes: Women's Theology from Latin America*, Maryknoll, NY: Orbis, 1989. Other contributors to this volume of essays included Ana María Bidegain (Uruguay/Colombia), María Clara Bingemer (Brazil), Tereza Cavalcanti (Brazil), Ivone Gebara (Brazil),

Notes

Consuelo del Prado (Peru), Nelly Ritchie (Argentina), Aracely de Rocchietti (Uruguay), and Alida Verhoeven (Argentina) who shared their theological reflections at a conference in Buenos Aires, Argentina 30 October – 3 November 1985.

323 Elsa Tamez, 'On milk and its derivatives', Theme Presentation 1, World Alliance of Reformed Churches General Assembly Meeting, Debrecen, 1997.

324 John Patrick Bell, *Crisis in Costa Rica: The 1948 Revolution*, Austin and London: University of Texas Press, 1971.

325 Leonard A. Bird, *Costa Rica: A Country without an Army*, Leeds: Leeds Community Press, n.d.

326 *Second General Conference of Latin American Bishops 1968, The Church in the Present-Day Transformation of Latin America in the Light of the Council: II Conclusions*, Washington, DC: United States Catholic Conference, Division for Latin America, 1973 and Gustavo Gutiérrez, *Teología de la liberación: Perspectivas*, Lima: CEP, 1971.

327 Franz Hinkelammert, *Las armas ideológicas de la muerte*, San José, Costa Rica: Educa, 1977 and 'Las raíces económicas de la idolatría: la metafísica del empresario', in *La lucha de los dioses: Los ídolos de la opresión y la búsqueda del Dios Liberador*, San José, Costa Rica and Managua, Nicaragua: DEI and Centro Antonio Valdivieso, 1980.

328 Boff, Leonardo and Elsa Tamez, *Teólogos de la liberación hablan sobre la mujer*, San José, Costa Rica: DEI, 1986.

329 See Elsa Tamez, *La sociedad que las mujeres soñamos: nuevas relaciones varón-mujer en un nuevo orden económico*, San José, Costa Rica: DEI, 1979.

330 Elsa Tamez, 'A mulher que complicou a história da salvacao', *Por trós da palavra*, Boletím do CEDI, 27 (March–April 1985).

331 Elsa Tamez, 'Reflections by Elsa Tamez', in Virginia Fabella and Sergio Torres (eds), *Irruption of the Third World*, Maryknoll, NY: Orbis, 1983, p. 184.

332 Elsa Tamez, 'Introduction: The Power of the Naked', in *Through Her Eyes: Women's Theology from Latin America*, Maryknoll, NY: Orbis, 1989, pp. 1–14.

333 Elsa Tamez, 'Introduction: The Power of the Naked', in *Through Her Eyes*, p. 13.

334 See for example, Alida Verhoeven, 'The Concept of God: A Feminine Perspective', in Elsa Tamez (ed.), *Through Her Eyes*, pp. 49–55; Leonardo Boff, *The Maternal Face of God*, San Francisco: Harper & Row, 1987; Rosino Gibellini, *La sfida del femminismo alla teologia*, Brescia: Editora Queriniana, 1980, and Rosemary Radford Ruether, 'The Feminine Nature of God', *Concilium*, 143 (1981), pp. 61–8.

335 Elsa Tamez, 'A Letter from Elsa Tamez to all Christians of Latin America and the Caribbean', 14 March 2003.

336 Rosemary Ruether, 'Letter to Elsa Tamez', 21 March 2003.

337 Elsa Tamez, 'La memoria de la caminada del cristianismo en América Latina y el Caribe' and 'Epístola de Priscila a los hermanos y hermanas reunidos en São Paulo, Brazil', 30 July 2003.

338 Gustavo Gutiérrez, *On Job: God-Talk and the Suffering of the Innocent*, Maryknoll, NY: Orbis, 1987.

339 Elsa Tamez, 'I Timothy and James on the Rich, Women and Theological Disputes', in Sean Freyne and Ellen van Wolde (eds), *The Many Voices of the Bible* (*Concilium* 2002), pp. 49–58.

340 The English translation *Bible of the Oppressed*, Maryknoll, NY: Orbis, 1982, incorporates translated materials from two works in Spanish: chapters 1–5 from *La Biblia de los oprimidos: La opresión en la teología bíblica*, San José, Costa Rica: DEI, 1979 and chapters 6–7 from *La hora de la vida*, San José, Costa Rica: DEI, 1978.

341 Unsurprisingly, she found a lack of a body of biblical studies on the theme of oppression in the Bible, see Elsa Tamez, *Bible of the Oppressed*, p. 4. However, for a more narrow reading using Marx and the Latin American context see José Porfirio Miranda, *Marx and the Bible: A Critique of the Philosophy of Oppression*, Maryknoll, NY: Orbis, 1974 and a related work by Hugo Assmann, *Opresión-Liberación: Desafío a los cristianos*, Montevideo: Tierra Nueva, 1971, translated in English as *Theology for a Nomad Church*, Maryknoll, NY: Orbis, 1976.

342 Elsa Tamez, *Bible of the Oppressed*, p. 1.

343 The word 'oppression' in the Old Testament has nine particular Hebrew roots explored in chapters 1–2 of *Bible of the Oppressed*.

344 Elsa Tamez, *Bible of the Oppressed*, p. 3.

345 Elsa Tamez, *Bible of the Oppressed*, p. 62.

346 Elsa Tamez, *Bible of the Oppressed*, p. 70.

347 Elsa Tamez, *Bible of the Oppressed*, p. 81.

348 Elsa Tamez, *Contra toda condena: La justificación por la fe desde los excluídos*, San José, Costa Rica: Departamento Ecuménico de Investigaciones [DEI] and Seminario Bíblico Latinoamericano [SEBILA], 1991; English translation published as *The Amnesty of Grace: Justification by Faith from a Latin American Perspective*, Nashville: Abingdon Press, 1993.

349 Elsa Tamez, *Santiago: Lectura latinoamericana de la epístola*, San José, Costa Rica: DEI, 1985; English translation published as *The Scandalous Message of James: Faith without Works is Dead*, New York: Crossroad, 1990, with study guide by the Women's Division, General Board of Global Ministries, The United Methodist Church, 2002.

Notes

350 Elsa Tamez, *The Amnesty of Grace*, p. 25.
351 Elsa Tamez, *The Amnesty of Grace*, p. 166.
352 Elsa Tamez, *The Scandalous Message of James*, p. 51.
353 Elsa Tamez, 'A Latin American Perspective', in K. C. Abraham (ed.), *Third World Theologies: Commonalities and Divergences*, Maryknoll, NY: Orbis, 1990, pp. 134–8.
354 'A Latin American Perspective', p. 137.
355 *Santo Domingo: Conclusiones*, Santiago: Conferencia Episcopal de Chile, 1993, §243–51, 299.

Chapter 9

356 Diego Irarrázaval, *Inculturation: New Dawn of the Church in Latin America*, Maryknoll, NY: Orbis, 2000, p. 117.
357 David Fernández Fernández, 'Oral History of the Chilean Movement Christians for Socialism 1971–1973', *Journal of Contemporary History* 34 (1999), pp. 283–94 at p. 287.
358 It was in the same locality of Chimbote that Gustavo Gutiérrez used the expression 'a theology of liberation' for the first time in the context of a talk to Peruvian clergy in 1968.
359 'Padre Diego Irarrázaval: Un misionero chileno en Perú', *Revista Iglesia de Santiago*, October 2004.
360 For an overview of the history of the Church in Peru see Jeffrey Klaiber SJ, The Church, Dictatorships, and Democracy in Latin America, Maryknoll, NY: Orbis, 1998, pp. 141–67. This work was originally published in Spanish as *Iglesia, dictaduras y democracia en América Latina*, Lima: Pontificia Universidad Católica, 1997.
361 Diego Irarrázaval, *Un Jesús jovial*, Lima: Ediciones Paulinas, 2003 and *Raíces de la esperanza*, Lima: CEP, 2004.
362 The term 'inculturation' should not be confused with the sociological word 'enculturation' that refers to societies' mutual influences in processes of change rather than to the process of inculturation as a mutual influence between the gospel, the Church and a particular society with its customs, history and symbolic systems of social action; see Aylward Shorter, *Toward a Theology of Inculturation*, London; Chapman, 1988. 'Inculturation' is also a different term and process from 'acculturation', whereby those who come from the outside try to open themselves to the local values and customs; 'inculturation' remains a process within a localized Christian community and their praxis and self-awareness; see Diego Irarrázaval, *Inculturation*, pp. 4–5.
363 Mario I. Aguilar, 'The social experience of two Gods in Africa', *African Eclesial Review*, 36 (1994), pp. 32–44.

364 IV Conferencia General del Episcopado Latinoamericano, *Conclusiones: nueva evangelización, promoción humana, cultura cristiana*, Santo Domingo, República Dominicana 12–28 de octubre de 1992, Santiago: Conferencia Episcopal de Chile, 1993.

365 Juan Pablo II, Discurso inaugural: Nueva evangelización, promoción humana, cultura cristiana, §22, cf. Juan Pablo II, Discurso al mundo de la cultura, Lima, 15 May 1988, § 5.

366 Juan Pablo II, Discurso inaugural, § 23.

367 Juan Pablo II, Discurso inaugural, § 24.

368 'Queremos acercarnos a los pueblos indígenas y afro americanos, a fin de que el Evangelio encarnado en sus culturas manifieste toda su vitalidad y entren ellos en diálogo de comunión con las demás comunidades cristianas para mutuo enriquecimiento', SD § 299.3.2.

369 SD § 251.

370 Aylward Shorter, *Toward a Theology of Inculturation*, p. xi.

371 Diego Irarrázaval, *Inculturation*, p. ix.

372 Diego Irarrázaval, *Inculturation*, p. 75.

373 Diego Irarrázaval, *Inculturation*, p. 117.

374 Diego Irarrázaval, 'Identidad polisémica', *Teología y Vida*, 46 (2005), pp. 615–24 at p. 615.

375 Some of these points have been highlighted by contemporary Latin American theologians, still unknown to the English-speaking world, for example, Juan Carlos Scannone, *Evangelización, cultura y teología*, Buenos Aires: Editorial Guadalupe, 1990; Fernando Torres *et alia*, *Teología a pie, entre sueños y clamores*, Bogotá: Dimensión Educativa, 1997 and Diego Irarrázaval, *Teología en la fe del pueblo*, San José: DEI, 1999.

376 Diego Irarrázaval, 'Identidad polisémica', p. 616.

377 'Las ciencias modernas explican la "identidad" como relación entre la persona y la sociedad (que se desarrolla por etapas); o bien como condición pragmática del actor social reconocido por otros/as; o bien como basada en códigos interpretativos y de validación comunicativa; o como no sujeto posmoderno, etc.', Diego Irarrázaval, 'Identidad polisémica', p. 616. Other related works on cultural identity in Latin America include the following: José Joaquín Brunner, *Chile: transformaciones culturales y modernidad*, Santiago: FLACSO, 1989 and *América Latina: cultura y modernidad*, Mexico: Grijalbo, 1992, Leopoldo Castedo, *Fundamentos culturales de la integración latinoamericana*, Santiago: Dolmen, 1999, Manuel Antonio Garretón, *Cultura y desarrollo en Chile*, Santiago: Andrés Bello, 2001, Jorge Gissi, *Identidad latinoamericana: psicología y sociedad*, Santiago: Andes, 1987, Hernán Godoy, *Apuntes sobre la cultura en Chile*, Valparaíso: Editorial Universitaria, 1982, Martín Hopenhyan, *Ni apocalípticos ni*

Notes

integrados: aventuras de la modernidad en América Latina, Santiago: FCE, 1994, Jorge Larraín, *Modernidad, razón e identidad en América Latina*, Santiago: Editorial Andrés Bello, 1996 and *Identidad chilena*, Santiago: LOM, 2001, Sonia Montecinos, *Madres y huachos: alegorías del mestizaje chileno*, Santiago: Cuarto Propio, 1991, Pedro Morandé, *Cultura y modernización en América Latina*, Santiago: Editorial de la Universidad Católica, 1984, Cristián Parker, *Otra lógica en América Latina*, Santiago: FCE, 1993, Ricardo Salas, *Lo sagrado y lo humano*, Santiago: Editorial San Pablo, 1996, and Eugenio Tirón, *El sueño chileno, comunidad, familia y nación en el Bicentenario*, Santiago: Taurus, 2005.

378 Diego Irarrázaval, 'Identidad polisémica', p. 618.

379 See for example, Francisco Varela, *El fenómeno de la vida*, Santiago: Dolmen, 2000.

380 Hugo F. Hinfelaar, MAfr, 'Evangelization and Inculturation', *African Ecclesial Review*, 36 (1994), pp. 2–18 at 6.

381 Marcella Althaus-Reid, *Indecent Theology: Theological Perversions in Sex, Gender and Politics*, London and New York: Routledge, 2000, *The Queer God*, London and New York: Routledge, 2003, Ivan Petrella, *The Future of Liberation Theology: An Argument and Manifesto*, Aldershot: Ashgate, 2004 and London: SCM Press, 2006, and Pedro Trigo, 'El futuro de la teología de la liberación', in José Comblin, José I. González Faus and Jon Sobrino (eds), *Cambio social y pensamiento cristiano en América Latina*, Madrid: Editorial Trotta, 1993, pp. 297–317.

382 In my theological taxonomy I am concerned with individuals as agents while I recognize that others have classified the theology of liberation movement through periods of gestation, development and challenges; see João Batista Libanio, 'Panorama de la teología de América Latina en los últimos veinte años' in José Comblin, José I. González Faus and Jon Sobrino (eds), *Cambio social y pensamiento cristiano en América Latina*, Madrid: Editorial Trotta, 1993, pp. 57–78.

Index

Index

Index

Index

Gospels, as creeds, Richard's views 87–8
Goulart, Joao (President of Brazil, 1964) 124
Gramsci, Antonio 64
Grande, Rutilio (parish priest of Aguilares, El Salvador) 109, 110
Gregory the Great, Pope 37
group work 56
Guantánamo Bay 103
Guatemala, rise of Pentecostalism 3
Gumucio, Esteban 155, 189 n. 177
Gutheim, Federico 188 n. 171
Gutheim, Miguel Ernesto 188 n. 171
Gutiérrez, Gustavo 9–10, 55, 57, 64, 88, 137, 155: biblical hermeneutics 147; and Christians for Socialism 76–7, 80; influence 178 n. 69; involvement with 500th anniversary of Columbus's discovery of the Americas 132; on liberation theology 15, 123, 203 n. 358; receives honorary Doctorate from St Andrews University ix; on religious practice 32–7, 38, 38–40; social ethics 48; *Teología de la liberación* 21, 22, 31, 164, 176 n. 58; theological investigation by the Vatican 125–6; on theology 21–2, 51 – as commentary 22–7; in the community 13; as history 27–32; as narrative 24–7; writings 176 n. 59

Hagar, Tamaz's understanding of 142
Hegel, G. W. F. 14, 52, 54
Henríquez, Silva, Cardinal 62, 187 n. 156
Hernández Martínez, Maximiliano, General (military dictator in El Salvador) 106
Hinfelaar, Hugo 167–8
Hinkelammert, Franz 139
historical thought, Dussel's views 48–9
history: Christianity's historical development as viewed by Dussel 44–6; God's intervention 27–9, 83, 90; role in theology 27–32
Holy Spirit, Boff's views criticized 128
human beings, relations with God and with each other, Oscar Romero's views 110
human person, centrality of 35–7
human rights abuses: by Argentinean

government 42–3; Roman Catholic bishops' responses in Argentina and Chile 187 n. 156

identity, and inculturation 167–9
idolatry 82–5, 173 n. 37
IMF (International Monetary Fund) 4
imperialism, effects on Christianity 87
impunity, and justice, Bonino's concerns with 69–70
incarnation 28, 160, 166
inculturation 75, 76, 160, 166: and identity 167–9; Irarrázaval's views 154; and liberation theology 160–4; theology 12, 157–9, 203 n. 362
India, civilization 53
indigenous peoples: fights for rights 4; place in liberation theology 12
individualism, and globalization 13–14
International Court of Justice, condemns Reagan administration's Nicaraguan policy 101
international dependency, and social justice 46
International Monetary Fund (IMF) 4
Iraq, second Iraq war 16, 76, 145
Irarrázaval, Diego 154–6: and Christians for Socialism 76, 155; on cultural identity 164–7; theology of inculturation 12, 133, 153, 158–9, 160–1, 161–2, 163–4
Islam, American attitudes towards 144
Israel, people of, God's involvement with 28
Iturbide, Agustín de (Mexican emperor) 91

Japan 53, 157
Jeroboam I (king of Israel) 83
'Jerusalem principle' 47
Jesuits 111, 114, 157, 179 n. 80, 196 n. 259
Jesus Christ: belief in 28, 67–8; Body, as indicative of the Church's role in El Salvador, Oscar Romero's views 111; Church model 127; incarnation 83; as liberator 121, 123–4, 149; Lordship, in conflict with divine status of the Roman Emperor 84; madness 135; ministry, Bonino's views 66; preference for the poor 47

Index

Richard's views 88–90; social generations 8–12; women's role 140, 142; *see also* theology
Liberation and Theology Series 184 n. 123
Ligas Populares 28 de Febrero (Popular Leagues of 28 February) 109
Lima Catholic University 155
Lima, Third Council (1582–83) 45
Liturgical Institute (Medellín) 44
liturgy, use of the vernacular 157
Llach, Lencho (Salvadorian Ambassador to the Vatican, 1978) 114
López Pérez, Rigoberto 92, 93
Lorscheider, Alois, Cardinal 128
love: divine love, Oscar Romero's theology 118; as the essence of Christianity, Cardenal's views 91
Lula (President of Brazil) 135
Luther, Martin 152

Madres de la Plaza de Mayo (mothers of the Argentinian disappeared) 60, 171 n. 10
Maipú (Chile), 'young Church' protests against proposed building of Catholic National Shrine (1968) 77
Maliaño, Francisco Urcuyo (President of Nicaragua, 1979) 99
Malvinas/Falkland Islands war 60
Mancarró (Solentiname archipelago), lay monastery 95–6, 97, 98–9, 192 n. 215
Mannheim, Karl 9, 172 n. 18
MAPU 80
marginalized: religious affiliation in Chile and Brazil 2–3; response to God's actions 32–3
Marian celebrations, importance for the Aymaras 156
Mariátegui, José Carlos 178 n. 72
market, effects in globalization 76
Maroto, Rafael (Episcopal Vicar of the Archdiocese of Santiago) 78
Martín, Juan 189 n. 177
Martínez Baigorri, Angel (Jesuit and poet) 93
Martínez de Perón, María Estela 59
Martínez de Perón, María Estela (wife of Juan Domingo Perón) 43
Marx, Karl 41, 48, 53–5, 184 n. 127

Marxism: Boff's views criticized 128; Cardenal's views 95, 96, 102–3; and Christianity 61–5, 96, 100, 102–3, 144, 193 n. 231; hermeneutics 85; influence on Europe 23; and liberation theology 6–8; Oscar Romero's attitudes to 196 n. 254; probable rejection of Dussel's views on thought 50
Mary Lawrence *see* Cardenal, Ernesto
mass media 166
Massera, Emilio E., Admiral (Military Junta, Argentina) 183 n. 115, 186 n. 147
materialism, and theology 11–12
'matter is music' (Cardenal's theme) 102
Mauss, Marcel 23
Mayorga, Silvio 193 n. 230
Medellín Conference (1968) 10, 17, 61, 77, 139: on the centrality of the person 36; effects, in El Salvador 107, 108; influence 31, 35, 180 n. 87; links with Argentinian guerillas 59; pastoral guidelines 57; on the role of the poor 37
mediated identity 166
men: domination of theology challenged 142–3, 144; male power sacralized 162
Méndez Arceo, Sergio (Bishop of Cuernavaca, Mexico) 79
Menem, Carlos (President of Argentina) 70
Merton, Thomas 93, 94, 95, 103, 191 n. 212
methodological paradigms, Dussel's use 42
Metz, Johann-Baptist 24–5, 50
Mexico, Enrique Dussel's exile in 44
militancy, Bonino's views 64
Military Junta (Argentina) 42–3, 44, 60, 183 n. 115, 186 n. 147: leaders granted clemency 70; violation of human rights 44; *see also* Argentina
military regimes: policies concerned with national security 42–3; relations with churches 3–4
milk, as symbol for hunger for Elsa Tamez 138
MIR (Movimiento de Izquierda Revolucionario) 79
modernity 52, 53, 160, 162

Index

Perón, Juan Domingo (President of
Argentina, 1970s) 43, 59
Peronist movement (*sindicalismo
peronista*) 43, 58, 59
person, exclusion from theology 24
Peru: Ayacucho Archdiocese 155–6;
Chimbote 27, 155, 178 n. 71,
203 n. 358; Chucuito, site of
Irarrázaval's parochial work
(1984–2004) 155; development of
liberation theology 155; Rimac 27,
178 n. 73
Peruvian bishops, support for socialism
(1971) 45
Petrella, Ivan 169
philosophical paradigms, Dussel's re-
elaboration of 41
Pinochet, support for evangelicalism 3
piqueteros 5
Plaza Libertad (San Salvador),
demonstrations (28 February 1977)
109
plurality, and inculturation 161
poetry 98: importance in Nicaragua
190 n. 207; and poverty, importance
for Cardenal 93
political power, idolatry 84
politics: Bonino's views 66–7; and
Christianity, Dussel's views 45–6; in
God's plan of salvation 27;
Gutiérrez's views 22; and neo-
scholastic theology 23; and post-
idealist theology 24; and religion
31–2, 38–9, 115–16; and
transcendental-idealist theology 24
Pontifical Justice and Peace
Commission 115
the poor: attitudes towards challenged
by Gutiérrez 35–7; biblical
understanding, Tamez's views 149;
Church's concerns with, Bonino's
views 64, 71; as evangelizers, Boff's
views 131; God revealed through,
Richard's views 89–90; involvement
with, as religious practice 30, 38–9;
and post-idealist theology 24;
preference for 30, 31, 47–8, 50;
response to God's actions 32–3;
Roman Catholic Church's neglect of
criticized 96; Romero's attitude
towards 107; Tamez's concerns with
140
popular religiosity 161

Popular Unity, manifesto supported by
Base Communities (1970) 77
Portuguese colonies, Jesuits expelled
from 179 n. 80
possession cults 3
post-idealist theology 24–6
post-modernity, Dussel's views 41, 52,
53
Pound, Ezra, influence on Cardenal
93, 191 n. 208
poverty: and poetry, importance for
Cardenal 93; Tamez's experience of
137–9
prayer, theology, Oscar Romero's
views 118
'preferential option for the poor' 30,
31, 47–8, 50
Priests of the Third World 59
private ownership, and the means of
production 182 n. 101
production, and private ownership
182 n. 101
prophetic thought, Dussel's views 49
the prophets, on social obligations 28
Protestant Evangelicals, in El Salvador
105
Protestantism, effects on Latin
American Christian communities
34–5
Puebla Conference (1979) 10, 17, 31,
35, 81, 117, 118, 161
pueblos originarios 153, 200 n. 314
Pujadas, Ignacio 79, 189 n. 177

racism, Enrique Dussel's criticisms of
German racism 183 n. 108
Ratzinger, Joseph (Benedict XVI) 125,
127–8
readers, contextual response to the
Scriptures, Richard's views 88
Reformation 150, 177 n. 65
Rega, José López (Peronist Minister for
Social Welfare) 44, 60
religion: Bonino's views 66; Castro's
views 127; centrality of the poor in
30; Gutiérrez's views 22; neo-
scholastic theology 23; organized
religion, Boff's views 135; and
politics 31–2, 115–16; and post-
idealist theology 24; religious
practice 28, 38–40; and science,
Bonino's views 67; and
transcendental-idealist theology 24